HOW COMPASSION MADE US HUMAN

HOW COMPASSION
MADE US HUMAN

*The Evolutionary Origins of
Tenderness, Trust and Morality*

Penny Spikins

First published in Great Britain in 2015 by
PEN & SWORD ARCHAEOLOGY
an imprint of
Pen and Sword Books Ltd
47 Church Street
Barnsley
South Yorkshire S70 2AS

ISBN 978 1 78159 310 3

Printed and bound in England
by CPI Group (UK) Ltd, Croydon, CR0 4YY

Typeset in Times New Roman by
CHIC GRAPHICS

Pen & Sword Books Ltd incorporates the imprints of
Pen & Sword Archaeology, Atlas, Aviation, Battleground, Discovery,
Family History, History, Maritime, Military, Naval, Politics, Railways,
Select, Social History, Transport, True Crime, Claymore Press,
Frontline Books, Leo Cooper, Praetorian Press, Remember When,
Seaforth Publishing and Wharncliffe.

For a complete list of Pen and Sword titles please contact
Pen and Sword Books Limited
47 Church Street, Barnsley, South Yorkshire, S70 2AS, England
E-mail: enquiries@pen-and-sword.co.uk
Website: www.pen-and-sword.co.uk

Contents

As a child I visited Rouffignac Cave and saw images of mammoths drawn thousands of years ago. There was nothing in the art that I saw there that bore any resemblance to the world I had been told of, a world where brutish cavemen struggled for existence. I couldn't help wondering what the art meant about the people of the time and perhaps about us.

Early antiquarians came across handaxes in river gravels and realised that they must have dated to a far distant period in the past. Such finds made them question what they thought they knew, and wonder whether there was anything human in this ancient past. More finds revealed more evidence. Yet no matter how much was uncovered, reconstructions of an ancient past seemed to be more about assumptions about what ought to be natural than the evidence itself. Could that be as true of our origin stories today?

Raymond Dart believed that aggression was innate to humanity and that he had found three-million-year-old archaeological evidence of the 'killer ape' that led to ourselves. A more detailed study of the evidence would prove him wrong, but these were not the only signs which might suggest to us that there was a violent side to our human past. Was it ruthless competition and aggression that made us human?

The archaeological record also reveals a different side to early humans. The evidence for people caring for the sick, grieving at the passing of loved ones, and demonstrating a remarkable sensitivity to aesthetics challenge the more violent view of our past nature. Could early humans have been kind and caring? Why would people care about objects?

What mechanisms can explain the evolution of human altruism? We consider the moral instinct of other apes and of our common ancestor. Forgotten ideas from the nineteenth century cast new light on the evolution of human morality while contributions from economics explain why it might pay off to be carried away by one's feelings. Could changes in human emotions have been the basis for our success, coming before increases in intelligence or the emergence of language?

PART THREE: A NEW STORY

Do the different strands of evidence lead us to a new story of human origins? We consider the path taken by *Homo erectus*, and how a particular turning point in evolution 1.8 million years ago may have led to the development of distinctively human emotions. What did Neanderthals feel for each other, and might it have been different from our own species?

What was life like in the Upper Palaeolithic? Popular images suggest that life was brutal, but is there any basis to these assumptions? Were modern human societies of the Upper Palaeolithic even more sensitive, kinder and more willing to help than our own? Might the societies of the Upper Palaeolithic have developed an emotional wisdom that we seem to have forgotten?

If we could travel back in the past would we understand what made humans different? Would we be willing to listen to what prehistoric hunter-gatherers could tell us? The history of our contact with modern hunting and gathering populations suggests that we might not. Is there something that we should learn?

Acknowledgements

Without Paul Mills this would have been a dull and probably rather confusing book. His 'just asking questions' always helped me see through to what I wanted to say, and how to express it in a more interesting way, and his poems are inspirational.

Thanks are also due to my family – their conviction that if I was writing something it was bound to be interesting may well have been biased, but was fantastically supportive all the same. Over the years the many students of human origins, with their enquiring minds and creative spirits, have always been an inspiration, as have so many of my academic colleagues who share a lifelong commitment to revealing the past – I hope I have inspired them as much as they have inspired me. Thank you also to a rural Yorkshire village for restoring my faith in humanity and to Chris for his constant support, and moreover for having the self-control not to mention the part of my illustrations which had obviously come out wonky-looking.

Thanks is also due to Phil Reynolds and Fulford Art class for teaching me to draw and to be sensitive to depiction – if I hadn't done my own illustrations within this volume it wouldn't have been the same. I'm not sure what possessed me to decide to draw everything by hand in pen and ink, however; much like making a handaxe, this means that the slightest mistake renders the end product useless, and there have been many mistakes! I'm sure that I've learnt something about patience, and an even greater respect for *Homo erectus*, along the way.

Thank you to Greg Currie, Francis Wenban-Smith, Ivan Briz i Godino and Paul Mills for finding the time and inspiration to say something that I could quote, Geoff Bailey for his consistent support of my unconventional approach to the material record of the Palaeolithic and for spending time to proofread the manuscript and to invaluable discussions of human compassion within the Compassionate Mind Foundation.

Thank you also to several proofreaders for their enthusiasm and careful copy-editing, and to Eloise Hansen at Pen and Sword for her unwavering commitment to a novel project which changed a great deal from its first inception.

Foreword

Until very recently – well into the present century – the idea that archaeological evidence might throw any light on past human feelings and emotions would have been dismissed by most archaeologists as impossible, irrelevant, or at best an exercise in subjective imagination better suited to the fictional novel than a scientific treatise. As one of my early archaeological teachers once succinctly put it: the soul leaves no skeleton. Similarly, emotions have played very little role in 20th century narratives of human evolution. Violence, it is true, has occasionally made an appearance, most famously in Raymond Dart's killer-ape hypothesis of human origins, but the evidence Dart used has long since been discredited. Otherwise, as Penny Spikins points out in the introduction to this interesting and important new volume, fashions in evolutionary explanations have ranged across a wide spectrum, from climate and environment, to technology, social relationships, economic processes, increased brain power and developments in cognition and language. Emotions, however, have scarcely made any appearance at all.

This is odd. We are an emotionally complex species, with characteristics generally regarded as distinctively human, not only in our ability to inflict cruelty, injury and death on members of our own species, but also in our capacity to identify with others through powers of empathy and acts of compassion. Are these qualities relatively recent developments in human evolution, qualities shared only by fully evolved *Homo sapiens* – 'modern' humans – along with other features such as language and symbolism? Or are they more deeply embedded in our evolutionary history? And if so when and why they did they evolve? And how important have they been in shaping the human evolutionary trajectory and how variable in their strength and frequency? Are they simply a hangover of an earlier evolutionary process that no longer serves any biological purpose, rather like the neuropsychological equivalent of an appendix, evolved over many hundreds of millennia in our supposedly early and primitive state as scavengers, hunters and gatherers living in small groups at low population densities? Or do they continue to play a vital role in our more complex and ever more crowded civilisation? And how can we go about answering these questions except by the rather dubious practice of extrapolating backwards in time from what we think we know of our present human condition?

That we continue to be emotional beings, that we define our distinctiveness as being human in these terms, and that these emotional qualities have persisted and developed over a very long period of time compels us to acknowledge that they must have some ongoing and positive role in an evolutionary sense, contributing to our overall success and well-being as a species, as societies and as individuals. Otherwise they would long ago have been eliminated by selective processes in favour of more efficient modes of survival.

In this fascinating and engaging survey, Penny Spikins tackles all these questions, drawing widely on evidence from archaeology, biology, psychology, animal behaviour, ethnographic and historical studies, and personal experiences. Once the questions are posed, it becomes clear that there are many types of evidence from the traditional archaeological fare of 'stones and bones' that can shed some light on the answers. This should come as no surprise after more than three decades of developments in archaeological research that have shown how material culture can be studied not simply as a fortuitous, fragmentary and rather poor-quality by-product of past social, economic and intellectual activities, but as an active and tangible embodiment and vehicle of their expression. It is but a small step to extend that thinking to the realm of human emotions. The approach developed here is informed by the scholarly apparatus of source evidence and an up-to-date and critical appraisal of established ideas and the wider literature. It is also illustrated with numerous line drawings penned by the author, and written with wit and humanity in a readable style that will engage the general reader as well as the specialist. There are, of course, many ambiguities in the evidence and challenges of interpretation, but also clearly a new field opening up for investigation, with new questions to be asked and new horizons to be explored. This book opens the door for us into this new universe of possibilities and leads us on the first steps of a journey that, like so many other human endeavours, is likely to have both emotional and intellectual qualities.

Geoff Bailey
Department of Archaeology
University of York
February 2015

PART ONE

The Mystery

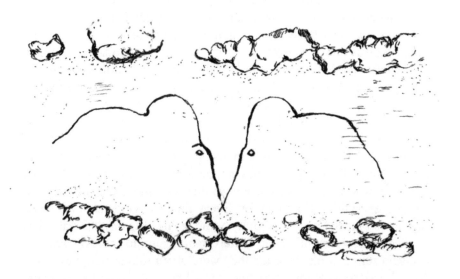

Depiction of two mammoths at Rouffignac Cave, France, around 15,000 years old.[1]

Prologue

Deep inside a long dark cave, I found myself in front of a remarkable image, 15,000 years old. I was eleven years old, on a family holiday and visiting Rouffignac Cave in the Dordogne. Television documentaries had painted a picture of human ancestors valiantly surviving in the harsh savannah. School books told me about grubby cavemen wearing skins, living harsh and brutal lives and I was desperate to find out more about this lost world.

I was determined to see for myself some of the Palaeolithic cave art sites that dated back to this far distant time. Going down deep damp caves on a sunny day was the least pleasant thing my parents could imagine, so I insisted I was fine by myself, was given my ticket and joined the throngs while they stayed at the entrance. I'd done this several times before at different caves and just as I hoped, it had never been so easy to fit into a tour group. If anyone looked at me quizzically I'd sidle up to the nearest French family and try and look as if I belonged to them. I was scared of the dark, so as we walked ever deeper into the caves I tried not to panic. As always, the blackness closed in and strange bodies pressed into me, far closer than I was used to, moving me forward. I was certain that if I showed how scared I was someone would return me to the entrance and I'd miss everything I'd come for. Every time the guide shouted some warning in French I would painfully bump my head against the stalactites overhead a few seconds later. It hurt, tears came to my eyes and the strangers stared at me. Worried they were about to question why I was alone, I tried to look confident, and if at all possible – and I wasn't sure how to do this – definitely French.

It was all worth it for that moment of awe I felt standing in front of a drawing of ice-age mammoths, seemingly entranced looking into each other's eyes. These almost cartoon-like depictions, with a few quick strokes of colour, were done so adeptly and preserved so finely that they looked as though they were made yesterday. Here was what I had come for. For at that moment I was presented with the existence of a different world, only a few feet away yet separated by many thousands of years. This was a place where people wore skins, hunted large animals with stone weapons and roamed among long-extinct species like mammoths, woolly rhinoceros and sabre-toothed cats. How could peoples desperate for survival, living such harsh and brutal lives be capable not only of fine artistic expression, but of capturing in a few strokes a sense of connection between two beings? How could the sense of tenderness and humanity I felt looking at this image possibly be in keeping with what I had been told about the world from which it came? While the guide talked in French, for me there was no explanation, no dates, no interpretations or theories, and perhaps that was part of the magic. I was simply eleven years of age and face to face with the vast depths of our existence, a moment that decided for me there and then that I wanted to find out where we had come from, to make sense of the bones, tools and fragments of art left behind all those thousands, even millions of years ago. Someone said something, people left, and I realised I had to follow them, wondering if I would ever return and if the mystery would make more sense to me when I did.

It was to be many years later before I myself excavated remains of the occupation sites of people from the cultures that had created this art, and had a chance to uncover even older finds dating to earlier species of human and further distant periods in time, even directing my own excavations of prehistoric hunting and gathering peoples. It was even longer before I would return to Rouffignac, contemplating everything I had found out.

There was a long journey ahead of me. I remember to this day the sense of awe I felt when I first uncovered and held a tool last touched by a Neanderthal around 60,000 years ago. By then I was a young student on excavation at a site called Les Tares in south-west France. As I turned the flint scraper around in my hand, the first to do so since it was abandoned, I couldn't help but notice how easily the maker had taken off flakes and formed a tool that was in so many ways 'beautiful' compared to my own recent stumbling efforts at making flint tools. The time separating us seemed at that moment slightly immaterial compared to my sense that we were both in many ways human. I felt then as though I'd been transported into some science fiction story, where different beings mingled together and talked about the everyday experience of making things. Only weeks before we had discussed the demise of the Neanderthals in class in the tone that was so praising of the success of our own species compared to our apparently less quick-witted or efficient Neanderthal contemporaries. We were rather pleased with ourselves that evolution gave us full marks and the Neanderthals got second place. It was clear to me in that moment nonetheless that this supposedly 'brutish' Neanderthal was a very great deal better at making elegant flint tools than I was. I couldn't help but wonder if our supposed 'superiority' might not have been a matter of chance and circumstance.

From the art to the everyday tools left behind by our earliest ancestors, the connection they give us to people who lived in far distant worlds thousands or even millions of years ago touches something inside us. Much as we look at the stars and feel a speck in the enormity of the universe, when we find ourselves face to face with the real physical world of our ancestors we can't help but wonder about our place in a great story which lies beyond our own lives.

We don't know if Neanderthals wondered about their place in the cosmos or sought explanation for their existence, but evidence from Neanderthal burials and from what we can gather from their brains suggest that they did. A need to understand who we are may date back at least half a million years, meaning that origin myths and explanatory stories will have been told around campfires for millennia after millennia. I'm sure that, like Greek myths or aboriginal dreamtime tales, these ancient explanations were colourful stories which held within them many important messages about how to negotiate the complex emotional worlds we build up with other people.

Only in the last two hundred years of our existence, the most recent moments of our time on earth, have we as a species been faced with the reality of our pasts and uncovered real objects we know to have been made by early humans. But what we find often seems a world away from engaging fantasies. At best, the real lives of our ancestors appear to us in nuggets of evidence, mostly discarded parts of everyday lives, tiny fragments of a larger picture which we piece together into the best explanation we can, despite the missing pieces. Unlike in myths or stories where we are free to imagine things the way we would like them to be, what we know about *people* can't be assumed or invented, and even less so the further back in time we travel and the more alien the people we meet become. Of course, the archaeological evidence for our real origin story appeals to us because of its promise of *hard truth*. Yet unlike the explanations we would like to find or stories we could invent, it is much more *gritty* and each new discovery is almost always a challenge to what we think we know, rarely if ever fitting in with what we would *like* to believe about ourselves. We are never quite sure if we want the past to tell us how innately good *we* are, how bad *they* were,

14

or how much better *we* have become and how far this colours what we say.

Thirty years later when I returned to Rouffignac cave much appeared to have changed. The gift shop sold many more knick-knacks and the toilets were newly tiled and sparkling. After many years of reading and research, not to mention writing my own books and papers, I had changed too. At least now I understood most of the conversations around me and was no longer so small as to be squashed. Now I was here as a specialist myself, visiting on a tour after a conference on human evolution. Of course I was still a bit nervous of the dark, that much never changed, and I still gritted my teeth to cover that up – heaven forbid that my learned colleagues would see me whimper. But when we reached the same spot the mammoths were exactly the same as they had been when I was a child, the same as they had been for thousands of years and will be, we assume, for many thousands of years to come. Once again, I still stood and wondered, and pondered who I was in the enormity of time, feeling that I could almost touch the hand of the painter it was so real. I still felt there was something to learn, but wasn't sure quite what. In this volume I'd like to take you with me on a journey to try to find out what the evidence from our distant past can tell us about who we are.

John Frere included an illustration of a particularly elegant handaxe in his letter to the Society of Antiquaries in 1797. The form of the handaxe had convinced him that it must have been made by human hands – people who must have lived in a very remote period from our own.

Chapter One

Origin Stories

Stories do not tell us what to do, externally, but transform who we are, internally. And the most powerful, or perhaps the most complex and ambiguous, or perhaps again the most flexible, of these stories become ... a vibrating string which sets in motion a hundred harmonic frequencies whose connections have been built up over many generations.[1]

Here we introduce the archaeological evidence as the hard 'truth' about our ancestors. However, archaeological discoveries rarely fit into the picture we would like to have of early humans and what we want to believe about what makes us 'human'. The interpretations which appear to fit into how we see ourselves can be given pride of place even when there are obvious problems with the inferences on which they are based. We follow this narrative through – from biblical versions that were believed despite the earliest finds of stone tools, to ideas which ignored the similarities between apes and humans; to the Piltdown, skull which was accepted as an ancestor because of its large brain; to the 'killer apes' theory accepted after the Second World War. Lastly, we consider how our current interpretations of human origins emphasise the efficiency and economic self-interest so highly regarded in our present-day culture.

Most societies have had the good fortune to feel comfortable about what it means *to be human*. Myths and legends made the world an understandable place. The actions of spirits or gods explained why the world was the way it was and what caused inexplicable things to happen. While these explanations might not have been *right*, they allowed us to get on with our lives without worrying about what we, as humans, were doing here.

Discoveries during the early nineteenth century were to shatter these comfortable beliefs and call into question where we came from, and why.[2] The uncovering of artefacts from what was to be called the 'Stone Age' marked the beginning of a long journey of self-discovery.

A find of a handaxe in sediments at Hoxne in Suffolk by John Frere in 1787 first sparked a debate as to its origins.[3] A few such finds could be ignored but during the first few decades of the nineteenth century flint tools in ancient layers were discovered alongside extinct animals more and more frequently. Such finds were a challenge – they must have been made by human hands, and seemed to call into question the accepted biblical story of human history. Were these really the work of peoples living thousands of years ago? What could these savages have been like? Early geologists were both awed and disturbed by such finds. Charles Lyell wrote:

> No subject has lately excited more curiosity and general interest among geologists and the public than the question of the Antiquity of the Human Race, – whether or no we have sufficient evidence in caves, or in the superficial deposits commonly called drift or 'diluvium,' to prove the former co-existence of man with certain extinct mammalia. For the last half-century, the occasional occurrence, in various parts of Europe, of the bones of Man or the works of his hands, in cave-breccias and stalagmites, associated with the remains of the extinct hyæna, bear, elephant, or rhinoceros, has given rise to a suspicion that the date of Man must be carried further back than we had heretofore imagined. On the other hand, extreme reluctance was naturally felt, on the part of scientific reasoners, to admit the validity of such evidence.[4]

Finding stone tools made by humans so clearly deposited alongside extinct animals might seem to us to be pretty conclusive evidence for the 'antiquity' of humans. At the time, however, it was difficult to overturn comfortable accepted wisdom for an idea so new and challenging. Anyone holding in their hands a handaxe, found deep in sediments alongside bones of animals such as mammoths, couldn't help but recognise a deeply subversive idea forming in their mind about where we had come from. It wasn't a welcome idea to voice.

For a while the 'Stone Age' was uncomfortably – and to our minds, slightly bizarrely – slotted into biblical chronologies. Debate over the 'Great Antiquity of Man' and how it could, or could not, be fitted into a biblical timescale raged on for many decades. The biblical flood might explain extinct animals, but what of the flint tools? Human bones associated with ancient animals were explained as coincidental. In 1824

Paul Buckland commented: 'the human bones are not of the same antiquity as those of the antediluvian animals that occur in the same caves with them.'[5] Even the first find of a Neanderthal in the 1820s, a species clearly *not human*, had done nothing to move the debate forward. Of course, the find, from Engis Caves in Belgium, was of a child's cranium and so was assumed to be unimportant. Such remains of Neanderthal children, often seen as insignificant compared with those of adults, have sometimes even been lost in museums.

Only by the 1860s did the sheer depth of sediments under which such tools were found and the range of animals they were found with become commonly accepted proofs of antiquity beyond that of the Bible. For the first time in human history the story of human origins became *an unexplained mystery*. There was little to go on except a few flint tools and perhaps the biology of ourselves and other species. Without myths or biblical narratives how might we imagine our ancestors or fit ourselves into a satisfying tale? What did these ancestors look like? Most particularly, how did they behave? Our desire to find out what marked ourselves as different could no longer be filled with stories and the mid nineteenth century was a worrying time. The very meaning of *being human* was up in the air.

Illustrations in Huxley's 1864 volume, Evidence as to Man's Place in Nature *demonstrated the relationship between humans and the other apes.*

GIBBON   ORANG   CHIMPANZEE   GORILLA   MAN

Science began to replace religion with answers that were not at all popular or comfortable. Indeed, so bizarre was the scientific explanation for the origins of humanity that few could be blamed for deciding to ignore or ridicule what scientists were saying. Our biology seemed to indicate that we were related to apes. Thomas Huxley's *Evidence as to Man's Place in Nature* (1864) illustrated in detail the clear anatomical similarities between humans and apes. While Darwin was entranced by the familiarity of the expressions of orang-utans in London Zoo, feeling convinced of our relationship to them, Queen Victoria preferred not to look – she found orang-utans 'disagreeably human'.

Darwin was mocked for arguing that humans were related to other apes – a cartoon published in the Hornet in 1871 portrayed him as an orang-utan.

Discussion of not just a relationship with apes but our evolution *from an ape ancestor* could hardly have met an audience less willing to sully their polite society with such an association. Darwin's 1859 volume, *On The Origin of Species*, and later 1871 volume. *The Descent of Man*, were more than contentious. Though eventually the evidence for our biological affinity to other apes could no longer be swept under the carpet, this was not before Darwin had been ridiculed in the press and in popular cartoons for his apparently bizarre ideas. We really don't like stories which don't fit with what *we feel must be right* about human evolution.

The final acceptance of our evolution *from apes* might have been a significant point, but there was as yet no real answer to why we evolved and who we evolved from.

What had happened *in between* ancestral apes and humans? Why were the other apes still eating leaves and picking parasites off each other while we sit in tea shops making polite conversation over cakes, or travel around the whole world collecting more and more knowledge? What spark made us human, and when did it occur?

The search for an explanation of human origins was to become a journey of dead ends, false assumptions, impassioned debate and careers made and lost. This was a story where preconceptions very often overrode the evidence, driven on by the pervading idea that there must be *some* predominent explanation that got us where we are today. That explanation, however, needed to be one we felt comfortable with. While fame and fortune lay ahead for someone with proof of what we wanted to be told, if Darwin was anything to judge by, ridicule was heaped on those with explanations – however correct – that we didn't like.

By the beginning of the twentieth century, substantial advancement was promised for the scientist who would fill the rather uncomfortable gap in the story of what made us human. Little was known about the so-called 'missing link', but it was felt that there were at least some things that could be reliably assumed. Given that our intelligence was acclaimed as marking us out from other animals, the missing link must have a large brain. Moreover, given the apparent supremacy of Europe within the nations of the world this 'Dawn Man' must be found in Europe.

It was with great acclaim that in 1912 Charles Dawson struck gold. He had found a fragmentary skull of a human-like ape from Piltdown in East Sussex. Piltdown fitted what was expected – a European ancestor (where else would humanity have evolved?) with a large brain but

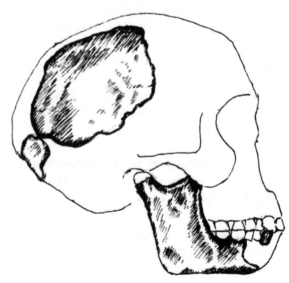

The Piltdown forgery, a simple combination of fragments of orang-utan jaw, chimpanzee teeth and human skull fragment, fooled science for decades.

otherwise ape-like characteristics. Outcompeting any of the apparently spurious evidence emerging from Africa of human-looking apes with small brains, Piltdown dominated the narrative of human evolution.

The Piltdown story left palaeoanthropologists who were working on early human remains in Africa struggling to gain acceptance. Some of the great names in palaeoanthropology, such as Louis and Mary Leakey, working in Olduvai Gorge where the African Rift valley exposed sediments several millions of years old, were beginning to reveal exciting finds. But sceptical audiences were convinced that human origins really ought to be in Europe and that humans really should have had the brains which showed that they 'thought human' before they looked it. Small-brained 'Olduvai Man', found by Louis Leakey in 1913, did not impress the scientific community. How could a small-brained ape from Africa be part of the story of human success?

'Piltdown Man' was, of course, a forgery and not even a good one. Yet Piltdown *fitted the expectations of the time*. The skull was a relatively simple combination of a human skull, orang-utan jaw and chimpanzee teeth, one of the most remarkable hoaxes in science.[6] It is still not certain who of the many possible candidates was responsible for the forgery, and it is even possible that Sir Arthur Conan Doyle, creator of Sherlock Holmes, was involved. Certainly, in its exploitation of the extent to which human imagination can override the evidence, to create our convictions it was entirely fitting. What was extraordinary was not its production, but forty years of uncritical acceptance. Piltdown had the advantage over 'real' human remains being found in Africa in that it fitted what was expected – an ape that would first become 'clever' and then afterwards become human-looking and, moreover, it came from Britain – a fine illustration of how we can be remarkably blind to things that we don't really want to see.

Once fossils of small-brained apes from Africa were finally, if regretfully, accepted as key to the human story, discoveries by people like Louis and Mary Leakey in Africa would build up our knowledge of what our real ancestors were like. Several human-like apes were recovered and the debates moved to whose fossil lay on the path to humanity, and whose was a sideshoot destined for extinction. Palaeoanthropology moved to passionate discussions about which of the many different ancestors were really 'us' and though there was little to go on, *what they were like*.

Despite the lessons of Piltdown, deep-seated preconceptions were never as removed from the science of human origins as we might have hoped. With a fossil record notoriously poor at giving us what we wanted, and while Piltdown was a deliberate slight of hand, the *power of conviction* could be equally as misleading.

A tendency to see what we think ought to be there was perhaps never best illustrated than in the story of Raymond Dart's *Osteodontokeratic culture* and his interpretation of its meaning for human nature. Dart was the key figure working on cave sites in South Africa in the 1920s. He began to discover early human-like ape remains preserved in cave sediments and was particularly famous for discovering the 'Taung child'. This specimen was a well preserved child's cranium belonging to a species of human-like ape that he called the australopithecines (or southern man-apes), which dated to around 3 million years ago. The australopithecines were tiny in stature and had small brain sizes, not so different from those of chimpanzees. They had bodies and brains that spoke 'ape', as well as long arms and curved fingers, but they also showed a number of human-like features of the face, such as a reduced set of canine teeth in comparison to other apes, and a rather flattened face shape. Most importantly, the australopithecines walked upright on two legs.

Dart describes finding the skull of the Taung child in boxes of fossils sent to him from the excavations:

> Even for an ape it was a big bulging brain and, most important, the forebrain was so big and had grown so far backward that it completely covered the hindbrain. But was there anywhere among this pile of rocks, a face to fit the brain? I ransacked feverishly through the boxes. My search was rewarded, for I found a large stone with a depression into which the cast fitted perfectly ... I stood in the shade holding the brain as greedily as any miser hugs his gold, my mind racing ahead. Here I was certain was one of the most significant finds ever made in the history of anthropology. Darwin's largely discredited theory that man's early progenitors probably lived in Africa came back to me. Was I to be the instrument by which his 'missing link' was found?[7]

Dart's australopithecine bones seemed all the more convincing for being surrounded by heavily fragmented animal bones, largely of gazelle which had apparently been sharpened to points – good early evidence, Dart surmised, as something that marked them as different.

Dart proposed that he had found the first human 'culture', dating to around 3 million years old. This was quite a turning point, and he called it the *Osteodontokeratic* or 'bone, tooth and horn' culture. He was struck by how effectively the sharpened bones, associated with his southern ape remains, would have been used as weapons. As he studied the bone remains in detail he came across finds of ancient baboons with characteristic depressed fractures on their skulls and similar fractures on those of the australopithecines skulls. This evidence rather chilled Dart as he realised that his early apes must have used their bone tools to kill not only baboons but also *each other*. These early humans stood out, it seemed to Dart, and set the pathway for the future of humanity, through a combination not only of intelligence and a capacity to think technologically, but also of aggression, and the use of technology to kill. He was looking into the face of a killer.

Holding the tiny Taung child in his hand, Raymond Dart saw the face of a killer.

In the same year that Piltdown was finally exposed as a forgery, 1953, Dart published his paper about the australopithecines and their role in the 'predatory transition from ape to man', no longer hampered by the assumption that human origins were in Europe. In the aftermath of the two world wars, with their abundant evidence for a human capacity for death and destruction, Dart's interpretations and the 'killer ape theory' fitted the mood of the time. The innately violent ape replaced the innately clever ape as our imagined ancestor. Australopithecines were real, but the story around the bones found beside them and their place in the world came more from what Dart believed should be there.

Origin stories have a tremendous power. Dart's killer apes were reflected in popular media, reinforcing the link between archaeological theory and contemporary culture which went well beyond the rather limited evidence.

Robert Ardrey, inspired by Dart, wrote in 1961 in his *African Genesis*:

Man had emerged from the anthropoid background for one reason only: because he was a killer. Long ago, perhaps many millions of years ago, a line of killer apes branched off from the non-aggressive primate background. For reasons of environmental necessity, the line adopted the predatory way. For reasons of predatory necessity the line advanced. We learned to stand erect in the first place as a necessity of the hunting life. We learned to run in our pursuit of game across the yellowing African savannah. Our hands freed for the mauling and the hauling, we had no further use for a snout; and so it retreated. And lacking fighting teeth or claws, we took recourse by necessity to the weapon. A rock, a stick, a heavy bone – to our ancestral killer ape it meant the margin of survival. But the use of the weapon meant new and multiplying demands on the nervous system for the co-ordination of muscle and touch and sight. And so at last came the enlarged brain; so at last came man ... that remarkable killer, Australopithecus africanus, the last animal before man ... our last direct ancestor in the animal world ... Man is a predator with an instinct to kill and a genetic cultural affinity for the weapon.[8]

Ardrey appealed to our sense of drama in his style of writing, though it is also hard to ignore that in many ways it is also rather appealing to think that our ancestors were so powerful and rather ruthless, elevated by their clever minds and aggressive instincts to a place of invulnerability above other animals. It is like finding that one is descended from a famous and influential figure; aggressively powerful ape ancestors make a good story.

The killer ape theory would also become part of a box office hit: *2001: A Space Odyssey*. In the opening scene of the film we see ancestral apes living in harmony with nature – vegetarians, they mingle among other animals searching for roots for food. However, after encountering and touching a black monolith (which in Arthur C Clarke's novel is sent by an alien race to help other species take key evolutionary steps), they realise that bones can be used as weapons. They batter an ape from a neighbouring group to death, and in jubilation throw up the bone, as the scene cuts to a future of space travel. The chilling implication was that propensity and capacity for violence appeared to be at the heart of what made us human.

Good stories which gel with our ideas about who we wish we were should really ring alarm bells in the field of human origins.

Certainly something didn't quite seem right with the killer ape theory, not to mention the worrying idea that 'innate aggression' might easily be used as an excuse for harming others. For one thing there was little to physically suggest that these apes *were* much different to any other ape, especially since australopithecines had similar brain sizes to chimpanzees. Moreover, any reconstructions of these early ape-humans cannot help but demonstrate that these were quite diminutive and vulnerable creatures. Indeed, australopithecines were not only tiny – only about three feet in height – but they had no natural defences, such as the claws or piercing teeth normally seen in predators. What's more, not only the australopithecines, but their earlier ancestors, such as the ardipithecines living around 4 to 5 million years ago, already had much smaller canine teeth (those usually used in aggressive encounters) than ancestral apes. It isn't easy to imagine how such primates could possibly attempt to compete with the savannah predators like the sleek big leopards or lions or packs of hyenas. Indeed, early human-like apes retained a compromise in their anatomy between the efficiencies of walking on two legs against the long arms and curved fingers that allowed them to still easily climb up and hang from trees. Physically, australopithecines don't evoke any sense of 'predator'. It is hard to ignore that they clearly needed to climb trees, which smacks a great deal more of the importance of 'getting away' than Dart was suggesting.

Killer ape theory had its period of influence, but by the 1970s and 1980s the time was up for Dart's killer southern apes. A series of researchers, including Sherwood Washburn and Bob Brain, were to demonstrate what might have been obvious, that Dart's weapons of sharpened bone were not actually made by humans. Bob Brain of the Transvaal Museum in South Africa carried out a careful study of how bone deposits in caves formed and carefully examined assemblages of modern bones that had been chewed and broken by carnivores. He demonstrated that hyenas trampling and crushing bones which they had brought back to their dens would produce 'artefacts' exactly like Dart's weapons. Also, the depressions which Dart had noticed in his baboon and human skulls matched those made by the teeth and jaws of large cats when they dragged away their prey. With no tools or weapons, and bearing clear tooth marks on their skulls from predators, it rapidly became clear that these early human-like apes were not the hunter-killers they had appeared to be. Far from it. Dart's southern apes were 'the hunted'.[9] Once again there was a challenge we had to face about ourselves – if Darwin's connection between humans and apes was rather humbling, the conclusion that 3 million years ago we were not the lords of the savannah but a tasty chunk of cat food was even more so. The explanation which might have been staring palaeontologists in the face had gone unnoticed in a wave of certainty about how humans *should* be.

Why were we so willing to believe in a brutal and violent ancestry on the basis of so little evidence, none of which would stand up to scrutiny? Many people believe it was the profound influence of the First and Second

World Wars which led Raymond Dart to see the evidence in front of him in a certain way. Perhaps unsurprisingly, viewing the horrors of war which were meted out not only on soldiers but on whole populations, women and children included, Dart felt sure that we must be innately aggressive.

The idea that aggression lay at the heart of our human evolutionary journey was left without evidence. The world wars were horrific, yet evidence that we were actually very poor killers had also been there all along. Studies of Second World War combat, as well as that in earlier wars, illustrated that despite the atrocities, it had been remarkably hard to make people kill others. Only 15 to 20 per cent of soldiers had actually fired weapons at the enemy, most preferring to risk their own life. In many cases soldiers would die on the battlefield rather than kill someone else.[10]

Far from the aggressive killers Dart had imagined, it would be at least a million years before Dart's southern apes would even be safe enough in the savannah to lose their adaptations for retreating to climbing and swinging in trees, and even longer before they moved up the food chain to make meat a normal part of their diet.

What set our ancestors on the path to being *human* was now rather up in the air. However, the critical pieces of the jigsaw of human *biological* origins had started to fit together during the 1960s and 1970s. Remarkable finds like Mary Leakey's flared cheekbone 'Zinjanthropus' (found in 1961) and Don Johansen's famous 'Lucy' skeleton (found in 1974) thrilled the world, and illustrated that the australopithecines were only one of a range of varied potential human ancestors – the 'muddle in the middle' of human origins. Indeed, a whole menagerie of potential human ancestors came to light, with different scientists playing the role of 'lumpers' or 'splitters' who attempted to piece together a tricky picture of who was who from fragmentary bone remains and, moreover, how each might fit into the picture of human origins. Putting one's own finds or species in pride of place on the path to humanity was an accepted part of academic endeavour, leading to lively debates and heated conflicts about which species was 'in' the human family and which was 'out'. However, what the 'missing link' *looked like* was still a much clearer picture than how they *behaved*.

The best clues came from the emergence of the first true 'archaeological sites'. Here, at sites like Olduvai Gorge and Koobi Fora in the Rift Valley, plate tectonics had pulled apart the landscape to expose sediments many millions of years old. Careful and meticulous excavation of deposits dating to around 2 million years ago by famous palaeoanthropologists Louis and Mary Leakey led to the recovery of what were more clearly *legitimate* deliberately manufactured tools made of stone, which were also associated with butchered animal bones.

From the earliest direct evidence for how early humans actually behaved, one species seemed to be most associated with the presence of early stone tools, and in light of this, *Homo habilis* (handy man) was first recognised in 1962 as the first true 'human'. 'Handy man' became the significant turning point in human origins as an interest in the australopithecines declined and sites in East Africa became the focus of attention.

The first true humans clearly made tools, albeit rather crude pebble tools, and were using them to butcher carcasses and eat meat from animals like gazelle and antelope. The use of humanly made tools to a *certain design* seemed an important indication of humanity, particularly in the 1960s era of space travel and excitement about the significance of human technological achievements. More than this, however, the combination of stone tools and animal bones seemed good evidence that humans had risen above other animals in the food chain, and had reached a certain dominance of the landscape, moving stone tools and animal carcasses together in an organised way. This stone-based 'Oldowan' culture, and not Dart's spurious interpretation of bones as weapons, was surely the mark of 'Man the Hunter' (and not a moment too soon).

Could we now, with real archaeological evidence, piece together what early humans were like, and what feature of their lives marked them out as special?

The most notable of the archaeologists who now set about telling a rather different story of what these first 'sites' meant about human behaviour was Glynn Isaac. Isaac paid particular attention to the patterns in the accumulations of animal bones and stone excavated by the Leakeys and the similarities he saw to the sites left by modern hunter-gatherers. In particular, sites like DK1 at Olduvai, with bones and stones distributed in a clear circle, caught his attention. These places, he reasoned, were *homes* and it was these home environments – where people were social beings and where vulnerable offspring were carefully nurtured – which turned protohumans into humans. Humans, he suggested, were special not only because they made tools and were clever, but because they worked together, or rather specifically because they divided tasks between men and women. Men went out hunting (or at the very least scaring top predators away from big carcasses) and brought meat back in order to provision females and young (who collected plant foods). This was certainly a far less aggressively focused interpretation of early humans and one that put collaboration, rather than killing each other, as key to humanity. Isaac's *home base hypothesis* became popular in a new 1970s climate of optimism about humanity.[11]

Many of the critical elements of Isaac's home base hypothesis remain valid today. Certainly most would agree that *collaboration* rather than constant and brutal conflict is a much better explanation for how early humans foraged for meat, protected themselves from savannah carnivores and raised vulnerable young. However, Isaac was far from free from the perceptions of the time and needed to create a comfortable story which didn't overly challenge the status quo.

Once again, what should be obvious had been missed because of the certainty that home bases *felt right*. Simply a better understanding of what happens to animal carcasses on the savannah put the Oldowan sites in a new light. Lewis Binford, famous proponent of processual archaeology, carried out detailed research, following on from that of Bob Brain, into *taphonomic processes* – how faunal remains and artefacts end up as part of 'sites'. He considered how hyenas and other carnivores kill or scavenge carcasses, and what those bone remains would look like, as well as examining the structure of carnivore dens and other ways in which bones came to be deposited, such as via natural stream channels. In his classic 1981 volume, *Bones, Ancient Men and Modern Myths*, Binford argued that a few of the so-called 'sites' (or homes) were not really real archaeological sites at all.[12] Like Dart's *Osteodontokeratic* culture, some so-called sites turned out simply to be natural accumulations. In most sites identified by Isaac, humans *had* played a role but Binford argued that they were not the primary agents, but the final scavengers arriving last to carcasses after the lions, hyenas and vultures had already had their pickings, using their stone tools to smash long bones to get at the fatty bone marrow. Any apparent pattern to the distributions was more plausibly explained as the effect of tree roots, movement by running water or other natural processes. Indeed, DK1 was much more plausibly explained as a concentration of material affected by the roots of a tree rather than any kind of structure. There was now no good evidence for the existence of homes, nor access to the quantities of meat that might have been worth bringing to them.

What about the accumulations of bones and stones? Even if they were only scavenging for leftover morsels of meat, were early humans not making these places particular to them, safe homes to return to? Careful analysis by Richard Potts illustrated that sites need not mean homes.[13] Though having larger 'mental maps' than chimpanzees, early humans had not so much created a home as simply remembered where the nearest stone tools were and returned back to them when they were needed. Using models of behaviour developed from economics, Potts illustrated, moreover, that coming back to the same place each day was not only a waste of time and effort but it was really not a sensible thing to do as it also meant hanging around carcasses in a savannah full of predators. The last place one would want to be with a vulnerable child was near to a fresh carcass. In a climate of growing recognition of the bewildering array of human species in Africa at the time, Potts's *resource transport model* not only clearly reflected the economic ideas at its heart, but also a growing acceptance that early human behaviour might be substantially more complicated to interpret than any watered down version of the activities of recent hunter-gatherers.

Some evidence, such as stone cutmarks on animal bones created *before* carnivore gnaw marks, illustrated that early humans were occasionally rather higher up the scavenging ladder, and many palaeoanthropologists reflected that Binford may have gone a bit far. A later theory put forward by Rose and Marshall, the *Resource Defence model*,[14] was to suggest that early humans might have defended carcasses that they had encountered. There may have been significant evolutionary selection pressures on early humans to be able to work together to scare off big carnivores and so exploit valuable marrow rather than having to run away if they approached. They might even have used tools to defend themselves, for instance, hurling cobbles, much as modern chimpanzees throw sticks in intimidation displays. Classic *home bases* were out, however, and a rather marginal scavenging by early humans who were making the best use of the carcasses quickly replaced them. Isaac's home bases were subject to the kind of ridicule that Darwin had endured in popular cartoons.

While much of Isaac's theory, particularly the importance of collaboration and food-sharing, remains the main explanation for early human behaviour, his enthusiasm about *homes*, *hunting* (or primary scavenging) and *men provisioning women* now looked like a naive version of modern social values superimposed on the past. What seemed to be sensible interpretations at the time had been shot down once again. Archaeologists had had their fingers burned by bringing to the public the apparent 'truth' about ourselves only to look faintly ridiculous later when the rug of evidence was pulled out from beneath them.

After the theories involving Piltdown, killer apes, and early human male providers and female homemakers, most archaeologists became cautious of any grand stories and focused on safer and specific areas of knowledge. Subsistence practices rose to the fore, with the greatest body of research into early archaeological assemblages being based on cutmarks on bones, the composition of animal remains and the issue of the role and significance of meat in diets, alongside the creation and use of stone tools. Discussions about the 'mind' stayed within safe areas of the thinking or planning skills displayed in the making of stone tools or the transport of raw material from natural outcrops. Motivations and emotions, the things we really wanted to know about our ancestors, were placed firmly in a metaphorical box marked 'do not open'.

Origin stories are powerful and we are right to be cautious. We would love to believe that today we are free from biases, that avoiding interpretations of any grand story keeps us safe from making inferences that are influential and dangerous.

Do we still interpret our ancestors in our own image? Or in our image of what we think is important?

Each year I carry out an experiment with my first year students and ask them to simply imagine a Neanderthal. I've done this experiment with a class of 300 on a joint course, more usually it is a class of 80 to 100 students. Remarkably no one imagines a woman, even though at least half the students themselves are women. Would I have done? Probably not. We all know women must have been there, the species wouldn't have survived without females. No one ever imagines a child either, yet because of life expectancies and demographics, around half of our ancestors any time would have been sub-adult. Perhaps we think our ancestors ought to have been stronger, more competitive, more aggressive – all of our cultural preconceptions about adult men.

I couldn't help but wonder how much it mattered.

There is little escaping a connection between what we think is important today and the possibilities we would accept or imagine for what early humans *could* be. Very often we assume that our ancestors would have been powerful, invulnerable, striding forwards alone, much like the image we see of human evolution – a man walking forwards, getting

32

bigger, stronger and more upright as he goes. Yet evolution, both biologically and socially, has been about groups of people, not all of them strong and powerful.

The last few decades have brought a wealth of new findings to the study of human origins, not just artefacts or the bone remains of our ancestors, but a whole battery of scientific techniques allowing us to map the genetic affinities (and differences) between us. By examining fragments of bone, we have been able to find out what types of food were eaten or understand precisely how tools were used. Despite all this evidence though, I'm not sure that our images of what our ancestors *must have been like* has become any less biased than they were in the last century. It is somewhat sobering that what we *think is either innate*, or *what we believe to be the basis of our success*, is often thus accepted as natural and innate whether or not the evidence is there to support this.

We often see what we want to see and then believe that this is the hard truth.

As a student at Cambridge in the late 1980s and early 1990s, I was soon convinced that any sensitivity I'd had all those years ago to Palaeolithic art had been a childish mistake. Rather than being at the whim of their emotions, Palaeolithic people were widely seen as behaving according to rational, analytical and self-oriented principles, and I'd been wrong to think otherwise. I was in a heady world where both the past and the present were places where opportunities were for the taking by the clever and competitive.

Concepts of the human world as one of a balance of costs and benefits, efforts and pay-offs, undoubtedly lead to major insights. An understanding of the economics of stone tool production explained why particularly good raw materials were often found greater distances from their sources – they had been worth the effort taking them there. That the main period of human brain expansion seemed to coincide with an increased dependence on meat in the diet made sense when we understand that brains were 'costly to produce' and needed more energy-giving foods to support them.

As a young student, however, I also found myself within a grander narrative that was underlying the specific sites. I heard how Neanderthals had died out because they were less efficient than modern humans, and how intelligence and cunning were the basis for human success. As individuality in the 1980s and 1990s took hold, with ideas of healthy competition and survival-of-the-fittest economics, our ancestors followed suit en masse and words like *costs, production, communication* and *economic* system became as much core to the human origins section of the library as in the outside world.

In making early humans rational self-interested actors, academics had emancipated them from their primitive state and made them active players, deserving their place in their world and research funds to study them. It isn't difficult, in the context of Dart's excesses, and Glyn Isaac's somewhat naive optimism, to see the appeal of founding our principles of early behaviour on emotionless principles of rational self-interest. Weighing up direct costs and benefits in an economic approach to behaviour has been safe, free from the dangers of rampant emotions, be they cruel or caring, and intuitively more scientific and right.

However, little by little in our imaginations early humans lost their soul.

What made humans successful came to be seen as neither the result of aggressive tendencies nor the existence of caring ones, but self-interested competition. Our ancestors were those with more practical communication skills and economic abilities to exploit new resources, and with the capacities to use flexible strategies when faced with risk. The development of our abilities to understand others became predicated on 'Machiavellian intelligence' (the ability to deceive others for one's own ends). Even the most complex and apparently the most sensitive of human behaviours tended to be seen in the apparently safe light of rational economic self-interest. Palaeolithic art was now explained as a means of *information gathering*, communicating knowledge about hunting practices.[15] The emergence of finely made decorative beads and shells transported along vast distances as our ancestors entered Europe is seen as part of an economic system of exchanging symbolic objects for obligations to help.[16] Kindness or caring, or being driven by any of our troublesome emotions became weaknesses. Our ancestors could no more have survived with such sensitivities as could top management executives or politicians. Early humans embraced the spirit of individualism almost as heartily as Margaret Thatcher had in maintaining that there was 'no such thing as society'.

Even if early humans had feelings, no one in their right mind would suggest that that such feelings were worthy of study or that emotions might have been important in our evolutionary story.

Was this calculated rational self-interest the 'scientific truth' about what our ancestors were like, or in our imaginations?

Were we once again seeing our ancestors in our own image? Could it be our own societies which were unusually rationally self-interested? Recent lines of research suggest that we might be. Anthropologists studying a range of different cultures came to the conclusion that those of us who are Western, Educated, Industrialised, Rich and Democratic are WEIRD in nature as much as in name. They found that we were far more analytical in our relationships with others, and far less likely to give without expecting anything back than people in other societies.[17] That's worrying. What's more, we aren't born that way. Two-year-olds are remarkably altruistic, most happy to help out someone who needs a hand.[18] As they get older in our societies they become more suspicious, reigning themselves in from motivations to help.

Was it *our societies* – rather than something innate to humanity – which made people more selfish and less trusting?

How fare are people influenced by belonging to a culture assumed to be based on rational self-interest. Robert Frank from Cornell University argues that they were. He first discovered the effect when considering how trust works to allow people to cooperate together. Frank was interested in the role of moral emotions as 'commitment devices' that gave a guarantee of future collaboration even if the costs become high or other alternatives more profitable (something we will return to in Chapter eight). In his 1988 volume, *Passions within Reason: The Strategic Role of the Emotions*, he illustrated how social emotions work to sustain in-depth collaboration precisely because they *prevent us* from thinking about relationships with people we are close to in rational self-interested terms.[19] He was shocked to find that though trusting others 'pays off', not only in an economic but in an emotional sense, an increasing tendency to see relationships in self-interested terms of cost and benefit meant that students of economics become progressively *worse* at trusting others the longer that they studied. Being surrounded in their mind by *models* of unemotional and self-interested people made them begin to believe that others really won't 'care', and if this is true then it isn't worth trusting people or being generous.

Was this just confined to students of economics? Research suggests not. The proportion of people who say that they generally trust other people dropped from 60 per cent in 1959 to 30 per cent in 2005 and it continues to decline.[20] Moreover, the effects of seeing a rational economic view of others as *natural* range from the obvious to the subtle. Simply by giving our children a scale on which they might be measured in terms of being intelligent, even if we tell them that they are 'smart', we turn them into a quantity, a fixed measure, which has a far-reaching effect on them.[21]

It seems as though what we believe about human nature changes us in profound ways.

Is it possible to see early humans outside of the modern lens which assumes a self-oriented perspective? Certainly rational self-interest as an explanation for human success has become deeply entrenched. I'd put away my thoughts about the Rouffignac mammoths very early in my career, and though posters of Palaeolithic art followed me from student rooms to offices, around Britain and Argentina, I focused on modelling environmental changes and safe analytically based calculations and interpretations. It would be many years before I'd look once again at Palaeolithic art and start to research the role of emotions in human evolution.

In 2010 I published a paper which reviewed the evidence for caring behaviour in early humans with two of my graduate students, making suggestions for the evolution of human capacities for compassion.[22] Jean-Jacques Hublin from the Max Planck Institute in Leipzig published a comment in a similar vein at approximately the same time.[23] The idea proved to be far more heretical than we had thought. In 2012 a key journal published an article which stated that these ideas were 'contentious for reasons the authors do not appear to understand' (which is academic speak for 'plain stupid'). Early humans, the reasoning goes, ought to be seen as innocent of any emotional motivations (particularly kindness, which smacks of weakness) until proven without doubt to be guilty of them. The alternative unemotional self-interest explanations for their care were that sick people were kept alive because others had calculated that they might be useful to them in the future. Self-interested rational logic was seen as *the truth* which had to be proved wrong beyond any doubt before anyone could consider that early humans were capable of feeling. It stood to reason that cold-hearted calculations of others' costs and benefits must have been the basis for human evolutionary success, and was felt to be blindingly obvious to any but the most cognitively challenged. A few years later, this research is still considered by many to be too contentious to even put forward for evaluation, not because of the content, the quality, how it was argued or the evidence used *but* because the subject itself was considered off-limits. I found that simply raising the issue of compassion or kindness in our early ancestors, and the scientific perspective on why it might have been important in our success, was considered by many to be *deeply subversive*.

Was there a very different story of human origins that had been waiting to be told?

*In a 3-million-year-old bone gnawed
by hyenas, Raymond Dart saw a
sharpened weapon.*

Chapter Two

The Killer Ape?

All knowledge is partial, infinitesimally partial. Reason is a net thrown out into an ocean. What truth it brings in is a fragment, a glimpse, a scintillation of the whole truth. [24]

Here we review evidence for violence and aggression in human origins, from the relatively limited evidence for violence in very early periods to clearer evidence for brutality in our own species. We consider violence in modern hunting and gathering populations and the difficulties in interpreting what violence means. Was violence in the prehistoric past more complex than simple aggression?

Was our prehistoric past a relentlessly harsh existence where only the ruthless survived?

For Raymond Dart it was an instinct for aggression which seemed the most obvious contender for marking out humanity. Bones split by hyena gnawing looked to him like sharpened weapons, the sign of killer apes. Thinking ourselves into a world full of dangerous predators and scarce resources, it isn't difficult to see how the aggression he imagined might pay off. It seems only to make sense that the strongest, most aggressive, most competitive might survive and the weak and vulnerable might not.

There is certainly little doubt that life for our ancestors was often difficult and survival far from guaranteed. Most of the bones of early humans, whether from Dart's australopithecines 3 million years ago or the latest of the Neanderthals around 30,000 years ago, show some evidence for patterns of injury, from breaks on leg or arm bones to more complex injuries. Key skeletons, such as the remarkably complete *Homo erectus*[25] skeleton nicknamed Nariokotome Boy from Kenya, dated to one and a half million years ago, is no exception. This young boy (aged about ten years old) had a dental abscess which probably led to his painful death from septicaemia. It is a familiar pattern with increasing evidence in later periods. Many of the remains of around thirty individuals of the later species related to *Homo heidelbergensis* from Sima de los Huesos, Atapuerca in Spain, dated to around 450,000 years ago, also display impressive injuries.[26] These range from another dental abscess and possible septicaemia to a fractured and deformed pelvis, to head injuries seen on three of the skulls. The most recent species before ourselves, the latest archaic human species the *Neanderthals*, show the highest levels of trauma of all, with most skeletons displaying injuries to the upper body.[27] One Neanderthal skeleton from Shanidar Cave in Iraq had so many injuries resulting in a withered arm, probable blindness in one eye and a damaged leg, it is hard to imagine how he lived at all. Life in the Stone Age must at times have been decidedly painful.

Nor was finding enough food always easy. Studies of the growth patterns on teeth and of areas where the enamel has not formed properly, known as *enamel hypoplasia*, illustrate that food shortages or illnesses were not uncommon. Around a third of the children at Sima de los Huesos had enamel hypoplasia and must have suffered from some form of dietary deficiency, illness or trauma that affected tooth formation,[28] with these effects seen in great numbers in Neanderthal children.[29] It is also common for leg bones to show effects from the wear and tear of a great deal of walking, seen both in Neanderthals and in early examples of our own species.[30] It was even typical to pass through several famines. Studies of the bones of a Neanderthal child found in museum collections of faunal remains from Shanidar Cave in Iraq, for example, showed that the child, aged about four, had suffered a period of stunted growth probably from lack of food at around nine months of age.[31]

It is difficult to imagine how any creature which developed in such difficult conditions would become the same as that which today sits in tea rooms, makes polite conversation, tends gardens or looks after the elderly.

We often hear the phrase that nature is 'red in tooth and claw' and in that frame of mind surely those who are the most willing to defend food or attack others for it would be the most likely to survive? There are certainly indicators that our ancestors were capable of violence towards each other. A Neanderthal from Saint-Césaire in France from around 36,000 years ago, for example, has a convincing head wound on the upper right area of his skull. The fracture to his skull had healed, and doesn't appear to have been severe enough to have caused his death. Computer tomography of the wound shows that it was probably made by a sharp implement – a classic indicator that this unfortunate Neanderthal was hit on the head with a weapon.[32] Similarly, there was projectile point damage on the ninth left rib of another Neanderthal from Shanidar Cave in the Near East. That this Neanderthal may have been 'shot' with a small projectile point, an action typically associated with modern humans, has been used to suggest that it was one of our species, rather than another Neanderthal, who attacked him – a sobering thought.[33]

In the absence of a 'smoking gun', these injuries are the best evidence we might get for violent confrontations in early species of human. Other evidence is more ambiguous and has been interpreted in different ways. Although many adult Neanderthals have a wealth of upper body injuries – indeed, few escaped some nasty knocks to the torso and upper body – these have typically been interpreted as a result of their dangerous hunting methods as they would get close up to large game like rhino or bison with only spears with which to attack or defend themselves. Certainly, the patterns of their injuries match those of rodeo riders, suggesting that close encounters with big game animals caused them.[34] However, Erik Trinkaus from the Department of Anthropology at Washington University has recently suggested that the upper body injuries might be the result of violence between Neanderthals themselves.[35] Others disagree, pointing out that there is little evidence of violence and that Neanderthals lived in small groups at such low population densities it is very unlikely they would ever be territorial.[36]

Some evidence of what might be a sign of aggression in early humans has, however, also provoked intense debate. Cannibalism, or at least the defleshing of other humans, crops up throughout the archaeological record of archaic humans. There have even been suggestions that cannibalism was so common in our ancestors that we have evolved some genetic protection against the prion diseases that may have been passed on through eating human brain tissue,[37] though this remains to be proved

36,000 years ago this Neanderthal from St Cesaire in France had been hit on the hard with a sharp implement which broke through his skull.

conclusively. Butchery and perhaps consumption of other human beings is something most of us find deeply repulsive. Evidence for cannibalism first emerges at the time of the australopithecines[38] and among the best known archaic human species, the Neanderthals, it seems to have been relatively common. At the 'mortuary' sites of L'Hortus in France, for example, the corpses of many Neanderthals were defleshed, perhaps well after death. We assume they were eaten and then deposited in a narrow cleft.[39]

How can we interpret such behaviour? It is remarkably difficult to judge whether eating one's fellows had brutal undertones or was by contrast even the normal way to treat the dead. Cannibalism appears rather 'grisly' as a cultural tradition. Yet the association of cannibalism (or at least defleshing of human corpses) with certain tool types suggests that for some Neanderthals such treatment might have been a cultural convention. There are many ethnographic examples of ritual defleshing of corpses and even cannibalism as a sign of respect, from Fiji to the Amazon basin. The anthropologist Caroline Aubry, for example, has described how cannibalism for the Wari of the Amazon basin was seen as an expression of compassion for the deceased and a means of reaffirming one's connection to close relatives.[40] Deciding what cannibalism *means* for the motivations of archaic humans is one of the areas where our own cultural prejudices make it hard for us to be unbiased. In the Western industrialised world we associate cannibalism with the appalling actions of deranged psychopaths. However, in law it is not the *eating of other humans* which is usually the crime of such people but the murder which precedes it. When we pause to consider where our moral sense comes from it becomes difficult to rationally explain why the cutting up, or even eating, of a human who is already dead, and so not able to suffer, *should* be considered repulsive, even if we might *feel* that it should be. It is probably impossible to be unemotional about cannibalism, but it is difficult to disentangle what seems brutal to us from what might once have been a normal cultural practice.

There are, nonetheless, certain sites where it seems unlikely that cannibalism was respectful. Here it has been more difficult to escape the brutal possibility that other humans were actually killed and eaten like prey. Evidence for such *nutritional cannibalism* comes from the site of Gran Dolina at Atapuerca in northern Spain at around 800,000 years ago. Here the highly fragmented bones of at least six individuals belonging to the species *Homo antecessor* were recovered, interspersed among animal bones and many stone tools. The bone remains, some of the earliest humans found in Europe, were those of two adults, two children aged between three and four years of age, and two adolescents aged between ten and twelve and thirteen and fourteen respectively. The human bones have been broken and cracked to exploit bone marrow and meat has been removed in exactly the same way as the meat has been stripped from the animal bones. In fact, with all the bones piled together, there is nothing to differentiate between the treatment of the two. The excavators find little other sensible explanation for this behaviour than that of nutritional cannibalism, the eating of other humans for food.[41] The age range of the specimens might even suggest that the most vulnerable members of another group have been picked off.

Potential nutritional cannibalism is also found in Neanderthal contexts, including that at Moula-Quercy in France where 100,000 years ago, two Neanderthal adults, two fifteen- or sixteen-year-olds and two six- or seven-year-olds were disposed of in exactly the same way as animals and used for food, with cheek muscles being filleted and skulls cracked to remove the brains and with the bones afterwards discarded alongside debris from butchering animals.[42] Fifty thousand years later at El Sidrón Cave in Spain, another group of Neanderthals who appear to have died in a rock fall were also broken up and cut apart in a way that was typical of how animals were processed for food. Genetic analysis reveals that this small Neanderthal group of twelve individuals were three brothers with females and children[43] – perhaps an entire close-knit family group. As with so much of the archaeological record, we are frustrated by what is missing, as it remains almost impossible to determine who was butchering other humans and why they were doing it. The possibility that at times and places archaic humans saw other humans as prey and a source of nutrition can't help but nudge at our sensibilities. It is difficult to be sure whether such acts were the result of desperate measures in a time of famine, something similar to acts of cannibalism recorded in modern crises, or a common approach to one's neighbours as potential food – something we find hard to imagine.

Chillingly, the only conclusive evidence that other humans were eaten as an act of deliberate and intentional *brutality*, rather than a practical need for sustenance, comes from our own species. At Gough's Cave in Somerset excavations revealed that around 15,000 years ago a group of Upper Palaeolithic humans, biologically identical to ourselves, carried

44

out a rather shocking massacre. They not only dismembered, butchered and ate at least five other people – we assume an enemy group – but also broke the bones from their skulls to make them into drinking vessels.[44] Human remains from at least five people – a child, two adolescents, an adult and an older adult – showed signs of skinning, defleshing and smashing of bones for marrow, and it was even possible to identify the gnaw marks from human teeth on human bones, which is pretty damning evidence for cannibalism. It is hard to escape the probability that this was some gruesome ritual celebration. Whereas we might excuse cannibalism at Atapuerca as an act of an archaic species who saw living human neighbours as food in a time of hunger rather than as feeling beings, Gough's Cave seems far more like a deliberately callous treatment of enemies.

Their action might remind us of cultures such as those in Melanesia or New Guinea which historically sought out human heads as trophies to celebrate their victories. For these people, capturing someone's head meant they might own the soul of the dead person. Even recently, as we shall see in Chapter seven, soldiers in Vietnam routinely took trophies, not only buttons or helmets but often teeth and ears, from massacred bodies of the enemy.[45] The reasons for such actions are doubtless complex, and Joanna Bourke in *An intimate history of killing* paints a picture of a kind of visceral pleasure. Others, however, suggest that by dehumanising victims, soldiers may be trying to resolve the moral tensions and sense of repugnance that they naturally feel at killing a living human being by deliberately seeing them as a mere object.

Evidence for what appears as *deliberate brutality* remains restricted to our own species but can also be found in other contexts. An act of perhaps similar highly symbolic violence has been recorded at Ofnet Cave

A 15,000-year-old skull cup from Gough's Cave in Somerset.

in Germany. Here, we see evidence for what may well have been a brutal massacre eight and a half thousand years ago. Thirty-eight skulls were found neatly arranged in a circle, almost a 'nest of skulls'. The skulls belonged to nineteen children, ten women and only four men. All had been decapitated by sharp blows to the neck, and several had cutmarks, suggesting that they had been scalped.[46] Though some archaeologists have argued that this may have been the result of some kind of ritual, the large proportion of women and children and the rather brutal decapitation and scalping might suggest a lethal raid on a community, perhaps when the men were absent.

Certainly, comparisons have been drawn between the Ofnet skulls and examples of lethal raiding in modern hunting societies. Skeletal remains at Saunaktuk, an Eskimo village in the Canadian Artic, were, like those at Ofnet, also dominated by the bones of women and children, many with injuries suggesting violent death, dismemberment and even cannibalism.

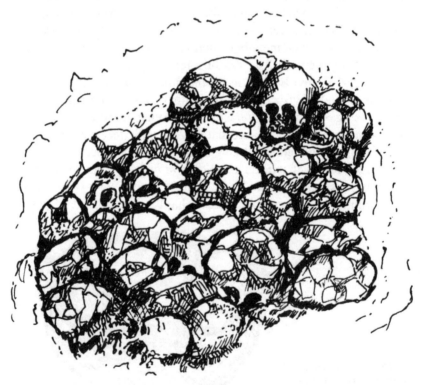

An 8,500-year-old 'nest' of decapitated skulls found at Offnet Cave in Germany.

Art from El Cingle de la Mola Remegia, Spain, showing an archer holding a dead or dying friend, probably 6,500 to 4,000 years old.

In this case, stories by the Inuvialuit explained these remains – it was the result of a vicious attack by rival Dene Indians when most of the men were hunting whales and not at the camp. We can imagine that the explanations for Ofnet might have been something similar had anyone remained to tell the tale.

Isolated cases of interpersonal violence are dotted throughout the Upper Palaeolithic and Mesolithic, with occasional burials of people with arrows in their spine or neck which are difficult to explain other than their having been deliberately shot. At Téviec in Brittany, for example, flint points were found in the spine of an adult male, and at Backaskog and Stora Bjers in Sweden, bone points were found in the chests of several men. We can only wonder at what provoked such an attack, and who these people left behind to mourn them.

One of the most evocative lines of evidence for aggression in our own species comes from the art of the Spanish Levant. Much like the drawings of mammoths at Rouffignac, art from the Mesolithic/early Neolithic of Levantine Spain looks as though it might have been produced yesterday. The message here, however, seems profoundly different. Various scenes are depicted, dating up to 6,500 years ago. Though there are the familiar scenes of animals, interspersed among them are scenes of conflict and violence. Such scenes are exceptional in any early prehistoric period, but within this particular region they are found in a number of caves. In the province of Castellón around the Gasulla and Valltota gorges we see scenes such as those of human executions by archers and in one case, a hanging, as well as scenes of conflict with rival groups armed with bows and arrows opposing each other.[47] The drawing at El Cingle de la Mola Remegia of an archer holding a dead or dying friend or relative particularly brings home the impact of such a kind of violent attack, while at the same time suggesting that the motives for such drawings were not necessarily to glorify feuding.

What can we conclude about violence in our early prehistoric past? Was a state of constant aggression the norm?

Skeletal remains are always rare, and evidence for deliberate violence only occasional. However, where we do find several people who have been killed violently we always wonder if this is an example of early warfare, symptomatic of the nastier side of human nature. Patterns of trauma in Mesolithic cemeteries in the Iron Gates Gorge region of the Danube between Romania and Serbia have been used to suggest that warfare featured highly in these societies for example. Several of the skeletons found in Mesolithic cemeteries of Lepenski Vir, Vlasec, Padina and Hajdučka have traumatic injuries or even arrows within their bones, which point to a violent death.

However, our reactions to the thought of violent encounters can colour our sense of perspective. It seems that violence leaps out at us from an otherwise stable archaeological record and Mirjana Roksandic of the Unversity of Toronto cautions us to put such violence within context. Violence stirs our imagination and attracts our attention, but the actual instances of violent interactions are few and probably represent sporadic conflicts rather than sustained violence within societies. Though arrow points in skeletons from the Iron Gates sites as well as evidence for traumatic injury exist, nearly three hundred skeletons are present in the cemeteries and only two to three per cent of the individuals buried there were victims of violence, certainly not a high enough percentage to justify the idea of constant warfare or even feuding. Much like the evidence from Spain of violence within cave art of a specific region for a specified time which stands out against a more 'usual' record of peace, any feuding at these Iron Gates sites seems to have been localised and short lived.[48] Like the rest of the evidence for violent confrontations in early prehistory, that at the Iron Gates remains relatively rare, certainly compared to what we might expect of Dart's bloodthirsty apes.

Our ancestors were capable of violence. But Raymond Dart's image seems something of an extreme fantasy, an image of raw primal instincts rather than the complex often highly symbolic realities we see archaeologically. The pattern of violence in prehistory certainly provokes us to think, however. If violence is *not everywhere*, but no doubt occurred *sometimes*, why might societies have been more violent in some contexts than others? Are humans naturally violent except where constrained, or naturally peaceful except where under extreme provocation?

The appearance of violence often seems to relate to pressures societies are under. One of these is climate instability, with climatic changes often implicated in the emergence of aggressive confrontations. The higher rates of violence recorded in skeletal remains found at prehistoric sites in the Colorado Plateau of the US, contemporary with the medieval climatic anomaly and period of drought (800 to 1350 AD), seem no concidence.[49] Likewise, violent deaths through projectile wounds affecting around 40 per cent of the skeletons at one of the earliest cemeteries, Jebel Sahaba in the Nile Valley at around 13,000 years ago, have been linked to a period of sudden extreme drought and famine.[50] Here, 40 per cent of fifty-nine burials, men and women alike, showed lethal violence, with projectile points found in their abdomens, back and skulls. It isn't difficult to see how shortages of food might lead to more of a fight for survival than is necessarily the norm.

However, we cannot always rely on climatic conditions as an explanation for violence. Nicolas Peterson of the Australian National University School of Archaeology and Anthropology is convinced that even before colonial contact the lifestyles of some Australian Aboriginal groups, such as the Arunta and the Pintupi, were dominated by bloody feuding.[51] Early photographs always show the men holding huge spears, and anthropological accounts, such as those by Walter Spencer and Francis Gillen in 1901, describe complex feuds where deaths are avenged. While none of the nomadic groups studied were ever recorded as seeking to dominate each other, their firm sense of honour and need to avenge a killing meant that sequences of revenge killings often took place. Even minor slights such as apparent deaths from 'sorcery', which could have been from any cause, or rumours of insults, could lead to a sequence of tit-for-tat

49

killings during which feuding parties travelled great distances to seek out the specific person who was believed to have slighted another or have been responsible for a past death. The anthropologist Fred Myers noted of the Pintupi that no adult man would walk around without his spear. Studies of skeletons in archaeological contexts support the notion that 'honour killings' happened frequently, with, at times, 10 per cent of skeletons showing damage to their arms from defending themselves (so-called 'parry fractures'). While far from a state of 'war', violence in feuding appears to have had an impact on these people's lives and Nicolas Peterson has suggested that 1 in 300 Aboriginal people in the area died in fighting. Many were keen to retreat into early mission houses away from violence.

Getting drawn into a feud was clearly dangerous, and likely to lead to one's own death. We might wonder why anyone would 'get involved' from a practical perspective. However, ethnographic accounts both of Aboriginal people and other societies where lethal feuding occurs illustrate that feuds are about complex concepts such as honour and loyalty to the family. In some cases revenge killings are even seen as being about compassion for the families of the deceased who would supposedly feel better if avenged. Peterson also explains that feuding may have been unusually prevalent among certain Aboriginal groups due to a particular social system of rules dictating marriage which left many men unmarried well into their later years. The average age difference between a wife and her first husband was around twenty years. Many young men were eager to display their courage and were willing to risk their life in bloody feuds, with no need to be concerned for wives or children. Theirs might have been a special case.

Modern and historically recorded hunter-gatherers may provide important clues as to how such peoples might have lived in the past, and about what motivated violence, at least as far as our own species is concerned, but the explanations are clearly not simple nor straightforward, nor easily related to any innate drive to hurt others.

In fact, anthropologists who have study modern nomadic hunting and gathering peoples, such as the Hadza or !Kung of East Africa, Baka of Cameroon or Inuit of Canada and the Arctic, agree that in almost all small-scale hunter-gatherer communities violence is remarkably rare. Feuding is recorded in some small-scale foraging societies, but only rarely so. In many such societies aggression is only rarely recorded with the overriding impression being that nomadic hunting and gathering peoples are actually gentle and non-violent, fiercely believing in sharing, equality and tolerance. For some groups, such as the Piraha of Brazil or the Maniq of Thailand,[52] violence is even documented as unknown. These societies could hardly be more far removed from Dart's bloodthirsty apes.

What explains the contrast between remarkably peaceful societies, and ones where feuds and violent death are more common? Are peaceful hunter-gatherers somehow innately non-aggressive? Anthropologists suggest that the answer may be more complex. For one thing, it may be that violence is something which tends to 'flare up' under certain contexts even if it is only rarely seen normally, and so on the timescales in which societies are studied might never be seen. However, more than this there does seem to be something about the structure of most small-scale foraging societies which keeps aggression firmly under wraps.

Why would nomadic hunter-gatherers live a remarkably peaceful existence? The first clues to the basis of such harmonious lifestyle came from their economic system. Widespread sharing and a firm belief in equality were ubiquitous in hunting societies. Indeed, nomadic hunter-gatherers everywhere believed that everyone is equal and all should be willing give to those in need. Food is always shared, such as meat from a kill, well beyond just their immediate families. This 'sharing ethic' was based on principles according to which anyone who has should give to those who have not, without expecting anything in return.

However much we might be impressed by such principles, from an economic perspective, the widespread sharing, particularly of meat, seems to play an important role in *survival,* perhaps explaining why such principles came to be so widely held. Through widespread sharing to those in need, hunting peoples even out shortfalls, as for each of them sharing what you have now becomes a kind of insurance for the future. Of course, individuals only see sharing as important in moral terms and as part of how things should be. However, when we look at this system with an analytical eye, we can see that it is by giving away food to those in need when they have it, such as just after killing an animal, people become respected and they 'socially store', guaranteeing that as respected and included members of the community they will be provided for in times of need. Given the vagaries of climate, resources and illness, such times of need are often just around the corner. Even the fittest and most able – the adult males – among the Ache of Paraguay were unable to hunt due to illness or injury around a third of the time and then found themselves dependent on others.[53]

Polly Weissner, working with the Jo'huansi, measured the amount of food which was given away or shared, and how much people relied on sharing to support them.[54] Of 297 meals eaten by eight families at Xamsa village between July 1996 and January 1997, 197 were provided by others families or included contributions from others. Such social storage even works *between* bands, with people able to depend on distant friends as an essential back-up in times of large-scale famine. In a time of food shortages following high winds and the destruction of the mongongo nuts in /Xai/xai, for example, half of the population moved in with distant exchange partners and would not have survived if this social support was not possible.

High degrees of 'give and take' make hunter-gatherers much more resilient to the whims of nature. In fact, it was probably not just a flair for making new technologies, but also such interdependence between and across groups which allowed our own species to occupy difficult and risky environmental extremes, such as desert fringes or the frozen Arctic. It isn't difficult to see how such a system would discourage anyone from falling out with neighbours – the very people who may one day be holding your life in their hands.

Nomadic hunter-gatherers also have many means of resolving conflicts before any potential violence, thereby stopping a fall-out from becoming a fight. The most obvious is that everyone can move to another group or 'vote with their feet' whenever they like; the most common way to cool off a dispute is just for the parties involved to avoid each other. Of course, serious conflicts (often arising over sexual jealousies) sometimes require other mechanisms to resolve them. Someone may step in to adjudicate, but there are other, perhaps surprising mechanisms. A set of traditions commonly called 'ritualised conflict' exist in many societies to prevent any conflict from spreading to a larger feud. The anthropologist Asen Balicki noted, for example, that the Netsilik have a form of ritual fighting in which they take it in turns to hit each other over the head until one gives in, after which the fight is all over. Other groups have an even less violent approach, taking it in turns to ridicule each other. It must take a great deal of courage to stand and wait for someone to hit you without defending yourself, and the participants gain in reputation from displaying the courage and self-restraint needed to resolve their grievances in what is seen as the 'proper way' (albeit violent!).

However, there appears to be more than economics or mobility at the heart of hunter-gatherer harmony, and while it was economics which first drew the attention of anthropologists, other less visible parts of their lifestyles may also be important. Hunter-gatherers themselves were unaware of how they related to others in economic terms, giving things away because they felt like it, and trusting others to be there for them. For them, it was how they *felt about those around them* that made them human. What was seen as naive to the wider economics of their survival can also be seen as a strength in the willingness to trust others, and give and take without weighing up consequences.

Barry and Bonnie Hewlett from the Department of Anthropology at Washington State University have for many years studied the Aka (traditionally termed pygmies) of the Congo Basin, typical of simple hunter-gatherers. They remain impressed with the close-knit emotional ties developed in such groups. They explain that a single hunter-gatherer group often all occupy a space the size of a typical dining and living room in the US, and whenever they sit they are usually touching someone. From infancy, children are held almost constantly, with three- to four-month-old infants held 91 per cent of the day (compared to around half of that in typical agricultural communities).[55] From an early age the most important things children learn are to share food, respect others and show self-restraint. Parents are exceptionally tolerant and rarely ever direct children to learn or do anything, they are simply free to learn. Perhaps most tellingly, children of hunter-gatherers cried almost half the time of that typical for those in agricultural societies.

Brian Wood of the Department of Anthropology at Yale University found the same environment among the Hadza of Tanzania.[56] Food sharing was taught from a very early age, and even very small children were taught to ask for and to give away food. Sharing food is not easy, especially when you are small and perhaps hungry, and children are encouraged to learn self-restraint. Highly valued food is often given to the young to share – it certainly demands self-restraint to wait for a toddler to divide up honey before you get your portion. Infants soon learn that not only food but material things are almost always shared between people, making their lives centred around their relationships with adults. Polly Weissner noted that the !Kung took beads from infants' necklaces for them to give to other people to enable them to learn about sharing[57] and Melvin Konner noted that mothers will stop infants from eating – when the food is on the way to their mouth – and expect them to give it to someone else so that they learn the self-restraint needed to share rather than eat the food.[58] Hunter-gatherer children are much less likely to get into conflict over possessions. Not only this, as adults they have learnt a level of self-restraint which allows them to give food away no matter how hungry they are, as well as to be tolerant and unreactive to anger. Putting others first is not just a nicety but essential to survival, and learning to live this way is a lesson not in economics but emotions.

The long road to adulthood in hunter-gatherers is not filled as ours is with a demanding routine of accumulating knowledge or developing skills, but rather the demands of 'emotional sculpting' – learning how to handle difficult feelings.

Many psychologists, including Bruce Charlton of the University of Newcastle, are convinced that the attention paid to emotional well-being and development, and the sharing ethic seen among modern day hunter-gathers implies that we must have been much *happier* in the sharing societies of the Palaeolithic than in the conditions of constant pressure we feel ourselves under today.[59] All too often we think of the Stone Age as a time of 'primal passions', men clubbing women on the head, but if modern hunter-gatherers teach us anything it is that it is us who, in emotional terms, seem 'primitive'. To them, we are alarmingly self-centred, and, moreover, prone to being 'carried away' by feelings of helplessness or anger, and unable to just calmly sit and accommodate such feelings. The anthropologist Hugh Brody describes many a sobering experience with the indigenous peoples of the far North. When he was out on a hunting expedition, he realised he might not return and was helpless to a sense of panic, yet he realised that his companions could deal with the possibility of death with total calm and acceptance.[60]

Jean Briggs, an anthropologist studying the Inuit, also described an unfortunate incident that made her realise how much more reactive she was to her emotions when she was working with them. When she was writing up her notes one day snow fell from the roof of the igloo onto her typewriter and all over her work. She reacted in frustration, throwing a nearby knife into a pile of fish in annoyance.[63] 'Losing it' in such a circumstance might not seem too unusual to us. However, the Inuit were greatly alarmed by this display of anger, seen as dangerous in such a small-scale interdependent group. They didn't speak to her for many weeks until they were sure that she could control her anger.

If such peoples are representative of our ancestors in our own species we would be wrong to think of stone-age people as ruled by their emotions; rather the reverse, for the Inuit it was Jean who was reacting like a child who had yet to learn to accommodate her feelings and show self-restraint.

Why would we see such violence occurring in societies apparently unlikely to get carried away with anger, frustration, envy or hatred? In our imagination evidence for violent confrontations supports our idea that stone-age people are driven by their feelings, quick to attack, to grab food from others for their own survival, to beat off competitors in order to survive. Yet modern hunter-gatherers seem, if anything, the opposite – they are less reactive to their feelings.

One explanation is a phenomenon termed 'moralistic aggression' or 'lethal levelling'. Moralistic aggression describes how we feel, for example, when we stand up against a bully who is hurting someone else. Christopher Boehm from the University of Southern California has studied moralistic aggression mechanisms in nomadic hunter-gatherers in depth.[62] He found that though remarkably tolerant in many ways, hunter-gatherers are surprisingly intolerant of 'upstarts'. He explains that peaceful harmony seems to be won through an uneasy dynamic between tendencies towards competition, and those towards collaboration, not only to survive but to defend principles of equality against those who would exploit, dominate or free-ride. Someone thinking that they are better than others, or that they can control or dominate them, threatens the survival of highly interdependent groups, so group reactions can be swift, not only in response to dominating behaviour, but even to dominating attitudes.

We might think it is natural for people to compare themselves favourably or unfavourably with others, but in a foraging society this is a dangerous attitude to take. Young men who start to become proud and egocentric usually find themselves ridiculed or ignored. If they continue, ultimate sanctions exist, with the group eventually throwing out or assassinating upstarts. Unsurprisingly, the wise take great care to display their humility and don't reveal any material signs of wealth or status or show off their accomplishments, thus taking great pains to be humble.

Richard Lee comments:

Say that a man has been hunting. He must not come home and announce like a braggart 'I have killed a big one in the bush!' He must first sit down in silence until I or someone else comes up to his fire, and asks 'What did you see today?' He replies quietly 'Ah... I'm no good for hunting. I saw nothing at all... maybe just a tiny one.' Then I smile to myself because I know he has killed something big'.[63]

Even so, members of the band may take great pains to put down the hunter. Lee adds that they might typically say jokingly:

> You mean to say that you have dragged us all this way out here to make us cart home your pile of bones? Oh, if I had known it was this thin I wouldn't have come. People, to think I gave up a nice day in the shade for this. At home we may be hungry but at least we have nice cool water to drink.

This is familiar banter in many a group of lads. At the same time I can't help but wonder if the all-too-familiar tendency among most of us to find it excruciatingly hard to show off our achievements to the world, to elevate our skills in interviews or be 'assertive' might not be rather more natural and normal than we might be led to believe.

Christopher Boehm notes:

> The widespread reports of leaders acting in an unassuming way, and of leaders being so generous that they themselves 'had nothing' do not necessarily mean that bands are choosing as leaders unaggressive individuals who just naturally tend to give away all of their resources. In this type of small society, in which the ethos is shared so uniformly, politically sensitive leaders know exactly how to comport themselves if they wish to lead without creating tension. Appropriate ways to assuage the apprehensions of watchful peers are never to give orders, to be generous to a fault, and to remain emotionally tranquil, particularly with respect to anger as a predictable component of dominance. Basically, one needs to avoid any signs of assertive self aggrandizement.[64]

Today, those school teachers who act in the same way, are often the ones who are most influential and listened to and can be contrasted with others who tend to dominate and control.[65]

The 'levelling' of upstarts is found right across different forager societies, from the treatment of shamans who exploit their power and position (such as in one case by insisting that the spirits would only improve the weather if he himself would sleep with two attractive young women) to people who take food and never give any to those in need. In some cases powerful upstarts might initially gain much power before the group has the courage to overthrow them. Boehm describes how a single shaman among the Greenland Inuit was feared to the extent that followers felt helpless to overthrow him and accepted intimidation for a long time until finally finding the courage to deal with him.

Our first reaction to seeing evidence for violence in early prehistoric societies, such as the point wound in the Shanidar Neanderthal, or the head wound from the Neanderthal at Saint-Césaire, is to assume that they were the victims of primal passions. Violence driven by moral motivations to depose a tyrant might leave similar traces to that motivated by an immediate hatred or blood lust. It is less easy to denounce any evidence for violence as primitive than it might first appear.

Is violence then even a certain sign that early humans lived by primal aggressive instincts?

I'm not sure that it is. Many people would trace the pattern of hunter-gatherer equality, tolerance, sharing and humility at least as far back as the emergence of our own species and probably much beyond. Mesolithic graves in Skateholm in Sweden, for example, suggest that a similar means of resolving disputes as we see today might have existed at least 5,000 years ago. Two of the men buried here had several head injuries markedly similar to those sustained by the Netsilik in ritual combat, each of which had completely healed. The simple material culture, and lack of displays of status throughout the archaeological record of mobile groups in the Palaeolithic and Mesolithic also suggests that hard-won equality, respect for others and widespread sharing was also the norm then. Many of the burials of individuals with arrow wounds in the back, or other indicators of their sudden death, have been interpreted as potentially a result of moralistic aggression.[66]

Yet we remain with the unavoidable conclusion that even in these most peaceful societies some are tempted to compete, overthrow others, take more than their share or feel the thrill of power. Moreover, feuds could arise, driven by a concern with honour or vengeance, and sporadic jealousies could lead to attacks. Does this mean that only the rigid systems to enforce sharing or equality that we see in modern hunter-gatherers keep this violence under wraps? Or are we innately kind, well designed to live together peacefully with aggressions flaring only on the odd occasion?

When we look closely at the evidence for violence in early prehistory almost everything we think we know about our ancestors seems to slip away. It isn't clear from this evidence that early humans were carried away by their aggressive instincts. At least where our own species is concerned, evidence from modern hunter-gatherers would even suggest that such peoples may have been less reactive to their feelings, less likely to 'lash out' than those in our own societies, and where violence does occur, it may be about defending a moral principle of equality, or upholding a sense of honour rather than fighting for something for themselves. An emotionally primal past might be a more a figment of a modern fantasy than a reflection of real stone-age lives.

The Makapansgat pebble, picked out and brought to Makapansgat Cave by an australopithecine 3 million years ago.

Chapter Three

A Prehistory of Compassion?

The sound of a kiss is not so loud as that of a cannon, but its echo lasts a great deal longer.[67]

In this chapter we consider the archaeological evidence for sensitivity, generosity and caring behaviour in early humans. Though subtle, the evidence for such behaviour is found to be widespread, with the extent of caring and generosity found in archaeological contexts going far beyond what might make any practical sense or be explained in terms of economic or material advantage. Hunter-gatherers, both past and present, seem to put considerable effort into being kind and generous, ironically most particularly in the harshest, least reliable and most difficult settings. Such effort expended into the well-being of others seems almost excessive, perhaps even, like the peacock's tail, well beyond what can be explained as practically useful.

A few seconds of aggression leave indelible traces, like the finds of early humans with broken bones or arrows in their spines. But in contrast, what evidence would we find of acts of kindness? Can we even identify *kindness* in early humans?

Of course, we know that among ourselves acts of kindness are subtle, and so might leave rather fragile traces – perhaps evidence that those who were vulnerable have recovered from debilitating wounds or injuries through being cared for, or evidence of a *reaching out* to do more than was necessary to make someone else's life better. The very idea of kindness contrasts with our image of our early humans – all too often one of people who were by necessity brutal, the very word *Neanderthal* conjuring up an image of thug-like insensitivity. These images are so strong that potential evidence for compassion, that early humans cared deeply about each other, is often disregarded. Yet despite its subtlety, evidence for a rather unique sensitivity persists in challenging our images of our ancestors and comes across even from some of the earliest periods of prehistory, markedly more widespread than we might suppose.

One of the earliest signs of a certain sensitivity comes ironically from the very same cave site that inspired Dart's ideas of killer apes. Here, amid the broken hyena bones and tooth-marked human skulls, lies a tiny but remarkable pebble. The 'Makapansgat pebble' looks a little like a baby's face. Of course, pebbles may often resemble faces of animals. What is remarkable is that this jasperite pebble has been carried several kilometres, brought back to the cave by an australopithecine around 3 million years ago. For reasons we don't understand, one of these ape-like early humans must have picked up this pebble and been so taken by this object that they took it with them and carried it until it was finally deposited in Makapansgat.[68] Did it remind them just slightly of a baby? Did they feel a need to protect and care for it? Or perhaps was it just interesting. It is difficult to tell.

This is not the only tantalising sign of something perhaps approaching tenderness. In East Africa another piece of evidence dating from the very earliest deposits associated with australopithecines captures an evocative moment in time. In 1976 Mary Leakey was exploring a site where mammal bones had been recovered when she came across a unique discovery – a trail of fossil human-like footprints, preserved almost as if they had been made the day before. Yet far from being recent, the Laetoli footprints were made around 3.5 million years ago and preserved by a rare occurrence of events, not unlike events at ancient Pompeii. After the eruption of a volcano had spread ash over the nearby land surface, rain had made the spread of volcanic ash into a soft surface which was easy to walk on, but a later ash deposit quickly sealed and preserved the surface. Among footprints of big cats, ancient ancestors of horses, extinct elephant, buffalo, antelope, giraffes, gazelles, hares and birds, those of remarkably familiar-looking human feet stand out.

The Laetoli footprints were made by two adults,

Footprints from Laetoli, Tanzania, 3.5 million years old.

around 1.3m and 1.45m high, and a smaller child following behind. The trail stretches for about 25m, with the pattern made by the soft parts of their feet, thereby showing that these human-like apes were walking at a leisurely pace. More remarkably, the prints seem to show that the smallest hominin walked in the footprints of the larger one. Though interpretations of these footprints as that of a 'nuclear family' – mother, father and child – are perhaps fanciful, they nonetheless capture something perhaps significant. The prints of the smaller hominin are difficult to interpret as other than a child walking in a parent's footsteps – an evocative moment. Rather than hinting at bloodthirsty aggression, the footprints instead suggest to us almost a playfulness in the way one walked in another's footprint, imagining themselves the other, finding a sense of security in the connection between their smaller feet and the larger ones.

We see more evidence for a certain sensitivity at various places in the archaeological record. At Tan-Tan in Morocco around 500,000 years ago, a quartzite rock appears to have been modified into a childlike form,[69] and at Berekhat-Ram in Israel around 280,000 years ago, a piece of stone

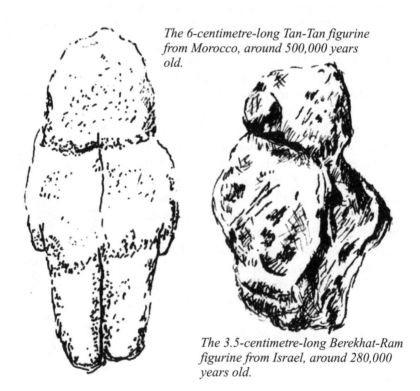

The 6-centimetre-long Tan-Tan figurine from Morocco, around 500,000 years old.

The 3.5-centimetre-long Berekhat-Ram figurine from Israel, around 280,000 years old.

has also been modified to accentuate a human-like form with infant proportions.[70] Whereas the Makapansgat pebble was a 'manuport' (a pebble which happened to look childlike and was selected and carried around), later 'figurines' have been deliberately sculpted. Miscroscopic analysis of the tracings on the Berekhat-Ram figurine by Francesco D'Errico and April Nowell confirmed that a stone tool was used to alter the shape and bring out the human-like form of the original stone cobble. Quite why early humans were interested in these infant-like forms remains an unanswered question, but not one that immediately speaks to us of aggressive instinct. It might almost seem as if they were trying to 'care for' infant-like stones by accentuating their form. Certainly, by this time they were able to see how to improve the form of the pebble towards what they imagined that it might be. This kind of imagination is not just artistic but a crucial element of an ability to empathise with (that is imagine oneself as) someone else. Stephen Porges, Director of the Brain-Body Center at the University of Illinois, certainly draws a connection between the physiology of human empathy and the creation of a sense of connection and safeness between us which allows us to be sensitive to aesthetic experience and free to be creatively playful.[71]

Of course, debates have always been heated over what makes 'art', what art implies and whether archaic humans prior to our species truly made 'art objects'. There is little doubt nonetheless that our archaic ancestors became increasingly more sensitive to the aesthetic, and yet more imaginative in how to create shapes, objects or colours which pleased them. From 270,000 years ago we begin to see pigments more commonly appearing on sites in Africa, perhaps used to decorate living areas,[72] and in Europe from 250,000 years ago,[73] becoming common by the time of Neanderthals.[74] By the time of the Neanderthals there is evidence that coloured shells and teeth were made into adornments (perhaps necklaces or sewn to clothes) and at Cueva de los Liones in Southern Spain pierced shells were decorated with bright red ochre.[75] Colourful feathers were also selected, again perhaps to decorate the body.[76] It seems a real possibility that Neanderthals decorated their homes and bodies with colour.

Perhaps the most intriguing 'art object' made by Neanderthals is the so-called 'Roche-Cotard mask'.[77] This tiny flint flake, only a few centimetres long, challenges the notion that many of the capacities which we hold to be unique to our own species were present in others. Around 33,000 years ago, a Neanderthal, sitting by the side of the river Loire, perhaps idly slotted a bone into a natural hole in this flake such that the bone made a pair of 'eyes'. We can be certain that this was deliberate since several small flakes were used to permanently secure the bone in place.

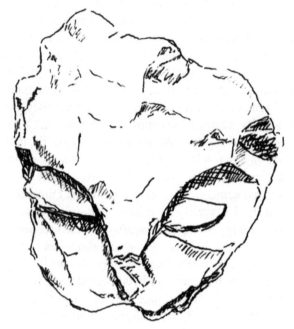

The 10.5-centimetre-wide Roche-Cotard 'mask' from France, 33,000 years old.

Once again, the proportions of the 'face' are notably childlike. Could this even have been a doll? (though perhaps your imagined Neanderthal was not the doll-making type?). Certainly, they, male or female, child or adult, cannot possibly have appreciated the enormity and significance of what may have been an idle act of creativity. At the very least it shows that Neanderthals were able to hold in their mind's eye an imagined creation in the image of a face, and use the flake and bone to make that image concrete. It is hard to escape the conclusion that, in being able to imagine another person and create an image of that person, they must also have been conscious of themselves. It is remarkable that we can hold in our hands the deliberate representation of a face made by a Neanderthal and feel the sense that its maker understood something of the relationship between themselves as creator and whoever else might hold it.

Not only what we consider art, but even the careful considered fashioning of more common artefacts can sometimes leave us in awe or respect for the people who produced them. A certain aesthetic sense or remarkable sensitivity can even be noted in the most apparently utilitarian of artefacts – stone handaxes.

Despite their tough image, handaxes or 'bifaces' marked a major threshold in the sophistication of how stone tools were made, which took place a bit later than 2 million years ago. Early Oldowan tools, crudely shaped pebble tools knapped using stone hammers to give sharp edges, were certainly able to to cut sinews, meat or bone. Indeed, such tools allowed early humans to get at precious fats and proteins in abandoned carcasses that may have been the basis of the first 'meaty' part of humans diets. However, when finely formed handaxes were added to the previously entirely functional tool set of early humans, something different seemed to be happening to the whole way that things were made. Producing a handaxe, following a process of knapping one side then the other of a nodule of flint to produce a symmetrical shape, demands being able to think in sequence and imagine both sides of an artefact at the same time. It is something that needs to be taught. More than this, John Gowlett of the University of Liverpool has shown that handaxes illustrate an understanding of an aesthetic which we don't see previously. They tend to fit the 'golden ratio' seen in architecture – proportions which we find aesthetically pleasing.[78] It seems almost excessive that early humans would choose to display a sensitivity to form, and a patience in making something which went beyond the practical simply to use to butcher carcasses.

Great effort went into biface production. Though many are neither finely made nor symmetrical, many are very carefully formed. The creator often goes to great lengths to make sure that imperfections in one side of a handaxe are matched in the other, or naturally occurring flaws or even fossils within the stone are placed centrally where they would feel most balanced. There must have been something intuitively wrong with a wonky handaxe. It is not only time but also considerable patience and a willingness to overcome frustration which is needed to impose a pleasing form on stone. Despite much practice, I'm still not good at handaxe production and that's not unusual – it takes modern students a long time and a lot of frustration to make something that seems to have been easy for an early human a million and half years ago. When you have shouted and sworn at your mistakes, and cut fingers on many occasions, you begin to develop a renewed sense of respect for our apparently primitive ancestors. Out of the harsh contexts of Palaeolithic survival we can't help but recognise that many handaxes are a reflection of patience, skill and more than this, a sense of beauty.

A finely made handaxe figures highly in a thought-provoking discovery in Spain. Only a few kilometres from the site where archaeologists were disturbed to discover that 800,000 years ago *Homo antecessor* brutally butchered their fellows, archaeologists led by Juan Luis Arsuaga of the University of Madrid made a discovery that would elevate the later occupants beyond what had previously been considered imaginable. By climbing through long underground passages taking several hours, archaeologists reached the base of what would have been a large rock fissure at Atapuerca 450,000 years ago. Here at Sima de los Huesos (the Pit of Bones) lay a huge deposit of human bones, corpses which must have been carried to the site and dropped in from above, probably as some kind of mortuary practice. Careful excavation of the fossilised material over many years revealed that among the bones was a finely made rose quartz handaxe. The handaxe, thereafter dubbed Excalibur, had been dropped from above with the corpses and was the first example of a 'grave good'. Whether their fellows had intended the handaxe to be useful in their concept of an afterlife, or it held some personal significance to one of them, or just felt like the right thing to place there, we will never know. It is hard to imagine Dart's aggressive bone-wielding ape-men either taking the time to 'make something nice' or to do something meaningful for the deceased.

That handaxe form means something is clear, and yet that something remains somewhat of a mystery. Indeed, it was the form and symmetry of handaxes which convinced early geologists that, despite how deep they were found in sediments, they represented humanity. Yet handaxes are an enigma. They remained in use for over a million years and throughout most of the occupied world of *Homo erectus/ergaster* and later *Homo heidelbergensis* from sites in Africa, such as Kilombe, to sites in England, such as Boxgrove near Chichester, and they seem to denote a certain stability, if not conservatism. Nonetheless, we think that many things were changing in the social world of these early humans. Humans started to make handaxes at a time when climates became more variable, oscillating radically between wet and dry or warm and cold. Therefore, food must have become more and more difficult to find. It can't have been easy. Yet at the same time, these humans seem to be thriving. The paradox is that as their surrounding resources imposed more risks and uncertainties, humans became larger and taller, bearing increasingly vulnerable offspring who were dependent for longer. Moreover, rather than conserving precious energy, they seem to have had enough to invest in new growth – indeed, brain sizes were increasing. The relationship between the excess time, effort, care invested in something that was used to butcher meat, and these other changes, has remained difficult to decipher.

The makers of handaxes, from *Homo ergaster* and *Homo erectus* to *Homo heidelbergensis* seem, on the one hand, touchingly like us in their willingness to go beyond the practical, yet at the same time, they were so unlike us in that the same commonly used object, the handaxe, remains the same, not just for a few generations but thousands and even a million years. It is hard to imagine ourselves happy with the same forms, resisting any temptation to tinker or make something new and interesting. We also see a contrast, which we find equally frustrating, in their treatment of the dead. The 'mortuary pit', created 450,000 years ago at Atapuerca, speaks to us of a shared grief at the loss of loved ones. There is a continued sense of connection to the dead bodies and the need to treat them with reverence. Yet tossing them in a jumbled heap at the bottom of a cleft seems non-human, echoed in a similar deposition of five to fifteen Neanderthals in a dark recess at Pontnewydd Cave in Wales around 225,000 years ago. As Paul Pettitt of Durham University argues, this is not yet reverential burial as *we* know it.[79] It is almost as if we can reach out and touch what we recognise as sensitivity or even compassion, yet even while we feel a sense that these humans are *recognisable*, we aren't entirely *comfortable*.

If we could go back in time, would we feel safe in the midst of these people?

At the very least, *caring for each other* seems to have had a long evolutionary history. Analyses of the pathology of ancient human bones often appear to tell us about a widespread willingness to care for those in need. If we could go back to experience life as an early human and be part of their group there seems every chance that we might have been at least looked after when we needed help.

The earliest evidence for care of someone far too vulnerable to look after themselves comes from around 1.6 million years ago in East Africa. KNM-ER 1808, an unusual female *Homo erectus*, was discovered in Kenya in 1974.[80] Her skeletal had an abnormal outer layer of bone, which had developed through excessive bleeding into the tissues for several weeks before her death. This condition matched one seen in wilderness explorers who had been forced to eat their huskies, often first eating the soft livers. The woman had suffered from hypervitaminosis A, a disease caused by excessive intake of vitamin A. Symptoms of this include a reduction in bone density and the development of coarse bone growths, both of which are present in KNM-ER 1808's skeleton.[81] The pathology present would have taken weeks or even months to develop, accompanied by symptoms such as abdominal pain, nausea, headaches, dizziness, blurred vision, lethargy, loss of muscular coordination and impaired consciousness. These effects

An outer abnormal layer of bone growth on the femoral bone of ER1808 attested to the considerable time, possibly months, that this person suffered the severe pain of hypervitaminosis.

would have greatly hindered her capacity for independent survival, yet she survived long enough for the disease to be identifiable in her skeleton, something which only occurs in the advanced stages of hypervitaminosis A. Alan Walker and Pat Shipman suggest that 'someone else took care of her',[82] and David Cameron and Colin Groves add: 'There is no way she could have survived alone for long in the African savannah...someone must have been feeding her, protecting her from carnivores.'[83]

From a similar time, at the site of Dmanisi in Georgia a very unusual jaw was recovered.[84] This *Dmanisi hominin*, probably also a *Homo erectus*, had lost all but one tooth several years before death, with all the sockets except for the canine teeth having been re-absorbed. They must have had great difficulty surviving and could only have consumed soft plant or animal foods, leading the excavator, David Lordkipanidze, to conclude that they had been looked after by the others in the group.

In later populations of early humans we see evidence which suggests an even more long-term care of others. The deceased deposited in the 'Pit of Bones' at Atapuerca, for example, included an elderly man approximately fifty years of age with a severe pelvic deformity. He must have been unable to walk without a stick (and even then only slowly).[85] We certainly never imagine our ancestors as elderly, walking with sticks and looked after by others. Ana Garcia[86] and her team have also published evidence from Cranium 14, a child mostly likely aged between five and eight years at death, nicknamed *Benjamina*, who suffered from lambdoid single suture craniosynostosis (SSC), a premature closing of some or all of the separate bony elements of the skull. This would have caused an increase in pressure within the brain in this child, had an impact upon their brain growth and also potentially on their mental capacity, as well as their facial appearance. However, despite this, they survived for at least five years, prompting Ana Garcia to note that 'her/his pathological condition was not an impediment to receive the same attention as any other Middle Pleistocene *Homo*

Figure 18. The 'toothless' Dmanisi hominin.

child'.[87] A Middle Palaeolithic woman from Salé, Morocco, also suffered from debilitating cranial distortion and muscular trauma related to a pre-birth physical deformity (congenital torticollis). She reached adulthood despite such obvious physical deformities.[88] The vulnerable seem to have been taken care of, regardless of how impractical or difficult this might have been. Feeling, an instinct to care, overrides any cold calculation.

Evidence for widespread care for others permeates the archaeological record ever more clearly through time. Shanidar 1, found at Shanidar Cave in Iraq, is perhaps one of the best known examples of a vulnerable Neanderthal who appears to have been cared for. This man suffered multiple fractures across his body, with the right side being particularly badly affected; the right arm has been described as completely 'withered',[89] with the forearm lost before death, and with degenerative deformities in both legs which is likely to have resulted in a painful limp.[90] He had also suffered from an injury to his skull, possibly causing blindness in his left eye,[91] and some have even hypothesised that there may have been some brain damage as a result of this injury.[92] Studies of Shanidar 1's injuries have suggested that the majority occurred in adolescence,[93] yet were largely healed, with little sign of infection, by the time of his death, some twenty to thirty-five years later, at the relatively advanced Neanderthal age of between thirty-five and fifty years old.[94] The man of Shanidar was not only looked after despite his injuries, but we might assume, given that he was elderly in Neanderthal terms, cared for by several different people, if not as a shared commitment to care from the whole group. As with a number of other Neanderthals, when he died this old man appears to have been carefully buried in a small grave.

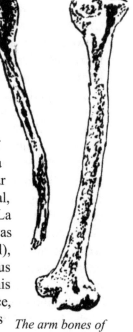

Other Shanidar Neanderthals were also cared for during a considerable time after injury or illness, including Shanidar 3, who had debilitating arthritis of the left ankle and foot joints,[95] Shanidar 4, who had a healed wound to his rib, and Shanidar 5, with a large scar on the left side of his face.[96] Another famous Neanderthal, the first ever Neanderthal burial found in 1908 at La Chapelle aux Saints in France, also survived until he was around forty (a considerable age for a Neanderthal), despite tooth disease and the loss of many teeth, plus arthritis or a similar joint disease severely affecting his jaw, spine, hip and foot.[97] At Bau de l'Aubesier in France, a similar lower jaw to that found at Dmanisi was recovered, dated to 180,000 years ago, and showing similar substantial dental disease and re-absorption of the teeth, which would have made chewing painful and ineffective. The excavator Serge Lebel is confident that this person must have been kept alive by others preparing soft food for them.[98]

The arm bones of Shanidar 1. While this Neanderthal's left arm is normal, his right arm is severely withered.

Perhaps most challengingly, the individual from Saint-Césaire, France, famous as illustrating clear evidence of a weapon injury to the head, must have been looked after following their attack.[99] Immediate effects would have included heavy bleeding and possible unconsciousness, as well as long-term effects, including brain damage. Publication of the evidence for apparent brutality has been extensive, while the parallel evidence for care hardly receives a mention.

Much of the Neanderthal world seems far more human, or at least 'humane', than the killer ape concept might imply. As well as evidence for extensive care of the sick or incapacitated, we see many different examples of burial practices across Neanderthal society, with at least nineteen burials recorded. Many are quite moving. One particular burial, for example, is that of a child and an adult female (perhaps their mother) laid out on a scree slope and covered with stones at Las Palomas in Southern Spain.[100] Children are those most likely to be buried with some types of grave goods, from flint flakes deposited with a newborn at La Ferrassie in France; to a red deer maxilla carefully placed in a crevice with a seven-month-old at Amud in Israel; to goat horns surrounding the burial of a child at Teshik-Tash in Uzbekistan.[101] The excavator of the child burial at Amud Cave, Erella Hovers, is convinced that this Neanderthal child was interred with a great deal of care.[102] It has become hard to reconcile the image of Neanderthals – and other archaic humans – as brutes with the evidence that they had a strong and abiding instinct to care for others and tenderness towards the vulnerable. The whole concept that early humans reached out to help others in need, were prepared to go to great lengths for those they cared about, speaks to us of words like love. That such a capacity lies right at the heart of human evolution and from an early date is inspiring, even what Jonathan Haidt, Professor of New York Stern University School of Business, would call 'elevating'.[103] It is difficult to deny that the evidence for sensitivity and caring, despite such difficult conditions, makes a convincing case that we inherit traits driven not by aggression or greed but by ordinary kindness and courage in the face of great hardship.

Where is cold calculation? A capacity for sensitivity, shared grief and, above all, compassion is also troubling. While the concept of caring and sensitive ancestors challenges common assumptions that early humans must have been tough and aggressive, we find that their willingness to reach out beyond themselves to give to others also challenges academic perspectives on what drove our evolution or made us successful. How, in a rational economic world driven by the survival of the fittest, could a tendency to give away what was often a great deal of time and resources possibly pay off in the harsh environments of the Palaeolithic? As Dachner Keltner from the University of Berkeley comments, many of us feel that *generosity is for suckers* (and such suckers should not survive, should they?).[104]

A disturbing tension arises. Our ancestors ought to be *competitive* surely, either driven by primitive aggressive urges to rise up above other species, or at least far more coldy rational, applying their superior intellect to conserve resources and create efficiencies? That would make them tough businessmen at heart. How else could they have survived?

Some have resolved the problem by suggesting that early humans might not actually have cared for others after all. Rather, they might perhaps have calculated their potential economic contribution, some unique knowledge or skills that they might impart through their survival rather than their demise, before deciding whether to help them. While not exactly comforting, this view at least makes some economic sense. Yet such thinking abilities are complicated, hardly even seen in our own species[105] let alone something earlier minds might have been able to handle (would any of us want or be able to calculate the economic contribution of elderly or ill relatives?). It is far more complex as an explanation for evidence for behaviour than simple emotional motivations. As Frans de Waal argues, it makes little sense to argue for complex calculations, extensive foresight and rational planning when the simple truth that they cared far more clearly explains why they would help each other.[106]

We *feel* like we *understand* – such sensitivity to others *feels human* – yet a rational part of our minds, a little like the unemotional beings, Spock or Data from Star Trek, nags at us, 'this is illogical Captain', and it *can't have worked*.

Evidence for extensive care despite the odds is even yet more troubling in our own species.

A remarkable archaeological site in South Asia, dating to around 3,500 years ago, goes even further in challenging our assumptions about how prehistoric people ought to be behaving. Here, within a cemetery of over ninety burials at the Neolithic site of Man Bac in Vietnam, archaeologists discovered the skeleton of a remarkable man. As they excavated the bones they were surprised by how incredibly thin and fragile they were. It was hardly possible to believe such bones could have supported someone. Actually they didn't. The report describing his condition is almost painful to read for this man was quadriplegic, I think, and had been since he was juvenile. Yet he did not die until sometime in his thirties, a normal age for the time. He was completely paralysed from the waist down, would have had only minor mobility of his arms if any, and a torsioning of his neck, with probable difficulties chewing. Various possibilities exist to explain his condition, probably a spinal cord injury. What is remarkable, however, is the level of care, attention and even respect with which he must have been accorded.[107] His survival required constant care, episodes of intensive nursing which will have included regularly turning. Not only this, but he required a specialised diet to counteract the effects of

72

immobility, needed regular cleaning and dressing, help with drinking and eating, and even regularly moved very, very gently to prevent pressure sores (of which there was no evidence). The excavators conclude that the community of which he was a part was not only experienced in looking after the sick, but had done so with compassion, respect and affection. They were committed to his survival, and given the psychological pressures that being so dependent on others entails, must have provided the kind of support for him that was emotional as well as the practical.

The Man Bac skeleton was an unusual case of an extremely rare condition. However, care for those who are vulnerable permeates early societies after the emergence of our own species throughout the world.

In Upper Palaeolithic Europe there are a number of burials which provide evidence for the long-term care of those with disabilities, despite the difficulties that such conditions might have imposed. Eleven thousand years ago in Italy, a child born with dwarfism was protected, cared for and given the same treatment as any other child, despite his disability. 'Romito 2' is the first known example of this condition. He was little over 1m in height and would have suffered reduced movements of his elbows, as well as the effects of bowing of his long bones, making many of the

Burial of a paraplegic man from Man Bac, Vietnam, 3,500 years old.

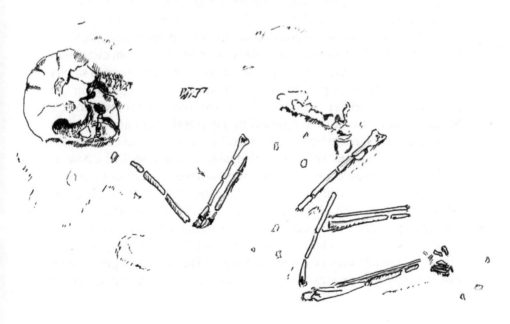

subsistence activities of the time (such as hunting large game animals) very difficult. Yet studies of his bone chemicals show that he ate exactly the same diet as the others in his group and must have been cared for throughout his life. This boy was buried alongside five others in a special burial site below a carefully painted image of a bull, and in the arms of a woman who many speculate may have been his mother.

Upper Palaeolithic burials are relatively rare and typically contain few grave goods, and disabilities are rarely seen. However, other burials of those with disabilities at this time tell a similar story of unusually careful support and respectful burial.[108] As well as the dwarf buried at Romito, at Sunghir in Russia around 24,000 years ago two young children were found – a girl of nine or ten with a marked deformity in her legs caused by a congenital disease, buried alongside a boy aged between eleven and thirteen. They were found with an unusual wealth of grave goods – mammoth tusk spears, engraved discs, perforated fox canines and even thousands of small ivory beads sewn onto their caps and clothing. This must have entailed many hours of careful preparation. They were clearly important. Another probable female from the same period 26,000 years ago in Moravia, was buried with two males and a wealth of grave goods of pierced canines, ivory pendants and red ochre. She also had a congenital deformity and shortening and bowing of the femur. As at Sunghir, the deformed woman was not only treated equally with others but perhaps even accorded particular respect at death.

Of course, people in the Upper Palaeolithic even with relatively severe disabilities may make some practical contribution despite their disability. However, several authors have speculated over why those with disabilities might have been accorded a level of attention which went beyond simply being cared for to help them survive. Perhaps surprisingly from our perspective, that either the man at Man Bac, the Romito dwarf or the Sunghir child was cared for would be no surprise to anthropologists working among modern hunter-gatherers. To consider the rational benefits of caring for someone would be unthinkable for these societies. Among the Baka, for example, people with severe disabilities, such as those who are wheelchair bound, are as much part of close-knit social groups as any others. What is more, they can take on a particular social role. They contribute practically where they can but also become a kind of social hub – someone available to talk to, with more social links to everyone in the group and outside than others might have.[109] The wealth of grave goods associated with those with disabilities in the Palaeolithic might reflect that far from being seen as a burden they can be regarded as being particularly important. This attitude is not, however, what we feel we would expect.

Other elements of Upper Palaeolithic societies challenge the idea that their behaviour was rationally defined, or even *sensible*.

By the time our own species reaches Europe there is widespread and elaborate figurative art, such as the 'lion headed man' statuette made of ivory and dated to 32,000 years ago from Hohlenstein-Stadel in Germany. Music is also in evidence, with flutes such as those from Hohle Fels from the same period. Indeed, any previous art, such as that of the Neanderthals, tends to be eclipsed by such a flowering of creativity. Yet such creativity, just like the extensive care for the vulnerable, is a challenge for us to understand.

The Ice Age brings with it almost unimaginably harsh conditions. Ice sheets move inexorably southwards through northern Europe, resources dwindle, much of the landscape periodically becomes unvegetated and whole areas of the north European plain become uninhabitable. Trees are a rarity. Yet it is in this climate, at the edge of survival, when huge time, effort and resources go into the production of art. We are awed and deeply moved by the sophistication of the Chauvet lions, or Altamira bison. Few can visit any of the cave art sites in Europe without feeling in some way changed by the experience. But we are also *perplexed* by its creation. It is not merely the time to create art, but more that it is clear that Upper Palaeolithic artists must have practiced a great deal to produce art of the sophistication that we see. The production of stone tools at the time was equally elaborated, far beyond what might have been needed. Something that we often see throughout prehistoric hunter-gatherer society. Finely and delicately produced tools were also recovered at my own excavations.

Anthony Sinclair from the University of Liverpool has calculated that learning to produce the (needlessly) elaborate Solutrean foliate points, and most likely the art made in Western Europe at the height of the Ice Age, must have taken many thousands of hours of sustained practice. Yet throughout Upper Palaeolithic Europe, when conditions were harshest and survival the most at risk, we see art, beads and ornaments, care for the vulnerable, and the sophisticated and elaborate production of tools. When the glaciers were knocking at the door of Palaeolithic societies, and when extreme climatic Heinrich events decimated the vegetation and caused widespread ecological disaster, art continued. Palaeolithic art is both moving and wonderful, and yet also seems excessive in the context of the societies which produced it. Sensitivity, generosity and care for others seem most obvious precisely when they are hardest to explain.

We love to see ourselves as some kind of pinnacle. The abilities of ice-age artists, or the compassion and commitment of those in the Palaeolithic to care for the vulnerable feels as though it is something to be truly proud of. Nonetheless, it is difficult to escape the conclusion that, in contrast to the economic self-interest we think we ought to find in our ancestors, it is apparent that the archaeological record tells us about an *extreme* of apparently irrational effort invested into looking after others who might never contribute to their well-being, as well as perfecting skills well beyond what is necessary.

Today we see modern hunter-gatherers behaving in the same way. Survival is by no means secure for the !Kung, with high infant mortality and frequent famine. Yet Polly Weissner observed that they would spend about a third of the year visiting close friends in distant camps, and about seventy-five to eighty days making gifts to give them.[110] Considerable long-distance movements of objects such as marine shells, even over distances up to 2000km, in Upper Palaeolithic Europe echoes similar patterns of visits and gift-giving that occurred thousands of years later in ethnographically documented societies.[111] In Poland exotic Slovakian radiolarite is found to have been transported into Polish early Upper Palaeolithic assemblages around twenty to thirty thousand years ago, despite its inferiority to the local chocolate-coloured flint.[112] Presumably even then, for those receiving a gift of flint raw material which was so much less useful than their own local flint and which had been carefully carried a great distance, 'it was the thought that counts'.

What was happening? Some archaeologists have argued that giving gifts has a practical rationale. Gifts may set up obligations to others, ensuring that they will help in times of need. At a certain level it is clear that distant friendships do help the !Kung survive when times are particularly hard, even if this is not something they are aware of. However, simply an agreed arrangement to help would surely be more sensible than elaborate gift-giving and visits? Moreover, psychological research on obligation suggests that far from helping them, we tend to avoid people who make us feel obliged.[113] A willingness to care for those who cannot ever help out in the future cannot be explained in terms of a fair exchange, any more than a desire to perfect skills, or inspire others through art.

Randolph Nesse, Professor at the University of Michigan, has an explanation for the extent of human sensitivity, generosity and willingness to care. He suggests that effort expended in being elaborately generous, helping others at great costs to ourselves, giving away what might be useful (or spending much time demonstrating our generosity in gifts), may be an example of *runaway selection* for altruism.[114] In small-scale societies, driven by a need to work together and where choosing a mate meant choosing someone to help raise a very vulnerable child for many years, finding someone generous with their time and effort became of prime importance. Natural selection may have so favoured the generous as to make more practical evaluations less important. Like the peacock's tail, so superbly unsuited to its practical survival, each of us ended up with a tendency to be generous so extreme as to hinder us, going well beyond any fair exchange, because other people liked us that way.

It is certainly an intriguing theory, and one which might also explain (as we will see in Chapter six) how we come to have such overflow of compassion which extends beyond even other animals into objects. Most of us almost can't help ourselves but protect even the least human-like things. Moreover, competitive generosity might provide us with an answer to how feelings like remorse or guilt – ones that actually punish us – might evolve.[115] Even today, people who self-punish, though feeling remorse most strongly, have more friends – quite simply we like them better because we can trust them not to exploit us.

We think our ancestors must have been competitive, self-interested rational individuals, fighting to make it in the world of harsh ice ages, dangerous predators and a struggle for survival. Were we generous, sensitive and caring to a fault?

Randolph Nesse explains that, much as humans accidentally selected wolves who were the most pleasing, affectionate and affiliative with humans to live within their homes and thus become endearing domestic dogs, we also accidentally selected the most pleasing, affiliative and easy to get on with of members of our own species.

Rather than the descendants of 'killer apes', are we 'domesticated apes', more willing to get on with others, be generous and tolerant and follow society's norms than our ape cousins?
Paul Gilbert of the University of Derby suggests that rather than being

entirely 'domesticated', our complex minds actually reflect more a tension between competitive and collaborative instincts. He explains that our *competitive* instincts come from our 'old brains', the product of our primate heritage where competition for places in an aggressive dominance hierarchy can be fierce. But we also have cooperative or affiliative instincts which are our 'new brain', the product of active selection for tendencies like empathy, generosity and tolerance.[116]

If our 'old brains' push us to compare ourselves to others (and who can resist that sometimes?), things rarely go well. We might feel we are better, but then we treat others with disdain. Worse still is that if we feel we are worse than others we may be scared, submissive or depressed. Our 'new brains', on the other hand, can push us to feel part of a greater whole, to connect to others and feel compassion towards them and ourselves, to stretch ourselves beyond our own skin and feel the benefits of caring for others and being cared for. Of course, it all becomes complicated and being able to imagine how others feel about us means that we also all tend to worry, get anxious, and stress about how we are seen. It is perhaps no wonder that the archaeological record of our own species is so full of demonstrations of sensitivity, patience and commitment in art, excessive generosity in gift-giving, and the widespread care for the vulnerable no matter what the costs.

Yet when and why did our minds become so emotionally complex?

Excavations in Africa had proved the origins of humanity millions of years ago yet frustratingly little could be gleaned about how these creatures thought. As we have seen, even the question of their violent or gentle intent seemed unresolvable. The question of what made us human seemed far beyond reach.

Where else could we look for clues? It would be the 'father of palaeoanthropology' Louis Leakey who first thought to turn to our nearest surviving cousins, the chimpanzees and other apes, to see if they could tell us what our ancestors were like and what made us human.

PART TWO

The Strands of Evidence

Jane Goodall and Freud the chimpanzee contemplate each other.

Chapter Four

Our Inner Ape?

You cannot share your life with a dog ... or a cat, and not know perfectly well that animals have personalities and minds and feelings.[117]

This chapter considers what apes can tell us about human origins and about the emotional capacities of the last common ancestor shared by apes and humans.

The earliest detailed studies of apes were set in place by Louis Leakey, motivated by his desire to illustrate the link between African apes and our early human ancestors. Jane Goodall was one of several ordinary women placed in an extraordinary situation who rose to the challenge. Decades of field research revealed remarkable similarities – well beyond any the Victorians might have imagined – between ourselves and our nearest living relatives. Golden barriers between apes and humans were broken down one by one. It became clear that apes formed close bonds, cared for each other and, most remarkably, were able to step in and help out others. A capacity for altruism seemed to be something we shared. But chimpanzees were also capable of ruthless self-interest and aggressive territoriality. Was this aggression part of a shared capacity for violence, or did the studies of apes also have another story to tell?

Are chimpanzees like us? This seems a ridiculous question; we surely know that they are *not human*. Chimpanzees, covered in a thick pelt of fur, knuckle-walk across the forest floor. They spend most of their days ambling around eating plants and grubs and show their closeness by picking parasites off each other. Yet so often when we look at them their expressions seem recognisable to us. When we watch infant chimpanzees playing with each other, or mothers holding their babies tenderly, they can seem remarkably human.

It was to chimpanzees, our nearest cousins, that Louis Leakey turned in his further efforts to prove that human origins *were* in Africa, the place where Darwin had been convinced that human origins were to be found. Huxley's anatomical drawings had illustrated the close similarities between humans and apes, with gorillas, chimpanzees, gibbons and orang-utans all sharing notable features of their skeleton with humans. However, although a close relationship between humans and apes had become evident, even by the 1960s there was so little fossil evidence that little, if anything, was known about the 'common ancestor' we shared with other apes. Even today, though we know that our closest common ancestor to chimpanzees lived around 7 to 8 million years ago,[118] there is still much debate about what this ancestor looked like, how they got around and how they behaved.

Louis Leakey realised it was in studies of ape behaviour that we have the best hope for understanding our common ancestor, what is innate to our own 'inner ape' and what might have driven the differences between us in the millions of years of our separation.

But how could he find out more about these elusive species, which were difficult to approach and as yet hardly studied? Though people had seen apes and knew what they looked like, finding out how they behaved in the wild demanded getting close to them and this was bound to be difficult. Louis was convinced that it would be *women* who would be best placed to cross the species divide and attempt to understand our nearest relatives. He set up funds to support detailed field research into how apes behaved. After testing many different candidates, Louis appointed Jane Goodall, with her mother Vanne, to go to Gombe on Lake Tanganyika to study chimpanzees, Dian Fossey to the Virunga volcanoes to study mountain gorillas, and Birute Galdikas to study orang-utans. Leakey's trio were dubbed *The Trimates*.[119]

The three women were ordinary people in extraordinary situations. Birute was a graduate student, but Jane had been a secretary and Dian, a physiotherapist. It may have been their emotional connection to 'their' apes untrammelled by too much academic preconception, or the different perspective they brought as women, or their individual personalities, but these women were to make history, not only in their field observations but in their drive to protect and conserve 'their' apes.[120]

It was Jane's work with chimpanzees, the species most closely related to humans, which would overturn ideas about what it was that placed our shared ancestor on the path to humanity.

Jane made up with determination, enthusiasm and conviction what she lacked in academic qualifications. She had wanted to work with animals in Africa since she was a small child. She trained as a secretary, hoping to use her skills to find employment there and in the meantime learnt everything she could about the continent. She was fortunate to get a job as Louis Leakey's secretary and at twenty-three years of age had a chance to visit Olduvai. As she explains: 'back then no human fossil had been found, just the fossilised remains of various animals and some pebbles which Louis and Mary Leakey were insisting were stone tools but nobody else believed them.'

For Jane it was the culmination of a dream of going to Africa that she'd had since childhood. She remembers that as a child of eleven years of age she had been fascinated by Tarzan:

I found the books about Tarzan. Everybody knows Tarzan today growing up because they watch TV. I don't think Johnny Weissmuller had appeared on the British theatre screens at that time. So, I read the books. And, of course, I fell passionately in love with this glorious lord of the jungle. And, what does he do? He goes and marries that other stupid wimpy Jane. I was extremely jealous. That was when my dream began. I will grow up. I will go to Africa. I will live with animals. I will write books about them. It seemed utterly impossible. Everybody laughed at me. I was always talking about it and they would say, 'Why don't you dream about something you can achieve?' ... At that time ... we didn't have any money ... World War II was raging. Africa was still the 'Dark Continent'. We really didn't know much about it at all except from some people who went out as District Commissioners and things like that. But, the most serious obstacle, the reason that everybody laughed at me, is that back then, girls simply didn't do that sort of thing.[121]

Yet not only did Jane get to work in Africa, she became the most famous of all primatologists and someone who would bring the world of chimpanzees to public attention as no one else before or since.

It was July 1960 when Jane Goodall and her mother Vanne arrived in Gombe, funded by Louis Leakey to find something remarkable about chimpanzees, but with no idea of the significance of these first few months of research. Jane was under tremendous pressure to discover something in order to have a good basis for carrying on the studies. It was not so simple, however. The chimpanzees were unused to people and elusive. Jane and her mother lived in a simple tent with animals and insects running in and out, and each day she tracked the elusive chimpanzees as well as she could and recorded their behaviour, often far in the distance, worried that she would let Louis Leakey down.[122]

Finally, with hardly any time left, and only records of movements to show for her effort, she saw something remarkable. David Greybeard, her favourite chimp, selected a twig, tore off the leaves and used it to fish in a termite mound. By sticking the twig inside he had made the termites bite and cling to it and could eat them from the twig. He had made a 'tool'. Up until that date tools had been seen as the sign of humanity yet here was proof that other apes also made tools.

Jane's first 'discovery' was the first of many to challenge the surety with which we construct thresholds between ourselves and our nearest living relatives. Chimpanzees appeared to be so different to ourselves, clearly inferior, yet as research progressed, each new understanding challenged the uniqueness of humanity. Were humans really the only animal to be capable of language? Were we unique in being self-aware? Were we the only animal to feel a sense of compassion for others? Over the next fifty years Jane and other researchers were to reveal many further ways in which chimpanzees would continue to challenge us, and break down most of the 'golden barriers' we set up to divide them from us. Tantalisingly human-like behaviours in chimpanzees often caught the public imagination, inspiring us to see in them, rightly or wrongly, what Jane Goodall termed 'the Mirror of Man'.

Perhaps most challenging of all was that much of their behaviour argues for genuine empathy to others, a drive to help and even perhaps a *morality* that had been seen as being unique to humanity. Seeing the bond between mothers and their infants in chimpanzees gives us an uncanny reminder of the same type of bonds in humans. Like

A young chimp 'fishing' for termites: Jane's discovery that chimpanzees used tools was to break down the 'golden barrier' between chimpanzees and humans.

humans, chimpanzee babies are born very vulnerable and take years to develop to adulthood, dependent throughout that time on adults. Mothers form a bond with their babies that goes beyond their practical needs. Infants love to play, inviting others with 'playful' expressions, and spend much time in rough and tumble play with their peers. Mothers even play 'peek-a-boo' as we would with our children. Chimpanzees ride on their mother's back for several years and it is from their mothers that they learn how to be a chimp. They learn how to use tools like termite digging sticks, leaf 'sponges' to drink water; leaves to use to scour out stomach parasites, and stones to crack nuts for food. Even as adults, at around seven years old, they still maintain a bond with their mothers and siblings.

Orphans cannot survive alone and perhaps one of the most remarkably human-like behaviours is the case of adult chimpanzees apparently being motivated by sympathy for the plight of orphaned infants and 'adopting' them as their own infants. Such foster parents are not only surviving relatives, such as older brothers and sisters, but even unrelated adults who continue in that role for several years. Jane Goodall herself documented the adoption of three-year-old 'Mel' by the unrelated adult male 'Spindle' at Gombe, and even the adoption of three infants by the adult female 'Gigi' who was barren.[123] Christophe Boesch from the Max Planck Institute for Evolutionary Anthropology and co-workers have more recently recorded eighteen cases of adoption in the Tai Forest chimpanzee group,[124] half of these by males, only one of whom was related to the infant. 'Porthos', an adult male chimp, adopted the orphaned two-year-old female 'Gia' for seventeen months until he himself died of anthrax. He carried her on his back, shared food with her and protected her from others, even carrying her in risky situations, for example, when they encountered neighbouring groups of chimpanzees. This adoption is costly for an adult chimp, but makes the difference to an infant's life or death as without a specific adult carer young chimpanzees cannot keep up with the group, typically fail to find food and will then die.

Chimpanzees form close bonds, which can often remind us of how we feel about those we love. Mothers appear to suffer a profound sense of loss when their infants die. At Boussou, Guinea, Dora Biro from the University of Oxford and her team recorded mothers who were so unwilling to be separated from their infant, even in death, that they carried around the carcass of their dead infant (which became increasingly mummified) for up to sixty-eight days.[125] A similar case of intense grief was also recorded by Jane Goodall at Gombe.[126] She documents the reactions of the male Flint when his mother, the matriarch, Flo died in 1972. Flint had always been unusually attached to his mother and found it hard to deal with the birth of his sister Flame. When his mother died, he stayed close to her body, listless and depressed until he eventually became ill and died himself three weeks later. Indeed, in a rather fascinating challenge to our accepted notions of a clear divide between ourselves and other apes, Flo was even given an obituary in *The Sunday Times* when she died.

Deaths can even affect a whole group of chimps in ways that can seem remarkably similar to those in human society. Traumatic deaths in chimpanzee communities, such as a chimp killed by a leopard, or falling from a tree, often result in shocked reactions from fellow members, aggressive displays and much mutual embracing and touching. Peaceful deaths, on the other hand, appear to provoke calmer and more respectful responses. James Andersen from the University of Stirling and colleagues illustrate the relationship between reactions to the death of fifty-year-old Pansy in a safari park and typical human reactions to such death (in brackets).

> During Pansy's final days the others were quiet and attentive to her, and they altered their nesting arrangements (respect, care, anticipatory grief). When Pansy died they appeared to test for signs of life by closely inspecting her mouth and manipulating her limbs (test for pulse or breath). Shortly afterwards, the adult male attacked the dead female, possibly attempting to rouse her [7] (attempted resuscitation); attacks may also have expressed anger or frustration (denial, feelings of anger towards the deceased). The adult daughter remained near the mother's corpse throughout the night (night-time vigil), while Blossom groomed Chippy for an extraordinary amount of time (consolation, social support). All three chimpanzees changed posture frequently during the night (disturbed sleep). They removed straw from Pansy's body the next morning (cleaning the body). For weeks post-death, the survivors remained lethargic and quiet, and they ate less than normal (grief, mourning). They avoided sleeping on the deathbed platform for several days (leaving objects or places associated with the deceased untouched).[127]

Other surprising similarities also challenge our notions of what makes humans different from other apes. At the Kanyawara community, in the

Kimbale National Park Uganda, chimpanzees, particularly young females, have been observed carrying around sticks which they cradle, holding them close and keeping them with them in their nests.[128] It remains unclear whether the infant chimpanzees are really mothering sticks as if they were dolls, or if they are just copying adult females with babies much as they also copy the use of sticks to fish for termites, but this behaviour doubtlessly adds to the human-like behaviours seen in chimpanzees. Until this finding we were convinced that only humans could care for inanimate objects by expressing a connection to things which goes beyond the purely functional.

By the turn of the twenty-first century, several decades of field research had shown beyond any real doubt that chimpanzees feel empathy for others. Frans De Waal from Emory University has recorded many different observations of chimpanzees and other apes reaching out to others to console them. Chimpanzees, for example, tend to feel sympathy for and 'hug' the loser of a fight rather than the winner where we might expect a selfish animal to 'side with' a winning chimpanzee. Apes console by touch and grooming, rush to those with whom they share close bonds for sympathy when they are distressed and show an understanding of others' pain.[129] Horacio Fábrega from the University of Pittsburgh has noted many building blocks of human reactions and care for the sick in chimpanzees.[130] When a chimpanzee is ill, a close relative may stay nearby and pay attention to grooming and cleaning wounds. In some cases, such as in captive communities where strong bonds may develop between unrelated individuals, and in the Tai National Park, where leopard predation is high, the whole community may be involved in the care of a sick individual, extending over months.

> Tai chimpanzees, however, totally independent of kin relationship, were regularly seen to tend wounded animals for extended periods of time ... Individual reactions tend to indicate that they are aware of the needs of the wounded, e.g., they lick the blood away and remove all dirt particles with fingers and lips, as well as preventing flies from coming near the wounds. In addition, empathy for the pain resulting from such wounds was clearly demonstrated by the reaction of other group members: After having received fresh wounds from an attack of a leopard, the injured individual is constantly looked after by group members, all trying to help by grooming and tending the wounds ... as wounds handicapped the

movements of the injured animal, group members remained with him as long as he needed before he was able to begin to walk again; some just waited whereas others would return to him until he started to move (three times the group waited for four hours at the same spot). Whenever he stopped they waited for him. Such a difference with Gombe chimpanzees may be explained by the high predation pressure Tai chimpanzees suffer from leopards.[131]

Apes, alongside dolphins and elephants, even show a level of self-awareness and understanding of others which means that they can truly 'step into another's shoes'. It may well be from such an understanding that these levels of care arise, as dolphins and elephants also attempt to help others who are injured. From around eighteen months of age both chimpanzees and humans also spontaneously help out others even where they is no expectation of any rewards, such as to reach objects, or pick up objects even where doing so involves considerable effort.[132]

The widespread evidence for a motivation in chimpanzees to care about and help others makes it difficult to argue that the evidence for any care in the early humans, such as that for the *Homo erectus* female with hypervitaminosis or for that of the toothless *Dmanisi hominin*, ought to be best explained by rational self-interested calculation. As Frans de Waal observes, reaching out to others is most plausibly explained in terms of an emotional motivation to help them, especially since rational calculation of any future benefits demands a much more complex level of thought.[133] If apes, like chimpanzees, gorillas and orang-utans, are capable of empathy and compassion, we should expect this motivation in early humans.

Observations of chimpanzees have also dispelled the myth that other animals are simply unwittingly *dictated to* by their emotions. We may be familiar with portrayals of Neanderthals or other ancient humans being driven by 'primal' urges, but despite these common perceptions it is clear that at least a certain capacity to control instinctive emotional responses has been present in apes for millions of years. Chimpanzees can deliberately hide their feelings to trick others. For example, they may control their anger and feign conciliation in order to fool an opponent into coming close enough to attack. Chimpanzee mothers may rein in their distress if a juvenile grabs their infant so as not to scare it into running away or going up a tree (though such mothers often attack the juvenile after having retrieved their infant). Subdominant males also control their desire to mate with a female while a dominant male is in view, including hiding their erect penis with their hands.

In humans terms we might say that chimpanzees are *cunning*. However, it is not only an understanding of others' beliefs which we note in such acts of deception but also impulse control. Being able to rein in the temptation for immediate action and control one's desire for a short-term reward in order to achieve a longer-term one is key to *delayed gratification*. Much of our society depends on delayed gratification on a far greater scale than we see in other primates, but both chimpanzees and human infants can overcome present frustrations or temptations for future gains. Given the choice between one treat now and several treats in the future, both chimpanzees and human infants can resist temptation, often by distracting themselves such as by playing with toys.[134] Sadly, advertising in modern societies often encourages us to opt for *have it now* rather than developing our far healthier abilities shared with chimpanzees to overcome immediate temptations in favour of a better future well-being.

Frans de Waal has even argued that chimpanzees have a type of morality which we might compare to our own.[135] Not everyone agrees, but at least the building blocks of some kind of emotional drive for fairness seems to be present in chimpanzee society. Those who attempt to steal food may find themselves threatened by several chimps who come to the aid of the chimp that they attempt to steal from (without expecting any reward). Those who are reluctant to share food will also tend to encounter aggression when they beg for food in the future. Chimpanzees

Chimpanzees console each other through touch.

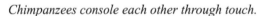

certainly have a rigid dominance hierarchy negotiated through power struggles; nonetheless, those alpha males who show greatest self-control and who concern themselves with fairness, such as by showing tolerance or breaking up fights among subordinate males, have a longer lived period of high status through support from the rest of the group. Excessively aggressive alpha males have even been known to have been thrown out from the group by the combined action of the others.

Chimpanzees are socially clever and can make judgements about those around them. They can mentally map the behaviours of different individuals, making decisions about who is likely to be a good collaborator as well as returning favours over long time spans, sometimes many months.[136] As we shall see in Chapter eight, it may have been characteristics such as these in the common ancestor between humans and chimpanzees that were critical to the evolution of a particularly human kind of emotional connection.

Of course, chimpanzees are no 'missing link'. From the times of our common ancestor they have also evolved along their own evolutionary path, adapting to the particular contexts in which they found themselves. There will be ways in which their evolutionary history may have given them certain talents which we never developed. Chimpanzees are physically several times stronger than us and though less intelligent in broad terms, may also have mental adaptations to their own particular settings. Experiments show that chimpanzees beat humans in games of visual memory. They are much better able to remember all of a visual image while humans are stuck focusing on what each part means in turn, trying to relate objects to their social context and how they might be used by someone, but in doing so missing something of the whole.[137] When watching a video of someone pouring a drink into a glass a chimpanzee will focus on the glass and the drink, remembering more details as they do. We, however, focus on what the objects might mean to the person holding them, watching their gaze and so missing details of what is happening. Visual memory must have been more important in the contexts in which chimpanzees evolved, but for some reason what objects may *mean* is more important to us. It is not all of their characteristics but only those which they share with us that are likely to have been present in our common ancestor.

Our shared responses to those we care about shows that early humans would have been capable of at least the level of compassion, perspective-taking and capacity to help others in distress that we see in chimpanzees.

But is chimpanzee empathy or compassion the same as that we see in humans?

It would appear that there are important differences.

The moments of empathy or compassion that astound us are not as common as they might appear. Moreover, empathy in chimpanzees seems to have a 'cut-off' point which is far more short-term and short-range than our own.

We may form a certain impression when we see moments of connection in chimpanzees, whether it is when they are reaching out to console another with a touch, or hugging a friend in distress. At that moment they certainly seem remarkably human. Yet such *moments* of connection are in typically few and far between in their predominantly self-orientated worlds, and only documented over many years of field research. Moreover, such empathy is very much *only to their friends* and *in the moment*, with no consideration for those outside a tight circle or for any long-term well-being.

Chimpanzees can often appear to be *impervious* to the well-being of other group members. Sharing of food is a rare event.[138] While chimpanzees at Tai Forest may be prepared to help injured friends, or adopt unrelated babies, these examples seem more of an exception, extremely rare or unknown in other groups.

Jane Goodall describes a moving incident at Gombe for example when the adult male Gregor contacted polio from human contact. Polio paralysed Gregor from the waist down and he dragged himself around by his arms, his loss of bladder control leaving him ridden with infection and followed by flies. Gregor tried to join the other chimps but he was shunned by them, even attacked by two of them. When he managed to drag himself to a circle of chimps who were grooming each other, holding out his hand desperately hoping for a touch from them, they fled away from him up into the trees.[139] Jane recalls that the ostracised Gregor sat motionless for several minutes, staring after them.

Jane wrote, 'As I watched him sitting there alone, my vision blurred, and when I looked up at the groomers in the tree, I came nearer to hating a chimpanzee than I have ever before or since.'[140]

Like Jane herself, we find ourselves more moved by Gregor's plight even just by knowing about it second-hand than were his closest friends and family who had lived their life with him. Such complete lack of compassion, common for any chimpanzee who looks or acts differently, upsets and angers us. Though Jane herself cared deeply about her chimps, we can't help but notice that the return feeling was, at best, only *tolerance*.

There is little room to be vulnerable in chimpanzee society. The rigid dominance hierarchy in which chimpanzees live means that status is highly tuned to physical power, and illness or injury radically affects social standing. Among the Tai Forest chimpanzees, the status of high-ranking Jomeo was substantially reduced when he injured his foot.[141] At Gombe illness reduced the previously dominant Faben to a submissive rank to his younger brother Figan when he lost the use of his arm through polio.[142] Indeed, adults normally become more solitary in old age as they are weaker and cannot keep up with the rest of the group. Though we have seen that there are cases where orphans *can* be adopted by another adult if their mothers die, this is the exception. It is normally only direct kin who *even respond* if infants are left behind or are whimpering, and orphans, no matter how vulnerable or whimpering, don't usually survive.

The social experience of a chimpanzee is profoundly different from our own. While chimpanzees live in groups, and are clearly 'social', their *internal experience* is largely one of making their way by themselves in the world in a way that seems lonely and isolated to us. We are driven to communicate our thoughts and feelings with others on an almost constant basis, whether we share knowledge, stories, gossip or dreams. Chimpanzees have no need for such connections. Though they can be taught sign language, they overwhelmingly use it communicate only about their physical wants and desires, even though able to use a limited set of emotion words (such as angry, happy or sad). It is not only *our ability to communicate* but *what we want to say to each other* which divides us from them.

Chimpanzee groups are not like human ones. While chimpanzees travel together, these groups are more loose coalitions than 'society'. There are no pair bonds, and the main close connections occur between mothers and young or in alliances made between often-related males. Such alliances can be dropped when they are no longer convenient. Trust has its role on some level, as a set of remembered favours, but power seems to be all-important, and we see little of any sense of shared feelings, or a common sense of what might be right or wrong.

John Mitani from the University of Michigan describes an incident among a group of chimpanzees:

A small party of chimpanzees gathers during the middle of the day. Bartok the alpha male, grooms quietly with his long-term friend and ally, Hare. The two rest comfortably beside each other, reaffirming their social bond while a third chimpanzee, the beta male Hodge, sits in the distance surveying the group. Just hours earlier the three joined several other males on a patrol deep into their neighbours' territory where together they encountered, attacked and killed a rival male. Suddenly another party of chimpanzees calls, having found a nearby tree laden with ripe fruit. Startled Bartok and Hare cease grooming and quickly move off in the direction of the calls to join the others. When they arrive at the fruit tree, they form a coalition and chase off Hodge, with whom they had earlier fought side-by-side against the neighbouring males.[143]

Bonds between chimpanzees might sometimes seem human, but they are easily forged or dropped depending on convenience, with little long-term trust.

Jane Goodall recounts another incident at Gombe. Sprout, mother to the adult male Satan, was a frail chimp, at least forty years old. When she heard powerful Satan being attacked by the adult males Figan and Evered she ran to his aid, throwing herself into the fray. Evered turned and began to hit her, giving Satan a chance to escape, which he gladly did. Sprout was hit a few times before she escaped.[144]

While the instinctive response of the mother to help her son reminds us of a certain human altruism, his own abandonment of her to her fate at the hands of the two adult males seems disloyal. We would have expected more solidarity and a willingness to stand up for someone dear to us, perhaps at almost any cost, rather than a bleak self-interest.

Perhaps the most shocking aspect of chimpanzee behaviour, however, has been their capacity for apparently heartless and calculated violence.

Chimpanzee 'warfare' first hit the news during 1974 to 1977. Until that point modern society had seen chimpanzees as the gentle cousins to humanity. This image was destroyed when at Gombe a splinter community consisting of several males and females split off from the main community only to be hunted down and killed over the subsequent four years. Chimps who had groomed each other and shared close bonds were killed brutally. First thoughts were that this was an isolated and unusual occurrence. However, research has shown that lethal raiding is a common element of chimpanzee social and territorial dynamics. During a decade-long study of chimpanzees at Kibale National Park Uganda, for example, twenty-one chimpanzees died in lethal violence leading to the eventual takeover of their territory.[145] 'Coalitions' of males form to raid neighbouring territories, attacking and killing their neighbours according to what have been shown to be chillingly rational decisions about whether such an attack is 'safe' or not, with unequal odds carefully avoided. This aggression is about *pay-offs*, not about honour or loyalties.

Lethal violence in chimpanzees is not easy to watch. It involves victims being brutally attacked, with adult males jumping on them and using their canines to tear off body parts such as ears and testes. In cases where humans have been attacked in such a way by chimpanzees, it appears that such 'territorial aggression' may well have been the cause. Most chillingly, perhaps, the protagonist chimpanzees seem to be in no

Two angry chimpanzees: chimpanzees can be remarkably violent towards other groups.

way disturbed by playing such a role in harm done to others. Chimpanzee hunting is equally a gruesome spectacle in which they tear apart monkeys or baboons with no apparent awareness of inflicting any suffering. Chimpanzees in their own way contributed to the idea that human warfare might be innate, and even *inevitable*.

Would we be right to jump to such a conclusion? Several lines of evidence suggest that extrapolating chimpanzee violence to a distant Palaeolithic past would be a mistake.

Violence in chimpanzees certainly appears to remind us of human violence. However, inferences about the behaviour of a common ancestor depend on *homologies* between related species. Homologies are behaviours (or genes) that species share that might reasonably have been present in the shared ancestor, and inherited in both branches of the family tree. For example, since a certain empathy is found in all apes, ourselves included, we can be quite certain that our shared ancestor with chimpanzees living around 7 to 8 million years ago also had a certain capacity for empathy and compassion (albeit perhaps fleeting and short-range).

Chimpanzees attacked their neighbours to take over their territory, and wasn't that exactly what happened in the First and Second World Wars? Inter-group violence certainly seemed to be *homologous* between chimpanzees and humans. While other apes are remarkably peaceful, if these two closely related species – chimpanzees and humans – were both aggressive to other groups, then this particular aggression – Dart's *killer ape instinct* – must have been present in their shared ancestor.

Violent feuding and competitions for dominance certainly seemed to support the concept that a high level of violence might be innate to humans. By being so aware of the shared empathy and altruism, were we only seeing what we wanted to see of our own ancestors in our chimpanzee cousins and ignoring the harsh reality of aggression?

A sad story, that of 'Nim Chimpsky', suggested to some that we *had* overly focused on our shared empathy with chimpanzees and failed to recognise the darker side of their nature. Indeed, nowhere were the dangers of *humanizing* chimpanzees, as well as the similarities and fundamental differences between ourselves and our nearest living relatives, better illustrated than in the story of this chimpanzee, *the chimp bought up to be human*.[146]

The story of Nim, the chimp, is possibly the most moving and certainly the most extraordinary story of primatology. Nim's life demonstrates how readily we can try to make other chimpanzees human, how close they can get to seeming like us, yet how wrong that can be. It also raised many ethical and emotional issues.

In order to test chimpanzee abilities at human language, Herbert Terrace from Colombia University ran a research project in the 1970s to raise a chimpanzee as a human. Nim was taken from his mother as a small baby and brought up by several different carers. He was taught sign language, would wear human clothes, eat at a table, and use the toilet. By the age of five, Nim used around 120 words, though little that might be called grammar or syntax. Alongside other experiments, those with Nim proved that chimpanzees could 'talk' in sign language, even if Nim's use of language, like other signing chimpanzees, was almost entirely pragmatic – to get what he wanted, rather than to share meaning, thoughts or feelings.[147]

However, the scientific insights gained from the experiment to bring Nim up as a human came at a great cost. Whatever his abilities to communicate, Nim didn't have the emotional capacities to live in a human world. As he grew older attacks on his carers became commonplace, one carer needing thirty-seven stitches and another being hospitalised. Did Nim care about his carers? Possibly. Certainly, it is clear that he loved human contact and to play. Yet he lacked the restraint necessary to limit his aggression or the capacity to understand the consequences of his attacks, or feel remorse for them. As is natural to a common chimpanzee, Nim was beginning to competitively assert his place in what he saw as a dominance hierarchy.

After four years and with no further funding, Nim was given back to the primate centre from where he came. Here, however, he struggled to fit in, getting into fights with other chimps and coming to the front of his cage, signing 'out' to anyone passing. It took Nim a long time to learn to be a chimp. Even more tragically, in 1982 Nim and at least twenty other chimps were sold to a Laboratory for Medical and Surgical research on primates, to be used in research into hepatitis. Here, he and his fellows would hang from the ceiling in cramped cages, while he repeatedly signed 'out' and asked for coffee, coke, cigarettes and pot. After a press campaign to free Nim, he was finally rescued, at least partly due to the efforts of an American lawyer who claimed that if he could speak he should be accorded human rights. His final home would be a horse sanctuary where it would be some time until any other chimp would join him. Nim died at the age of twenty-six of a heart attack.

In his enclosure in the horse sanctuary, Nim had two cherished possessions which he hid away. One was a children's book, a *Sesame Street* volume with a section on how to learn sign language. The other was Terrance's published volume on the Nim project. This featured many photographs of Nim when he was young, images which Nim often pored over. We can't help but wonder what it meant to him. Chimpanzees are self-aware and he will doubtless have recognised himself. Did he wonder why he was put in such a situation and ponder on the motives of the people who appeared to have cared about him?

Can we blame Nim for his acts of aggression? As in the case of other common chimpanzees who have attacked and maimed humans, often their owners or carers mistakenly thought of him as *almost human*, though he was only *being a chimp*. We would not have expected him to have any conscience, nor a shared sense of a greater whole, nor a common understanding of right or wrong or sense of loyalty or trust or responsibility. His aggression was innate to an animal evolving in a physically competitive world and he rarely had the self-control which might prevent him from acting on his impulse to attack.

The infant Nim: an ape expected to be human.

Had Jane stumbled upon an uncomfortable truth about humanity while studying chimpanzees? The callousness of inter-group conflicts at Gombe, as well as Nim's inability or unwillingness to control his aggression, suggest that a brutal and aggressive past lay just under the surface of our civilised exteriors. But was the basis for chimpanzee aggression unique to their particular context?

The emotions at the heart of chimpanzee aggression seem different from those that fuel human conflicts. For chimpanzees, members of other groups seem not to exist – they are *dechimpified* even if they used to be friends. Humans *can* fail to see any feelings in others, but as we shall see in Chapter six, only in certain specific circumstances. Humans conflicts are complicated. We are more often fuelled by a need to defend and protect loved ones, or by an active hatred for another group. We experience jealousies, pride, patriotism, loyalty, and a host of other deep-seated emotions – seen as both morally good or ill – which are infinitely more complex and more *other-focused* than in chimpanzees. Human conflicts are much less immediate. We might get angry at those around us, but only toddlers lack the self-control to prevent them from hitting out.

Even the fiercest and most violent ethnographically documented population, the Yanomami peoples who live by hunting and gathering and horticulture in the Amazon, are violent for entirely different reasons than those seen in chimpanzees. Their inter-group feuding takes the form of longstanding and very specific retaliations for previous personal attacks. Moreover, the Yanomami see attacks on specific members of another group as motivated by compassion, a selfless desire to show courage and put oneself at risk in order to alleviate the suffering of relatives of someone who has been hurt or killed.[148]

Chimpanzees' internal social systems are fundamentally different from ours – they are dominated by aggressive competitions for positions in a rigidly defined dominance hierarchy. There are constant conflicts over power within a hierarchy where regular displays of aggression instil a climate of tension as males compete to be an alpha male. Some might see some parallels in human society but most researchers disagree. There is good reason to think that the chimpanzee social system is *derived*, that is, developed after the split with the hominin (human) line and so not homologous at all.

The social systems of all the apes are remarkably different and seem to adapt quickly to different ecological situations according to varying environments. Chimpanzees seem to be a particular case. Orang-utans living in forests where food is thinly distributed are solitary or live in female-infant pairs; gorillas live in harems with only one adult male and several females; gibbons live as lifelong monogamous pairs. Though all apes share a quick mind, empathy, sense of curiosity and social orientation, the way that they organise their social groups and its implications for aggressive encounters could hardly be more different. Moreover, such systems adapt quickly to changing environments.

Rob Foley from the University of Cambridge argues that the early human social structure, adapted to a more open savannah environment, was unlikely to be like that of chimpanzees. He argues that human groups were potentially made up of many individuals within which males and females formed serially monogamous bonds in order to protect vulnerable offspring.[149] Andrew Whiten from the University of Aberdeen also argues that egalitarianism might have been the key to avoiding the constant conflicts (with its waste of energy and constant risk of injury) seen in chimpanzees.[150] Collaboration rather than constant conflict may well be the secret of human success compared to chimpanzees.

In an evolutionary sense is chimpanzee violence in a camp of its own?

We have always thought of chimpanzees as our nearest living relatives, and their behaviour the best model we can have for that of early humans. However, this may have been wrong.

Further evidence against seeing the aggression of chimpanzees as equally part of a human past comes from the *forgotten ape*, the bonobo.[151]

What makes bonobos, or pygmy chimpanzees, important is that they are as closely related to us as common chimpanzees. Both species share a common ancestor living around 2 to 3 million years ago, from which common chimpanzees (*Pan troglodytes*) and bonobos (*Pan paniscus*) evolved.

Bonobos have rarely been considered as a model for a human ancestor. They are rarer than common chimpanzees, restricted to the Congo Basin, thereby making them harder to study. We rarely see them in zoos as their frequent use of sex with different partners and in different positions to appease conflicts and forge bonds with each other, was certainly not suitable for Victorian eyes. Most particularly, they are *less overtly impressive*. Though captive bonobos proved to be the best at picking up how to use stone tools and how to use sign language, of which Kanzi is the most famous example, in the wild they rarely hunt or use tools. Moreover, with their somewhat more gaunt bodies, tufts of hair on their heads and a greater degree of baldness, they are *less attractive looking* than chimpanzees. Bononos are also gentle, tolerant and non-aggressive. Precisely due to their gentle nature and emotional tolerance, they have been seen as far less relevant to the human story. By being less intimidating, less powerful and less aggressive they didn't seem to fit the bill for a model of how to take over the world.

Bonobos certainly tell us a slightly different story of an ape society, and one which might be a much better analogy for early human societies. Many researchers believe that our common ancestors' emotions might have been more bonobo-like in important ways.

Bonobos are, if anything, more altruistic than common chimpanzees. Frans de Waal documents an incident with a group of bonobos at San Diego Zoo:

> The two-meter-deep moat in front of the old bonobo enclosure at the San Diego Zoo had been drained for cleaning. After having scrubbed the moat and released the apes, the keepers went to turn on the valve to refill it with water when all of a sudden the old male, Kakowet, came to their window, screaming and frantically waving his arms so as to catch their attention. After so many years, he was familiar with the cleaning routine. As it turned out, several young bonobos had entered the dry moat but were unable to get out. The keepers provided a ladder. All bonobos got out except for the smallest one, who was pulled up by Kakowet himself.[152]

Bonobo social systems are also subtly different. Bonobos are far less competitive than common chimps – they are much more tolerant of outsiders, as well as much less aggressive within their groups, with inter-group violence almost unknown. As Jane Goodall documented, common chimpanzees live within highly political social systems with rigid hierarchies. Males are top of the heap, forever putting much of their efforts into competing for dominance. Females, living under risk of aggression from males, live for much of their lives less connected to each other in their small family groups around the related coalitions of male chimpanzees. Like common chimpanzees, bonobos live in groups of related males and unrelated females. However, bonobo hierarchy is *female dominated*, with females forming strong bonds. Moreover, the ability of bonobos to handle their feelings in order to console others, to collaborate through shared understanding, or to resist the temptation to lose their tempers, are more finely tuned than such abilities in common chimpanzees.

Why don't the most aggressive bonobos rise to the top and dominate the others as we see typically in chimpanzees? It seems that for bonobos, being helpful and likeable is a better way of attracting and keeping friends and allies and being influential rather than being dominating. Being *likeable* is important to some extent to all primates. Research has shown that even monkeys tend to shun humans whom they have seen being mean;[153] it matters to them who they can trust. Being liked rather than feared seems to be the most important social principle in bonobos, however. Zanna Clay and Frans de Waal have shown that those bonobos best able to handle their own feelings, and so best able to console others when they were upset, had the closest circles of allies.[154] Having allies for bonobos seems to be more about being empathetic and liked than being strong, powerful and competitive, and bonobo society itself reflects

Are gentle bonobos a better analogy for a common ancestor with humans than common chimpanzees?

these rather different priorities than we typically see in common chimpanzees. More stable and collaborative societies make sense from an evolutionary perspective – it frees up the effort, stress and risk otherwise expended in aggressive encounters.

Brian Hare and his team from the Max Planck Institute in Leipzig recently demonstrated a remarkable similarity between bonobos and humans but not common chimpanzees – one that for certain interesting reasons we also share with dogs.[155] They noticed that while common chimpanzees are relatively poor at particular cooperative tasks that involve shared attention, and understanding 'what the other individual is getting at', human infants are relatively good at this. Pointing, or other more subtle indicators of where food is hidden, work well with infants. Remarkably, the only other animals with this ability are dogs and bonobos. What appears to govern this ability is the selection for reduced emotional reactivity. In dogs a reduced tendency to be afraid of or aggressive towards humans has been promoted through human selection. However, the same ability also appears to have been selected for naturally by the social environment of early humans and bonobos alike. Brian Hare calls this the 'self-domestication' hypothesis.[156] Since it didn't pay off to be aggressive in either bonobo or early human groups, these were the 'kinder' and more tolerant contexts where shared understandings thrived most easily.

Did chimpanzee violence develop after bonobos and chimpanzees split, around 2 to 3 million years ago, following its own evolutionary track unrelated to ours? Or are the similarities in the emotional tolerance of members of their own and other groups seen in bonobos' and humans' adaptations to similar conditions, much as a similar tolerance developed in dogs under selection from humans? As yet there isn't enough evidence to know.

One thing that is clear is that evidence from bonobos shows that we can't make a direct parallel between the aggression we see in chimpanzees and what might have structured early human societies. Both chimpanzees and bonobos seem so human in some ways and so unlike us in others, and it is no wonder that it has been so difficult to resist the temptation of jumping to conclusions every time we see something, like violent feuding, that seems at least on the surface to feel *human*. Yet both Nim's behaviour and chimpanzee feuding prove to be *less human* than we had assumed.

Research in primatology has gone a long way to revealing how the societies of our nearest living relatives work since Jane Goodall's first footsteps in chimpanzee behaviour. From having almost no information in the 1960s, research into chimpanzees and bonobos has provided fundamental insights. Evidence for empathy, compassion and an ability to reach out to others in our nearest living cousins and across other apes – something we all share – gives us a tantalising picture of the potential capacity for altruism in early humans. Through being able to see the world through others' eyes, we've seen that both chimpanzees and bonobos can achieve a bond between kin and close friends, and are able to console each other in distress, and they can, at times, even step in to help those who are vulnerable and defend each other from threats. Other apes give us a basis for how we might imagine something of our human past.

Whatever they can tell us, nonetheless, modern apes are neither the same as us, nor can they give us more than *glimpses* of what early humans might have been like. We can study them in detail, but they are still far removed in time and in genetic makeup from our ancestors. Fascinating as they are, the emotional capacities of neither chimpanzee nor bonobo are truly *the same as ours,* nor the same as early humans also separated from them by millions of years of evolution.

Some key emotional differences can't help but stand out. No chimpanzee or bonobo has ever looked after another adult even for *days* let alone the *weeks* for which the *Homo erectus* female with hypervitaminosos was cared for, and nothing approaches the months and years of consistent long-term care for the vulnerable that we've seen in *Homo heidelbergensis* or Neanderthals. No chimpanzee or bonobo creates anything we can call confidently refer to as true *art* or which shows the concern with form and aesthetic that we see from shortly after 2 million years ago in humans. There are no finely worked pieces, no precious objects that are carried around. There are no pair bonds in chimpanzee society, and even while friends remember favours, their own self-interest remains paramount in their minds. Chimpanzees seem to care about each other in their own way, yet Hare was let down by his allies and Sprout by her son without any of them giving a second thought. The entire group at Gombe was killed one by one by their previous friends. Bonobos may be less aggressive, yet there is also something missing in terms of any long-term *trust*. Why are they not appalled at any callous treatment? Where is the ripple of emotions that turns a crowd? Can they even understand a moment of ordinary kindness, self-sacrifice, bravery, or supreme control that inspires us all? Where is the sense of consciousness about who they are, about what others think? Where is the shared feeling of *chimpanzeeness* to compare with what we see as human? Both chimpanzees and bonobos who learn human sign language use it to talk about things they want, not about how we or they might feel.

Seven to eight million years ago our ancestor may have been the same, but chimpanzees and bonobos took their own paths since then. We will have to turn to other evidence to tell us when, where and why our distinctively human minds and emotions emerged.

Was it something about the environments in which we found ourselves, how we found food, the dangers that we faced or how our groups were structured that made us human? Was there some spark which set us along our own unique path to human feelings?

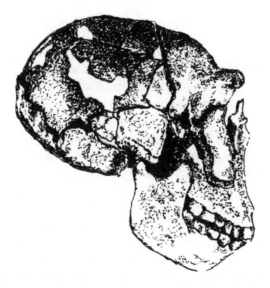

The cranium of WT15000 (Nariokotome Boy)
illustrates the enlarged brain size of early
Homo erectus.

Chapter Five

Minds Preserved in Stone

And the bones said
these had the gliding hip-roll of all fours
hands as feet in a sort of crawl
and these erect straighter
this cupula of a skull in sticky mud
this pelvis balanced for running movements
and energy pours through it alert fingers
limbs that dance these voices together.[157]

We can never ask our ancestors what they felt, and living primates only provide us with some glimpses, rather tangential clues to early humans themselves. Here we focus on what appears to be the best and most direct evidence of ancient minds, that from the size and shape of fossil crania and from other hard evidence for our early ancestors. Over time, our brains have become larger and larger, but what did early humans need these large brains for? Could what is inside their minds be interpreted from what is left of their skulls? Our preconceptions often seem to cloud our judgement of even this apparently hardest of evidence, making it even more difficult to interpret. We consider interpretations of Neanderthals based on fossil evidence and reflect on how easily we respond to what our gut reactions tell us we ought to see.

If only our ancestors could somehow tell us how they felt, what motivated them to either look after their fellows or hurt them. Were they protecting their loved ones, maintaining equality when they attacked another human or, like the common chimpanzees in their violent attacks, did they not see others as human at all and care nothing for them? Did they care deeply for people close to them when they looked after them or carried out some ritual at their death or was it just something that they did that did little to move their hearts? What would we feel if we looked in their eyes?

All that is left to us is the dry and dusty remains of their fossilised bones and the hard evidence of their stone tools or food remains. Yet sometimes even the humblest of evidence can transport us in time and that which seems the hardest and most direct evidence can be the most misleading.

The artefacts more than any others that speak to us most directly about how people in the Palaeolithic might have *felt* are often not found on display in museums. They are not beautiful, skilfully made or aesthetically pleasing, though certainly these finely made creations often fill us with awe. These other artefacts instead, are deeply evocative of how it felt to be a Palaeolithic hunter-gatherer, at least for a few moments of time. When I was excavating as a student at the Upper Palaeolithic site of Combe Saunière in France I found one such artefact.

I'd been learning to knap flint, a long and difficult process. In fact, I never seemed to get beyond making the typical mistakes of the learner – step fractures and hinge fractures where flakes I wanted to take off right across the flint core had broken part way. I had a tendency to optimistically keep on going, attempting to take pieces off even when it ought to have been obvious that the piece I was working on had been ruined and was useless, and I had a deep sense of frustration at how difficult it was, leading to ineffective bashing of the edges. I depended on the skilled flint knappers at the site to show me what to do. It was a bit humiliating to make so many mistakes, but I really wanted to learn so I stuck at it.

It was one day, when excavating in levels 20,000 years old at the margins of the site, that I uncovered an artefact that stopped me in my tracks. It was a flint core. This one was not perfectly worked, not finely made, but instead, a mass of *oh so familiar* mistakes resulting in nothing of any use being produced – the same step and hinge fractures that I had made, the same frustrated useless bashing even when things had gone wrong, just like the mistakes I'd made the day before. The core may well have been thrown away in frustration, lying well beyond the main part of the site. Holding it in my hand I knew *just how they felt*. Like the other cores and artefacts made by novice knappers, this core would never find its way to the museum display. Unlike the finely made artefacts in museums this was a mess, its final form far from impressive, but nonetheless it spoke directly about a very human determination to learn, as well as about defeat and frustration.

Evidence for novice knappers, often at the periphery of where skilled knappers were working, comes from many sites in the Upper Palaeolithic and even in the Middle Palaeolithic and earlier.[158] At Oldeholtewolde in the Late Palaeolithic of the Netherlands, for example, refitting analysis of flint flakes has shown that experts had knapped finely made blades and flakes from their cores before passing the used central core to learners, probably children. The learners would use the cores for practice, knapping clumsy flakes that were of no use. Novices have also been identified at several Neanderthal sites. At the site of Maastrict Belvedere Site K, a majority of cores are covered in incompetent mistakes, some even showing repeated and pointless bashing at the flint edges. These have been interpreted as being made by young Neanderthal children – typical of a frustrated child taking their temper out on their toys. Several of the artefacts at Boxgrove dated to half a million years ago have also been interpreted as having been made by learners, probably children. The conscious attempt to get better, to develop a skill, the grim determination to continue despite the odds, and the sense of frustration at failure seen in such poorly made artefacts seem so entirely human.

The messy and imperfect tools made by children often receive the scarcest attention yet they tell us much about how people might have felt.

Often it is the most intimate moments of connection between peoples which leaves the least impressive-looking evidence. My own excavations at Mesolithic sites five to ten thousand years old in the Pennines were no exception. Here, we found among the smallest flint assemblages in the world, tiny finely made microliths (the barbs for hunting weapons), often only a few millimetres long. Sometimes made of black chert and found in Pennine peats, they are among the most challenging artefacts to excavate. Over four years, my

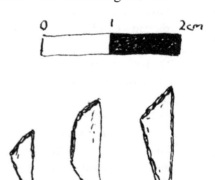

Microliths from March Hill – these diminuitive tools can be seen as unimpressive and unimportant no matter how finely made simply because of their size.

team of ten to fifteen people had to use the most careful and meticulous methods for excavating and recording sites, the location of the tiniest flint flakes recorded to millimetres of accuracy. It was more than worth it though as we revealed the location of a series of hearths around which prehistoric hunter-gatherers had sat knapping flint, knocking old damaged barbs from their arrows and replacing them with new ones, most likely while looking out across the Pennines and the surrounding lowlands for new game.[159] Their precise sitting positions were even left to us, like a Palaeolithic Pompeii, as gaps in the distributions, and their flint cores could be re-fitted. Once everything was excavated we all wanted a turn to sit in a Mesolithic bottom print and look out across the moors, of course.

These sites are uniquely well preserved, studies showing that the artefacts had moved no more than a few centimetres from where they were deposited.[160] They are always hard to interest people in or protect from damage however, simply because the finds themselves are small and seem unimpressive.

We can't help but wonder how these Mesolithic people felt. Sitting on those hillsides in the wild Pennines, often shrouded in mist, we seemed ourselves to be living and working in a wild and prehistoric landscape yet one from which we could see the cities at the heart of the Industrial Revolution, cities like Huddersfield and Manchester. Scarcely could there be a greater contrast. It seemed so bizarre that so many people in the distance hurried about their frantic lives with no knowledge of the ancient landscape beneath them or these so different ways of being. We could almost feel the ghosts of Mesolithic hunter-gatherers watching our world.

Our basic human emotions link us to past hunter-gatherers from the Upper Palaeolithic and Mesolithic, but how do we understand or even imagine the feelings of earlier humans? These Neanderthal children no doubt felt a frustration similar to mine when their attempts to knap didn't go their way. But did they also feel embarrassed at their mistakes? Proud when things finally went right? Were adults sympathetic? Was it the understanding, example and patient guidance of adults that helped them get there in the end?

Did earlier species feel these same emotions or other emotions that seem so particularly *human*? Which of these early human species would our hearts tell us was human? Could *Homo heidelbergensis* at Boxgrove half a million years ago *admire* or *respect* someone else? Did they feel *grateful* or *remorseful* or *ashamed* or *embarrassed*? Did they blush with embarrassment or cry when upset, both evolved physiological responses

111

to give honest displays of how we feel?[161] What of darker emotions, *revenge* or *spite*, seemingly so lacking in chimpanzees? Did these early humans feel *betrayed*, and were they driven to take revenge? And were they aware of how they felt?

If only the minds of these ancient people could be preserved. They can't, of course, and there is little direct material evidence left to us to tell us how the brains of these peoples worked. However, one clue, excavated from sites across the world, comes from the fossil crania, human braincases which once housed ancient brains.

The famous palaeontologist Louis Leakey was in little doubt that the best direct evidence for our earliest ancestors would come from their own bones – the preserved fossil evidence of early humans. Meticulous excavations over many decades built up a better and better record of the anatomy of ancient human species and how they related to each other, which of the different human-like apes were on the main branch of human evolution and which were side branches that never survived. Painstaking research allows us to now hold skulls in our hands and look into the face of human-like apes living millions of years ago.

Could these fossil skulls tell us what ancient humans thought or felt?

The clearest pattern we see is that of *an increase in brain size* throughout human evolution. Much as Victorians had delighted in the large brain of Piltdown Man, the increasing brain size through evolution seemed to confirm that humans were more and more clever, technically intelligent, better able to think and solve problems and that *thinking skills* were at the heart of our human journey.

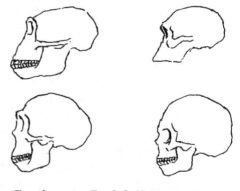

Fossil crania: Top left: Homo erectus *Top right:* Australopithecine, *Bottom left:* Neanderthal, *Bottom right:* Modern human.

Brain size, and most importantly brain size *in relation to body size*, hasn't increased entirely gradually. Around 3 million years ago, australopithecine brains, around 450cc in size, were not so different in size than the 350cc of our chimpanzee cousins. However, 2 million years ago human brains began to get significantly larger and the period of infant

112

dependency correspondingly greater. Those of *Homo ergaster* living at this time were of the order of 900cc and by the time of *Homo heidelbergensis*, around half million years ago, our brains were almost the size that they are today (1000ml, compared with modern brains of 1200ml). Today, our brains are around three times the size of those of our nearest living relatives, the chimpanzees.

Size isn't everything, of course. The diminutive *Homo floresiensis* or 'Hobbit', living on the island of Flores, apparently survived with a brain size of only 425cc until as recently as perhaps 12,000 years ago. Nonetheless, something happened to the main branch of the human evolutionary tree which allowed us to break what scientists call the 'grey ceiling', a limit on how much energy could normally be invested in the brain in proportion to our bodies. Opinions vary over what was used to power such large brains, whether such energy came from increasing the proportion of meat in diets,[162] or the advent of cooking which released more energy from foods.[163] However, it is clear that there was intense evolutionary pressure on brain expansion from around 2 million years ago.

Was the increase in brain size just about intellectual intelligence, our capacity to think through problems or reason scientifically which so impressed the Victorians?

Recently, researchers have appreciated that it was not just the size but the *shape* of the brain which may have been most important. Those changes in shape cause us to question whether it was really *intellectual abilities* which were of critical importance. Studies of changes in the *shape of the brain* and what brain shape means in other primates suggest that that it was something to do with our social lives which drove brain enlargement.

Robin Dunbar from Oxford University has studied the shape of human and other primate brains, and found a relationship between the size of the neocortex, the front part of the brain, and size of the social group that different primates live in.[164] Getting on with lots of individuals is mentally much more taxing than only a few for those primates which develop many complex bonds. Since our neocortex size has progressively increased in proportion to the rest of the brain throughout human evolution, Dunbar suggests that our move into open grasslands, with all the dangerous predators, meant that we had to live in much larger groups to survive, and that we needed more and more social brain power to get on with everyone

113

else and avoid being excluded. Along with the philosopher Nicolas Humphrey,[165] he believes that our big brains, our complicated areas of thought like our *consciousness*, our ability to think through what other people think about us or how they might react to what we do, even our drive to gossip, read novels or watch Eastenders, were driven by an evolutionary need to get on with other people.

The shape of human brains, inasmuch as they are preserved from so many million years ago, may suggest that what made us unique had something to do with social lives. But sadly, the study of crania revealed nothing that might indicate emotional capacities or complex thoughts, no one area for *morality*, *compassion* or *intellect*. We don't really know what element of being more social was particularly important.

Was a drive to understand others all about improving their well-being, or was it about being more cunning and manipulative to further our own welfare?

In the 1980s the obvious answer seemed to be that large brains were about being better at deceiving people and exploiting others to gets one's own way. So-called Machiavellian intelligence theory was named after the highly manipulative politics described in Niccolò Machiavelli's book, *The Prince*, in the sixteenth century.[166] It put being cunning and political at the heart of the evolution of human minds. Early humans would have *thought* their way to the top through cunning deception.

Chimpanzees can be cunning, and humans likewise. But was the theory of Machiavellian intelligence simply a reflection of the climate of the time? It may well have been. In recent decades others have argued that the social drive in human brain expansion is far more likely to be related to *collaboration*, being better able to work together to survive.

There is no lump or bump that might tell us. The only part of our brains that we can identify as becoming much larger at a certain time is a region called *Broca's area* in the front part of the brain. This region is enlarged in the crania of *Homo habilis* around 1.9 million years ago. Since people who suffer damage to this part of the brain have their abilities to speak and understand language impaired, its appearance suggests that spoken language might have emerged at this time.

Language might not at first glance seem to have much to do with our feelings towards others, but many academics argue that it does.[167] Robin Dunbar suggests that language developed as a way of maintaining contact

114

with many different friends as group sizes got larger.[168] Dean Falk from Florida State University believes that language was important in reassuring our young. Words may have developed from the melodic vocalisations that many mammals use with their infants.[169] The cooing way that we all talk to babies, something psychologists call *motherese*, certainly has more to do with feelings than any intellectual thought. Perhaps most importantly, language helps us to be aware of our feelings, bringing them into rational thought. If we don't have a chance for our feelings to be understood as a child, something called *validation*, as an adult we will tend to react impulsively. Research has shown that people involved in violent fights often can't put their feelings into words; anger *makes them hit out* where the act of bringing feelings into thought through the use of words would tame angry impulses.[170] We don't just depend on those around us to learn language to communicate practical things as we grow up, we depend on them to help us use it to *tame* our emotions, to exercise self-control.

Other than Broca's area however, little of the internal structure of the brain shows up on crania. Moreover, aside from the expansion of the neocortex, many of the changes in shape that we see in different periods of evolution are difficult to decipher.[171]

Paranthropus boisei, for example, the so-called 'nutcracker man', from around 5 million years ago, has huge flared ridges on the top of his skull. Rather than anything to do with thinking (and *boisei* seemed to have a rather small brain), these are most likely to be attachments for vast chewing muscles. We still don't know if *Paranthropus boisei* needed all these muscles for chewing grasses or nuts or exactly what they ate, but it must have been something very difficult to chew. Had we evolved from *boisei* we might have looked very different.

Other archaic human species don't look as radical as *boisei* did. However, there are still distinctive features in the size and shape of their brains which suggest that they might have thought or felt in their own particular way. Neanderthals, for example, evolved separately from our own line for 600,000 years and though their brains were as large or even larger than our own, their brain shape is longer and lower. As separate species adapted to their environments, their bodies are more robust than their Homo sapiens cousins, better suited to enduring cold climates and travelling and hunting in rugged terrains. Was something missing in the minds of the Neanderthals that we were uniquely endowed with? Conversely, did Neanderthals have mental abilities that we ourselves lack?

Robin Dunbar and his student Eiluned Pearce have concluded that part of the difference in shape is related to an enlarged visual cortex in Neanderthals.[172] The dark and sometimes forested environments of Europe seem to put evolutionary pressure on Neanderthals to develop better visual abilities than those of our species.

As well as the visual part of their brains, other elements of how they thought or felt may well have been different from our own and more finely adapted to the worlds *in which they lived*. Even closely related species of primates, such as common bonobos and chimpanzees or different species of New World Monkey have evolved to be subtly different in emotional terms.[173] Separation often leads to random differences, so called *genetic drift*, but different emotional capacities might also have been important in terms of survival. Some New World Monkeys have adapted to a diet of sap extruding slowly from trees and are more patient than others, better able to wait without getting frustrated. As we saw in Chapter four, bonobos are more tolerant of each other than common chimpanzees and being less prone to react angrily to others, they are noticeably better co-operators. Emotional capacities seem to be able to change remarkably quickly. Our own selection of the most pleasing puppies radically changed the temperament of wolves into those of domestic dogs, whose tolerance towards humans is a far cry from that of their Palaeolithic ancestors. Experiments in Siberia show that this process can happen in only a few generations in wild foxes.

Frustratingly, the direct evidence from fossil crania tells us much less than we might expect it to about human emotions. Simply the hard bones themselves couldn't answer any of the questions about what emotions early humans were feeling, when they emerged and how they evolved.

That archaic human brains were *different* in size and shape to our own reminds us that these people might have been distinct not only in cognitive but also in emotional terms. But what do these differences mean? How can we begin to understand the emotions of species like Neanderthals, and ones of those earlier species ancestral to ourselves?

We can't resist coming up with theories about what set Neanderthals apart from us. Steve Mithen from the University of Reading thinks that Neanderthals may not have been able to connect different types of thoughts together in the same way that we can.[174] The different realms of

116

their thoughts might have remained separate – thinking about practical skills, like making stone tools, never overlapping with thoughts about people. Of course, it is possible but there is little evidence to prove or dispute the idea. Other researchers have suggested that Neanderthals could not conceive of the future, or had limited abilities to communicate with each other. The idea of a species of human so near to us, yet subtly different, fascinates us.

Sadly, in the case of Neanderthals any suggestion of difference is easily interpreted as inferiority, a *lack of human feeling* rather than more subtle differences. Simply the way that Neanderthals looked, from their big brow ridges to their robust skeletons, has had a major impact on how we interpret their remains and on what it might mean that an ancient human could have a brain that, though as large as ours, may have been structured differently.

The first reconstructions of Neanderthals were hardly complimentary. The palaeontologist Marcelin Boule described them as dull-witted, and his reconstruction of a Neanderthal in 1911 showed them with their heads thrust forwards, thuggish, stooped and hairy. Much of that image has stuck. He may have based his reconstruction on the hard evidence of fossil

The skeleton which Marcelin Boule used for his reconstruction of a Neanderthal, that from La Chapelle aux Saints, had a pronounced curvature of the spine and other deformities most probably caused by osteoarthritis.

remains but he ignored the fact that the fossil he had used for inspiration from La Chapelle aux Saints was not only elderly, but his bones had been badly affected by osteoarthritis or extreme strain causing curvature of his spine and other deformities. Boule's tendency to envisage beings that were not human as brutish and inferior coloured what he saw. Even early illustrators would rotate the crania of Neanderthals to make them look smaller brained and with bigger brow ridges in comparison to our species – emphasising differences in a way that was hardly scientific.[175] It was almost as if they couldn't help themselves.

Our tendency to see Neanderthals as thuggish, based on how we feel about how they look, lasts to this day and is hard to overcome.

Have we been as biased in making assumptions about how Neanderthals felt?

For many years researchers have avoided the subject of emotions. However, we can't help wishing to know what motivated our nearest fossil relatives, a species which contributed to our own genes. Thomas Wynn and Frederick Coolidge for example conclude that we *can* begin to interpret something of their

Marcelin Boule combined a vivid imagination with biased skeletal remains in his reconstruction in 1909 of a brutish, hunched, hairy Neanderthal.

The Neanderthal cranium illustrated in Huxley's 1863 Man's Place in Nature (left) had been inclined and drawn from very close, which emphasised the brow ridges and made the brain case appear small; had it been drawn face-on (right), Neanderthals would have been shown to have been far more similar to our own species.[176]

personalities on the basis of archaeological evidence. In reviewing evidence for patterns of injury from fossil skeletons, they argue that even though Neanderthals certainly looked after those who were ill, and with his few teeth and debilitating arthritis Boule's old man from La Chapelle was no exception, we should not believe that they were kind. In their view, Neanderthals were in actual fact notably *callous* and *hard-hearted*.[176] A damning conclusion – callous hard-heartedness is something we normally find hard to forgive. Chimpanzees fighting for dominance may be described as 'aggressive', failing may be to respond to pleas for food or support as 'pragmatic', but rarely as 'callous' or 'hard-hearted'. Somehow, people who feel nothing at another's plight almost seem lower in our eyes than any driven by fear or aggression.

Were Neanderthals truly callous? Wynn and Coolidge base their conclusions on the evidence for traumatic injuries seen in fossil bones. A relative abundance of serious upper body traumas over those to the lower body in the skeletal record suggests to them that even though all the individuals who were preserved in the archaeological record had been cared for and allowed to heal, there were others for which we have no evidence. *These* were the ones who were treated callously. According to Wynn and Coolidge, if we don't find people who were injured in the legs and couldn't walk, they must have been abandoned, never making it back to the rockshelter sites where human bones are typically recovered.

Did harsh conditions, cold, famines and the difficulties they had finding food, force Neanderthals to become hard-hearted in response? Paul Pettitt takes a similar approach from reviewing the fossil bones of infants and children found on Neanderthal sites. He sees Neanderthals as brutish, a little like hyenas in the way in which they used their home spaces, perhaps even callous with their young, commenting that teeth and small skeletal fragments of infants and juveniles 'litter caves'.[177]

Such interpretations influence us. No need to feel sympathy for such folk who, even if they did look after their wounded, must have been driven by practical concerns when doing so, ready to abandon the vulnerable at other times. Survival of the strongest? The image of a Neanderthal injured in the leg when hunting with the group, vainly trying to keep up with the others but being ruthlessly abandoned, while friends and family make their way back to their cosy home is an evocative one. How could they be so cruel? Carcasses of babies heartlessly discarded in caves like rubbish is an equally chilling image.

Can we be a little quick to jump to conclusions where Neanderthals are concerned? A little too influenced by the assumptions we inherit from a highly competitive modern world? If we wish to make inferences about emotions we might need to be careful about our biases. As we shall see in Chapter seven we judge people on what we think *motivates them*, and Neanderthals are no different. We can be remarkably quick to make assumptions about people who we feel might not really belong to *our* group or who seem to reflect forms of behaviour about which we feel particularly anxious.

Any interpretation that Neanderthals *must have been callous* requires further scrutiny. Take the bones of infants littering caves. Bones of infants *are* found in the sediments of Neanderthal cave sites. However, similar infant bones are also found equally frequently littering sites of much later periods. Is it really a human trait to be so careless of our infants? Two of my students, Andy Needham and Gail Hitchens, and myself suggest it is far more likely that, as in later periods, the fragile bones found within cave sediments are what remain after what was the careful deposition, now disturbed, of some type of ritual, the young buried in the safety of home.[178] As with hunter-gatherer sites of later periods, many processes disturb archaeological deposits and lead to a mixing of tiny infant bones with the general sediments of the cave. Infant burials are easily disturbed by burrowing animals, as well as being difficult to identify in excavation. Recent finds support this idea. A tiny burial of a newborn infant from excavations over a century ago at the site of Le Moustier in France was found recently in a box labelled as animal bones in the Smithsonian museum collections[179] and two newborns were only recently identified in the faunal collections fifteen years after excavations at Saint-Césaire.[180] Far from littering the cave, the presence of infant bones in cave deposits probably means that they were kept close when they died. Where they are possible to identify in excavations we see that Neanderthals took particular care over infant burials, with the infant at Amud Cave in Israel carefully placed on a ledge with the jaw of a red deer, and those at la Ferrasie placed in carefully made grave pits.

The evidence for Neanderthals *being left behind* if they were injured also seems to fall apart with only a little scrutiny. Wynn and Coolidge make their inference on the basis of research by Thomas Berger and Erik Trinkaus on the skeletal remains of a sample of Neanderthals skeletons.[181] Some lower limb injuries were present in the sample. However, no lower limb injuries were judged to have prevented any Neanderthal from walking (even if painfully). The only injuries which caused limbs to be completely immobilised (and so useless) were indeed in upper limb and not lower. However, only seventeen Neanderthals were studied. Two of these had upper limb injuries which would have immobilised these limbs, yet none had lower limb injuries as severe. Does this mean that only those who could walk were looked after (these two individuals with serious upper limb injuries being the example) and those with severely injured lower limbs were callously left behind?

Isn't this far too small a sample to make this inference? The probability that the two particularly serious injuries in our small sample would happen to be in the upper limbs rather than lower limbs is high in any case just by chance (around one in four). But even *if* we had enough skeletons to make this a real pattern in which severely injured lower limbs were lacking, we don't know what the typical pattern of injury when facing an angry mammoth or woolly rhino is. It is very likely that the upper part of the body is more *in the line of fire* so this pattern is only what we might expect. For me, however, the most damning counter-argument comes from where the skeletons were recovered. These seventeen individuals were recovered from rockshelter sites – the only places in the landscape with the unique type of preservation that allows bones to be preserved for so many thousands of years – whereas bones located in low lying open area sites don't tend to be preserved. Rockshelters are not easy places to reach. Access to Shanidar Cave involves a long scramble, for example.

Would it not have been foolish to attempt to take someone with a lower limb injury to a rockshelter site? These are people who had a choice about where to stay, rather than relying on a definitive home that they must reach. Might they not have been looked after nearer to where they were injured, a group deciding to make camp there rather than travel back to a cave? That we have not yet found individuals who were *so seriously injured that they couldn't walk to difficult-to-access rockshelters* seems hardly surprising. If we did, would we not conclude that Neanderthals were rather stupid?

The pattern of upper body and lower body injury in this small sample of Neanderthals is not for me any kind of evidence for hard-heartedness, but simply that people are very ready and willing to believe such claims. We can't help but reflect that if there is any evidence in the Palaeolithic archaeological record for people being *callous*, surely the Gough's Cave skull cups made by our own species is a much better contender?

In the case of Neanderthals there is no real evidence that they did ever abandon anyone, even if to do so might at times be understandable. Who knows, there might have been Neanderthals who were left behind to their fate, but there is no evidence in the archaeological record for them. I'm not sure that I would even blame a Neanderthal who abandoned someone, let alone conclude that the whole species were callous. We know that their lives were hard, famines were frequent and finding food involved great stamina and endurance. Modern hunter-gatherers, have been known to sometimes abandon their newborn babies. Yet this is not because they don't care for them – such abandonment is extraordinarily hard to do – but because they are aware that neither they nor their existing children would survive if they tried to nurture another.[182] Such decisions, made by the mothers themselves, are by no means callous or ruthless; they reflect a harsh reality of life and responsibility for others.

I worry about how quickly we jump to conclusions where Neanderthals are concerned. John Speth, Professor of Anthropology at the University of Michigan, agrees. He suggests that we are often far too willing to convict Neanderthals of being fundamentally inferior with very little evidence, that 'Neanderthals have been so readily convicted of so much on the basis of so little'. We seem to be particularly biased against them, largely because they looked a little different. We are hardly able to view the evidence objectively. As Speth notes, we mostly judge Neanderthals by what they didn't do, but this is rather an unfair perspective:

> Neanderthals are no more cognitively impaired for not knowing how to paint their cave walls or to carve bone than ... our great grandparents for not knowing how to blow their neighbours to smithereens with an atomic bomb or do their holiday shopping online, or ourselves for not knowing how to 'Beam Scotty up' yet.[183]

Joao Zilhao of the University of Barcelona is a firm supporter of Neanderthals. Far from being callous, Neanderthals, he believes, were fundamentally the same as ourselves, filled with the same emotions, feelings and motivations. After all, as a species they survived for far longer than we have to date.

I suspect that after all those thousands of years of separate evolution Neanderthals might have been different, they might not feel *exactly the same* but we need to be careful what we accuse Neanderthals of with little evidence, especially when it makes a difference to how we feel about them and often, by implication, about ourselves.

Even the hardest evidence, that from fossil crania or from trauma patterns on fossil bones, is far more open to interpretations which are based on our own preconceptions than we might think. Fossil crania can give us some insight into how early humans felt. We know that there were evolutionary pressures to develop larger and more social brains, but not what people used these brains for. We know that Neanderthals might have felt differently, but not how they felt.

How can we begin to understand archaic human emotions and motivations? How can we escape falling for elements of apparent evidence which seem to make sense and give us what we expect to see?

Sometimes the most stunning and impressive evidence tells us the least, and the most humble can be the most honest and the most informative.

It might be the smallest and subtlest of clues that can tell us the answer. While Raymond Dart looked in South African caves for the answer to how we became human, Louis Leakey dug into sediments hundreds of metres thick in East Africa, and Jane Goodall sought to understand chimpanzees in the depths of the forest, over the last decade scientists have begun to look far closer to home – somewhere far less exotic. A whole new class of evidence came from *within our own minds*. Some of the subtlest of clues *in the way that we treat objects* might be of the most important.

A tweenbot – urban art by Kacie Kinzer. Why do passersby stop and help it on its way?

Chapter Six

Small Things Forgotten

It has long been an axiom of mine that the little things
are infinitely the most important.[184]

*Why would people care about small things? What makes us want to
defend or protect inanimate objects that appear to need our help? Why
would we become so attached to personal possessions which have no
value, can't do anything practical for us or repay the effort we put into
looking after them?*

*Here we look at what experiments in psychology and neurobiology
can tell us about our tendencies to be altruistic, not only to people but
even to things. We seem to have evolved a variety of different responses
to objects – from those that seem vulnerable, to those that appear to
protect us, to those who make us feel a certain way. Why would we evolve
such complex responses? Could the small things around us, which we so
often ignore, and our reaction to them have been important in our
evolutionary past?*

People walking through Washington Square Park in New York have
been surprised to see a small cardboard object trundling along by itself,
the poor thing frequently getting stuck. The odd-looking cardboard
character, called a tweenbot,[185] can only trundle forwards in a straight line.
Attached to it is a flag to tell everyone where it wants to go. Yet this little
cardboard robot will be rescued whenever it is stuck against a curb or
under a bench and set off in the right direction again, some of its rescuers
even speaking to it to reassure it. Such *humanly assisted robots*, an
example of urban art, always reach their destination. There can hardly be
a more alienating setting than a big city. It seems particularly heart-
warming that even here people will stop and help a vulnerable tweenbot.
Yet we cannot help but reflect that this kind of behaviour is also rather
strange. If you asked the rescuers why they stopped to help they wouldn't

be able to explain – it isn't as if they really thought such cardboard boxes on wheels were actually alive, just that they couldn't help themselves but reach out to help something in need.

Scientists have been baffled. We so easily seem to care deeply about some objects almost as if they were alive, but why would we? All of us at some time or other display a rather bizarre affection and attachment to certain, often small, material things even if they have no use or economic value. It doesn't seem at all rational.

Other examples come from the field of robotics. In one experiment volunteers are given a torch and a simple mechanical toy bug which moves towards the light. They play with this simple robot toy for a few minutes, then the experimenter instructs them to smash it up with a hammer. The volunteers find this a real challenge, possible but not easy. They feel guilty, and show high levels of stress, which is picked up on monitors of physiological arousal,[186] when they smash the mechanical bug to pieces. It's not that they have any delusions that this simple piece of metal and plastic is really a living being, but even so, they find it hard to bring themselves to damage it. Most people said that they had to *convince themselves* that they weren't harming a real creature; even so, they felt distressed. When instructed to destroy even the simplest and most buglike of moving machines, many people say such experiments are 'inhumane'. In another experiment volunteers play with a small toy dinosaur, Ugobe's PLEO. When they later watch a video of the little

Ugobe's PLEO – the robot dinosaur which people felt strongly should be protected from physical harm.

dinosaur being hit and abused, held by its tail and its head knocked against a table, they are often deeply upset. Astrid Rosenthal-von der Pütten, head of the research laboratory in Duisberg-Essen, found that people even tend to agree with statements such as, 'I do not understand how people can treat the robot like this', and 'watching the robot in this situation has made me angry'. They feel a deep-seated need to protect it.

Our odd connection to inanimate things starts very young, seemingly to be hard-wired into our psyches. We all feel attached to certain treasured possessions. Children of only two years of age will flatly refuse to swap their own cherished toy for any copy, no matter how identical. They feel that *their* toy has a soul, and another would not be the same. Our favourite toys feel alive to us, remembered as living things with personalities. Many adults keep their childhood teddy bear, unwilling to part with it, no matter how battered or worn it has become. There is something almost offensive about harming such objects. Forty-six per cent of young children asked in one study felt that it wasn't morally right to put a robot toy in a cupboard.[187] If adults weren't prepared to protect such toys, they felt that they should.

We believe ourselves to grow out of a *delusion* that objects have feelings as we get older. However, the economic value we attach to things shows that our sense that objects *must* carry some kind of essence continues well into adulthood. Paul McCartney's first guitar or Abraham Lincoln's travelling shaving mirror both have a value and attraction entirely beyond that of any similar object with a more ordinary background. Do we really believe that these objects are physically any different from any similar items, that by association or touching them we might pick up some of the qualities of their owner? Rationally, we might not, yet most of us have treasured possessions of no material worth which we would be distraught to lose. We found in our own research that people who are most attached to precious objects or personal mementoes score most highly in self-compassion, a measure of emotional well-being.[188]

Even if we can't explain *why* we cherish certain possessions they seem to truly have a profound effect on us.

Our tendencies to care for objects emerge even in the most unlikely of places. Soldiers in World War One sometimes had tiny 'sweetheart bears' which were given to them by their mothers or girlfriends. With eyes placed at the top of their head, they would be put into top pockets where they could see out. These sweetheart bears went into battle, and perished, with many soldiers.

We can hardly imagine teddy bears being important in war and yet they appear to have been. Leanda Harwood tells the story of a particularly remarkable bear, Grubby, given to David Campbell by his grandmother. David always took Grubby into battle with him ... until the day that he was captured at St Valery in France. German soldiers laughed at David for having a teddy bear and cruelly took Grubby away. However, a German officer was upset by what they had done and stepped in, insisting that David was allowed to keep his bear. David and Grubby kept each other company for three years in a prisoner of war camp.[189]

It is hard *not* to smile at such a story. Both David himself and the German officer who rescued Grubby for him seem more *likeable* for their tenderness even towards an inanimate bear. We tend to feel a little nervous of any soldiers with weapons; yet we can't help but instinctively expect both David and the German officer to be *kind-hearted*.

A sweetheart bear carried by soldiers in the First World War and designed so that it could look out of their top pocket.

Perhaps the most moving wartime bear story is that of the treasured teddy of a small girl called Aileen Rogers. Aileen lived in Canada and was ten years old when her father enlisted as an army medic and was sent to the Front in the First World War. Fearing for his safety, she sent him her cherished teddy bear, believing that it would protect him. Lawrence Rogers kept the bear with him at all times. Although there was a dressing station where he would have been safer, Lawrence, like many medics, chose to place the wounded in safety and risk his own death by dressing wounds in the battlefield. He was killed at Paschendale in 1917 tending the wounded. What remains of the teddy bear was chosen as the most significant of all the 3,000 or so First World War artefacts which were submitted to the Memory Project of The Globe and Mail and the Dominion Institute.

Aileen Rogers' bear. Her father in his letter home before his death in battle said, 'Tell Aileen I still have the Teddy Bear and I will try to hang on to it for her. It is dirty and his hind legs are kind of loose but he is still with me.'

Eileen's bear is far more than just a toy. Certain objects seem to be able to be a conduit for the feelings between us, passing love or compassion through them, almost as if the person we miss were there with us. It isn't really the bear that Eileen's father speaks to us about in his letter but the value he places on Eileen herself, and it is in some sense *her* that he takes with him everywhere until he dies.

Where does our tendency to see a certain life in things, to reach out to objects, and even to people through objects come from?

The archaeological record suggests that a focus on material things and a certain tendency to care beyond the practical is no recent acquisition. The earliest signs might start to appear 3 million years ago. Were australopithecines moved by the apparent vulnerability of the Makapangsat pebble? They certainly might have been. Perhaps the australopithecine who picked it up 3 million years ago took it home because of a felt need to look after and protect this infant-like stone, even if they couldn't quite explain why.

By 1.8 million years ago at least, if not before, there is abundant evidence that material objects can be cared for in ways that go well beyond the practical. Great care is taken to create a pleasing form in handaxes, far beyond any practical purpose. Early humans couldn't seem to help themselves but care about what they made. Even the supposedly practically minded Neanderthals made entirely impractical objects like perforated and stained shells or used decorative bird feathers. It seems no coincidence either that the earliest art from the Berekhat-Ram figurine and the Tan-tan figurine to the Roche-Cotard mask have infant-like dimensions. Were early humans nurturing forms that looked a little vulnerable?

Objects and things could clearly conjure up powerful feelings many thousands of years ago.

No other species shares our unusual relationship to the material world. Chimpanzees don't give each other gifts, or attach any emotional significance to objects. The only suggestions of objects appearing to have a significance come from reports of female chimpanzees seeming to use sticks as dolls,[190] taking them to their nests at night, cradling them in their arms. Even these observations have been much debated – it isn't clear if the chimps imagine a personality to the sticks they use or if they are just copying the behaviours of adults with young.

For other animals the material world around them is a means to source items to eat or to shelter from the elements, but nothing else. Why should it be? Why care about things? How might this tendency have been significant in our evolutionary story?

Our drive to look after, care for and protect objects cannot help but be related in some way to our tendencies to care for people. These at least are better understood. We only need to look at the rest of the animal world to recognise a certain drive to care, to nurture and protect in all mammals. From cats nurturing their kittens, to polar bears playing with their cubs, there is something familiar about the way mammal mothers treat their young. No other mammals care about inanimate objects, but we can't fail to see something familiar in the tenderness and care they feel for their young, a sense that their babies are *cherished.*

It is our shared evolutionary history as mammals that gives us our emotional motivation to care for and nurture our infants and other things besides. Mammalian young are vulnerable and only those mothers who were most sensitive to their needs, most responsive to their distress and most willing to put themselves out to look after them passed on their genes. Particular pathways in their brains evolved to motivate them to care for their young and to feel good when they did so, prompting a flood of hormones like oxytocin. We feel the same.

Much of our modern drive to *care for, protect and look after* – whether we express it in giving blood, giving to charity, helping a stranger or falling in love – may seem a million miles away from the maternal affection shown by mammals to their young. However, as Jean Decety of the University of Chicago Social Cognitive neuroscience laboratory explains, brain imaging shows us that even the most complex of our capacities to care for other people are deeply rooted in exactly the same parts of our brains.[191] The very parts of our mind designed to motivate us to be *sensitive to something vulnerable that needed our help*, and to *be generous in helping them without counting the cost* are essentially the same.[192] For some reason doing good in all kinds of ways, and even helping out and caring for *things*, helped us survive so selection pressures made us feel good in a wide range of settings now far removed from dealing with young.

Many of our affiliative feelings, those that give us pleasure at being with others, also have their basis in our past as mammals. Social mammals, like dogs, elephants and lions, feel good about being with others and intensely bad about being excluded because their evolutionary past has been one in which they needed each other to survive and needed to keep in the group. These social mammals, ourselves included, have brains with a larger neocortex – the area particularly devoted to social thinking – than mammals that live more solitary lives. We all like to feel we belong, are accepted and liked by those around us, and use all our social skills to make sure that we are. The feelings we get at bonding with each other are thus not so different. The brains of both dogs and their owners each generate oxytocin when dogs are handled, the hormone which gives us a warm fuzzy feeling,[193] and dogs can even function as attachment figures, promoting emotional health and a sense of security in their owners.[194] The similarities in our minds, giving us shared motivations to connect to others, to be part of a group and to show affection provide pleasure to both.

We recognise a tenderness with young, a desire to cherish and a warmth of affection in other mammals. Why are we so different?

A lot has happened to our motivation to care for others and to form strong bonds over the last several million years of our evolution. Some of the most important changes came with our transition from lower primate to ape[195] around 15 million years ago.

Apes think and feel in remarkable ways. Even clever and sociable animals like dogs are separated from us by many million years of evolution and don't think in quite the way that we do when it comes to helping out someone in distress, no matter how much their sense of affection seems similar to ours. I remember as a child taking our dog to play in a field with a friend and losing my shoe in a muddy pond. No amount of telling the dog to go home and fetch help (and in particular another shoe) seemed to do any good. I was sorely disappointed as Lassie on the TV rushed home to fetch help all the time and brought back useful things as well. Why couldn't our dog see what I needed? It was a long and rather resentful walk home with only one shoe.

Dogs may be affectionate, but constructive helping is usually beyond them. While we might share a sense of warmth and affection in their company, and often a remarkable emotional understanding, only we can translate that feeling into *looking after them* in practical terms. They may be affectionate and eager to please, we get pleasure from looking after them, but we have to *train them* to do things that might help us.

Only certain mammals can help constructively when others are in distress. As Frans de Waal explains, this is an important transition. Monkeys sometimes accidentally drown their own babies because they can't *see* what they need – when they swim across a river their baby's head can happen to be under water as they swim, with tragic consequences. Apes, however, can see the world from another's point of view, think through what to do and realise that their babies have to have their heads above water, so they will carry them in such as way as to enable them to breathe.[196] Chimpanzees can see what others might need, at least to a certain extent. They may help another chimp down from a tree when they are stuck, for example. Infant humans and infant chimpanzees will both reach out to open a door, or pick something up when someone needs it.[197] They both feel good about helping out and have the ability to see what to do to make things better.

Is it precisely this combination of a motivation to respond to distress, an ability to help out, and a feel-good reward which explains evidence for care of vulnerable early humans in the archaeological record?

Certainly, the same basic neurological and cognitive response must be in action. The care for others we see in the archaeological record is not as new or unique as we might think it to be. Early humans must have had a strong desire to care for those they were close to and felt a *warm fuzzy feeling* in caring for their loved ones much as we do. Like our closest relatives, they could see what to do to help.

There are important differences between the care we see in chimpanzees or bonobos and the care we find in the archaeological evidence, however. By 1.8 million years ago we were already on our own evolutionary track towards developing a far greater depth, extent and range of cues to trigger compassion than in any other animal.

Chimpanzees tend to help *in the moment*, giving food or protection, but they don't think through any long-term needs. Injured chimpanzees will be left behind when a troop moves, there being no intention of changing a route taken or making any adaptations to accommodate them.[198] We can't help but recognise that the care given to the *Homo ergaster* female who died 1.6 million years ago goes well beyond this. Someone must have stayed with her, taken her somewhere safe, fetched food and water. Long-term care of the toothless *Dmanisi hominin* may also imply planning to find and prepare the right types of food. Of course, as we saw in Chapter three, even these examples seem minor compared to the care we see in later periods. The care taken over the Shanidar Neanderthal with a withered arm, withered leg and probable blindness must have involved the whole group and over many years and he was only one example.

We almost get the impression that not looking after someone was *unthinkable*. Quite a transformation.

Given that only the tiniest fraction of our compassionate instinct towards other people will ever leave archaeological evidence, then what we do find seems to tell an important story. Even our early ancestors must have had substantially stronger ties and been far more willing to put themselves out for each other than anything we see in our nearest living non-human relatives.

For whatever reason, *our* evolutionary journey intensified our drive to connect with those around us, to be sensitive to how they feel, to be driven to help when needed. No other animal even approaches the range of triggers which prompt us to care for someone, or even *something*.

We all feel a little cynical about humanity sometimes, we can doubt whether people really care about others. Experiments on human altruism convince us otherwise however.[199] Though our societies may be rather less inclined to be as generous as many others,[200] most of us are still remarkably willing to go out of our way to help others most of the time. As long as we have an emotionally secure background and we don't feel under threat, we are remarkably generous with our time and efforts, even to strangers.

Isn't this just for a calculated reward? It seems not. Brain imaging illustrates that actually we help others because it feels good. We feel as good *giving to charity* as *receiving the same funds ourselves*, activating the same part of our mind.[201] We feel good when we care for principles by standing up for what we believe to be right. Most of us are even willing to take on pain to help out a stranger in need, preferring that we should take the place of someone having to put their hands in iced water rather than watch them suffer.[202] We can't help ourselves, it is in our neurobiological make-up to think about the welfare of others as well as ourselves. Dacher Keltner calls this basic hard-wiring to help others our *compassionate instinct.*[203]

Could it be that as *our drive to care* went rather out of control it over spilled into areas that make little rational sense, material objects just one of those? No chimp would help out a tweenbot, neither do they care about any chimp who isn't their kin or ally. Yet an overspilling of compassion beyond what might ever seem to make practical sense seems to typify much of what motivates *us* to help – it hardly makes sense to give money to charity, give blood to unknown others, or care about what disasters befall people we might never have met. Perhaps in this context, our unusual tendency to *warm to* objects is no surprise.

Could our relationship to objects simply be an overspilling of motivations to nurture? Has their form simply tricked us into responding as if they were alive, vulnerable, infant-like? Is our response to objects just an accident of our overgenerous nature?

We certainly respond to anything that remotely resembles a human infant, even if that resemblance is remarkably slight. Any face with big eyes and a round image is something that we find *cute*.[204]

There is a good argument that in our evolutionary history a tendency to *overrespond* to any cues of vulnerability in face shape, facial expression or movement would be a better bet for passing on our genes than to fail to pick up such cues. With highly vulnerable young it will have been those adults with *an excess* of kindness who responded to the slightest of signs of need who were more likely to pass on their genes successfully than those who didn't respond. Human babies are particularly vulnerable and savannahs would have been particularly dangerous places. In such a context it is perhaps no surprise that cuteness, whether in our own infants, in young mammals, or in material objects, affects us emotionally. It was better to err on the side of keeping vulnerable things safe than risk failing to respond to the needs of one's offspring.

Cuteness certainly affects us. Seeing cute things even makes our fingers tingle – we have evolved a neurological response that makes us more careful and more dexterous when we see cute things so that we are better able to respond to and handle fragile babies.[205] It is perhaps no surprise that the Makapansgat pebble or the Tan-tan figure drew the attention of our ancestors with their infant-like forms.

However, cute is more complex than we think. Our brains respond differently to robots, no matter how cute or even emotionally expressive, than anything that is truly alive.[206] We might act as though objects are alive, but we don't actually think that they are, and our brains don't react in the same way. Moreover, Gary Sherman and Johnathan Haidt from the University of Virginia have shown that our response to cute things goes beyond nurturance.[207] They found that seeing cute things doesn't just make us a little more tender, it makes us more playful and more socially orientated. When we respond to cute things we are a little more fun to be with. There is something sociable about being primed to respond to something that looks cute.

There is more to our emotional relationship to our material world than a compassionate reaction to anything vulnerable.

Objects can appear to be vulnerable, but we can also ourselves be vulnerable to the effects objects have on us. As Ian Hodder from Stanford University explains, our lives and feelings become *entangled* with the things around us.[208] Many of our treasured possessions are not at all vulnerable, and certainly in its later days Eileen's bear was far from cute. Objects affect us in many different ways.

Precious things can provide us with comfort. Mario Mikulincer from the Interdisciplinary Centre at Herzlyia in Israel and Philip Shaver from the University of California have demonstrated that holding photographs of people who care about us makes us feel supported and secure, prompting those parts of our brain which pick up on social cues and making us likely to be much more giving.[209] We experience the same effect when we hold or look at other objects which strongly remind us of people we trust. People whose difficult development in their childhood has left them more anxious will feel more secure when they look at photographs of people to whom they are close. Immersed in memories of warm experiences with others, they will be more *trusting* and so generous to those around them who are in need. Like the attachments we form to our pets, do some of our most precious possessions function a little like attachment figures to help us feel more safe and secure? They certainly seem to.

Objects can affect us deeply. One explanation for the power of objects in our lives comes from the difference between our memory systems and those of other animals, even our closest relatives. Horst Steklis and Richard Lane from the University of Arizona explain that at best other apes can remember things such as *what happened, where* and *when,* through *episodic memory* – flashes of remembered experience.[210]

136

However, only humans seem to relate events and the feelings associated with them as happening *to me*. It is through this *autobiographical memory* that our uniquely human memories affect our hormone system and emotions.[211] We can mentally time travel to the past to *re-feel* an event as happening to us or *forward feel* to the future. Just like stories or conversations or even a touch or smell, objects around us can become a remembered part of our lives and prompt us to feel again past experiences or imagine future ones. As far as our minds are concerned, this *mental time travel* has transported us from *now* to another time, place and feeling.

As much as objects can support us emotionally, our sense of attachment to them means that they can also be used to hurt us.

Who as child hasn't felt that sense of humiliation when a playground bully destroys something we own, stamps on a book or pencil case, or runs away with something? We feel hurt even if such things aren't all that valuable or precious. Inanimate things can also be used to hurt us in more sinister ways. By restricting the personal possessions of soldiers we reduce their sense of identity and make them more compliant. In the same way, people in prisons routinely have their possessions checked and gone through, so nothing is entirely private or personal to them. Doing this makes them feel more powerless.

Few things evoke stronger feelings in us than the inanimate bodies of our loved ones. We feel a strong need to protect the bodies of the deceased, even if decay is inevitable. It is not just that we respond to the vulnerability of a corpse, even if it is not alive, but we also respond to the memories we experience seeing someone we love. Their physical presence or material reminder seems to help us feel that our memories are real; physical signs, from photographs to their possessions, continue to remind us of them. How often do we keep as precious, carry with us or keep safe, things which belonged to people who were important to us? Like those objects which have value, just because they belonged to a famous figure, such objects – much like Aileen's bear to her father –

A human molar tooth 35,000 to 30,000 years old found at Isturitz in the Pyrenees, and made into a pendant, is polished due to substantial wear. It was probably worn close to the skin. Was this a memento of a loved one?

have an intangible value *to us*. Whether it is a broken penknife or a scratched watch, certain things have a power to give us some sense that *something* still exists of someone who is no longer there.

Was it just this type of attachment that prompted someone to wear the human tooth pendant dating back to 35 to 30,000 years ago found at Isturitz in the Pyrenees? It certainly seems to have been. Signs of wear on the pierced hole shows that the tooth must have been worn for something like a year at least.[212] We can't help but imagine someone all those thousands of years ago carrying a memento of someone they loved that they never wanted to let go of, remembering them each time that they touched it.

Such objects have a tremendous power over us but they also make us vulnerable in a way entirely alien to any other species. Deliberate desecration of a corpse or our cherished mementoes harms us almost as if it were us who was being hurt. Other animals can experience a sense of loss, even be drawn to the physical remains of their loved ones, but material things associated with the dead don't hold anything like the same power for them.

Was it this attachment to the material remains and reminders of our loved ones, the power they began to have over us, that provoked the emergence of mortuary practice? From the pit of bones at Atapuerca almost half a million years ago to the many different examples of careful burial of Neanderthal dead, it mattered to people to dispose of a corpse in the right way, to carry out some shared ritual to help them deal with their grief. The development of a need to take care of the dead from hundreds of thousands of years ago through to our own times must reflect the increasing strength of our connection to our loved ones, our capacity to *remember* what they meant to us and the ever extending power of the material signs of their presence to move us even when the living soul has gone.

Our emotional responses to our material world go much deeper than those of our nearest living relatives and affect us in many different ways.

Jean-Pierre Changeux, Director of the Pasteur Institute, explains that an expansion of our empathy circuits has been central to making it possible to be moved by art.[213] Neuroimaging shows that we have developed connections in our pre-frontal cortex that are sensitive to artistic representations.

Part of our sensitivity to art comes from a response to form and symmetry that we know dates back to at least 1.8 million years with the careful production of fine symmetrical handaxes by *Homo erectus*.[214] However, our response to art is about more than a pleasing form. It also includes a combination of surprise, a sense of harmony and most of all, the use of *depiction* to manage other people's sensitivities and share an understanding or perspective on the world. Visual art can affect our emotions deeply, as can music. Our response to art is embodied, our sensory circuits through the action of mirror neurones stimulate us to feel *as if* we were part of a picture or sculpture that we see,[215] and our understanding of someone else's perspectives allows us to imagine ourselves as the artist or subject.

The oldest human portraits, here that of a man, were found at La Marche in France dating to 14,000 years ago. Because of our empathy circuits and our evolved sensitivity to depiction we read this art as far more than a series of engraved lines.

Because of our evolved sensitivity to visual depiction we can feel *transported* by art. The effect of Upper Palaeolithic art is no different even though it was made thousands of years ago. When I look at the roughly sketched portrait of a man from La Marche in France my mind still imagines that I am there in the place of the artist. There is something in this depiction not unlike the tenderness of the Rouffignac mammoths. I can't help but wonder what this person meant to them. It seems a rather gentle portrait.

More harrowing feelings can be communicated in other art. Picasso's *Guernica* is an image few can forget. It instils in a single glance a sense of the trauma of innocent lives lost in war. Was the intention of the artist we saw in Chapter two who painted the Mesolithic rock art depicting an archer holding their dead comrade in their arms not so different? Both of these artists were *sensitive* to the effect that they were creating in us, wanting to tell us something of the futility and pointlessness of the violence and loss of life that they had experienced.

We can draw what we see, but to communicate *a feeling* in art we need

139

The Hall of the Bulls, Lascaux, 13–11,000bp.

to sense a connection to those who will view it, know how they will feel about what they see.

No one can doubt that the Palaeolithic artists creating the depictions of the famous cave art sites like Lascaux, Altmira or Chauvet understood the impact of the images that they created.

Can we trust our feelings about what Upper Palaeolithic art was meant to communicate to us? Our common neurobiology would argue that we can.

Could there have been some unique selection pressure on our evolutionary journey to communicate how we feel in material ways?

It is difficult to see how our emotional reactions to things could have been an advantage Why would we want to be moved by material things, troubled by intense feelings? So many of our human emotions seem to make our lives more difficult rather than easier. Yet we are far more dependent on our emotions than we tend to think. We rely on them even when we think we are at our most rational.[216] We can't plan ahead or make decisions without the emotional parts of our brains.[217] Even in the most economic of circumstances we often make decisions which are far from rational as emotion and intuition play such an important part in our lives.[218]

Many of our uniquely human feelings are quite bizarre when we consider them objectively – often they even benefit others more than they benefit ourselves. Our 'social' or 'moral' emotions depend on our understanding of how people around us feel about us. However, while emotions such as *embarrassment, shame* and *remorse* play a vital role in

140

our lives, they are hardly pleasant.[219] Why would such emotions evolve? *Gratitude* might feel more tolerable, pleasant certainly, yet it motivates us to show our willingness to give things away, to be generous through displays such as elaborate thanks or giving gifts.[220] *Altruistic anger*, our evolved response to wish to punish cheats or bullies to our own detriment, even prompts us to put ourselves at risk for no clear gain to ourselves.[221] Why would we evolve often painful motivations to put others first? It is almost as if we needed to be seen to suffer for the sake of others.

Much of our emotional minds seem to do more to hinder than to help us. While our moral emotions direct us to act in ways that are against our own interests, our conscious awareness of how we feel also seems more of a curse than a blessing. Being able to reflect on what we feel means that we alone and no other animal can feel *ashamed* of our own feelings, most of us often engaging in a complex and often self-critical self-talk about what we *ought to be feeling*, how *we should be*.[222] We can feel embarrassed simply by *thinking about what we might do*, or reflecting on something that happened in the past or what someone else might think of us. We might feel a momentary pleasure of anticipation of another's response when we give a gift or make an elaborate gesture. But what if the gift is too great, so as to cause embarrassment? What if our intentions are not understood? What if our gestures are too small? We so frequently feel the pain of shame, guilt or remorse just by *imagining* something that might or could have happened.

Was it always this complicated? We saw in Chapter five that there must have been intense selection pressures on our abilities to understand social situations, with significant expansion of our neocortex around 1.8 million years – social life was already complicated back then. We don't know when people first gave each other gifts, though sharing food with each other must date back to at least the same time. However, the widespread presence of non-functional objects (such as beads) within the last 50,000 years, transported over many hundreds of kilometres, illustrates that gift-giving is not new. Beads and shells were material objects with far more power than their small size might imply, and troubling over making and giving gifts has been part and parcel of our lives for thousands of years. As we saw in Chapter three, modern hunter-gatherers like the !Kung may pass through many famines and live in harsh and difficult environments yet they spend about eighty days a year making gifts and a third of their lives visiting distant friends and taking gifts with them.[223]

Why waste time making and giving gifts? And why would such gifts be things that are not in any way useful? Wouldn't it make more sense to give people something that they needed?

Gift-giving may be bound up with a specific emotion unique to humans – gratitude. Our capacity to feel *grateful*, a highly complex emotion which depends on us being able to interpret whether another's actions have a genuinely altruistic motivation or not, may well have been an important part of the extension of our social worlds from a small group of kin to many hundreds of people. The movement of gifts over large distances may tell us something important about how people felt about those they didn't know well.

There is no doubt that our social worlds have exploded in size over the last 2 million years.

One clue to how the size of our social networks has increased comes from the distances over which flint raw materials used to make tools have travelled. Before 2 million years ago raw materials were never transported much more than 1km – social worlds were small. After this time the social landscapes of early humans seem to have expanded somewhat, with most raw materials up until 1.2 million years ago coming from up to 3km away and some even travelling 15km. It was only after 1.2 million years, however, that materials travelled beyond these distances, implying some connections or relationships with neighbouring groups. Hereafter, maximum transfer distances increase to 100km – several days' travel at least – and well into the territories of other groups.

The big increase in movement of raw material occurs with our own species. Arriving in Europe around 40,000 years ago, modern humans transferred a whole range of materials great distances, often over 800km – not only raw materials for things that are needed, but also marine shells or other aesthetic objects which seem to have no functional purpose... gifts.

It may have been changes in our emotional minds which allowed our worlds to get larger.

Jean Decety argues that there must have been changes in the make-up of our brains which allowed us to form bonds with people outside our group whom we perhaps only rarely saw. One of the mechanisms is likely to have been changes in our hormone responses – a damping down of our threat-based reactions to those we didn't know well. An increase in the production of oxytocin, the hormone associated with bonding and trust, would allow us to feel affiliative feelings with people we didn't usually spend time with. Without such an oxytocin response, our contacts with strangers or people we didn't know well might have been limited to our threat responses of attack, flight or freeze. We could never put a group of chimpanzees who don't know each other in a cage together, but thanks to our evolved minds and our far more tolerant responses to strangers, we can navigate trains, buses, concert halls and cities without attacking everyone around us or being frozen in fear.

Feelings like gratitude may have been another adaptation. We only feel grateful in certain situations. We feel gratitude more strongly with strangers, and it binds us to those who genuinely care about us, prompting us to display our gratitude in helping them out or giving them gifts, supporting the types of bonds that mean we have people there for us no matter what.[224] Whenever anyone is generous to us, if we judge that they *genuinely mean to help us out without any thought of their own interest*, we feel grateful and we warm to them and wish to help them out in the future. These are the types of alliances which we saw in Chapter three that make it possible for modern hunter-gatherers to survive serious famines or other catastrophes – they know they have people in distant groups who they can trust to look after them. Gratitude drives large-scale connections with genuinely altruistic acts being *passed on*[225] – generosity provokes a motivation to be kind to someone else in turn. Though archaeologists used to talk of 'networks of obligation' along which gifts passed in the Palaeolithic past, we know from research that any feeling of obligation makes people avoid each other – indebtedness in uncomfortable. Only a positive feeling towards distant friends could motivate people to do everything they could to make sure that they make it through.

However, showing that you care is complicated. If we judge that the person who gives us a present or does us a favour does not have our interests at heart, or is trying to make us appreciate them and oblige us to help them out in future, we feel annoyed or even *spiteful*. *Currying favour* makes no one popular. Making sure that others don't think we have ulterior motives for giving gifts gives us something else to worry about. The difference between an appropriate and inappropriate present is something of a tightrope, one worried about by the !Kung and their gift-giving seen in Chapter three as much as in the present day. This may be one reason for the rise of transfers or gifts of non-functional items in the Palaeolithic – they are things that are less likely to be interpreted in terms of a desire for economic benefits.[226]

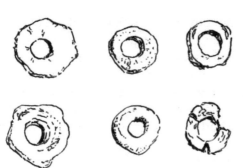

Ostrich eggshell beads have been given as gifts in the Kalahari for at least 40,000 years. Gifts which clearly have no functional use are more likely to be interpreted as reflecting genuine care than anything which might imply an economic transaction.

Social networks of people who genuinely care about others help us to survive, but unless our emotions are genuine and we are good at showing them appropriately we won't be able to create such networks – everyone has an astute sense of the difference between someone *who wants something from us* and someone who is genuine.

Why couldn't life be simpler? So demanding are our peculiarly human emotional worlds that our minds show extensive physical adaptions to dealing with all the difficult, problematic and often conflicting emotions our social lives throw at them.

Many of the physical changes in our brains which separate us from other animals relate to evolved ways of *better handling* our intense and complicated feelings in relation to those around us.

The biggest physical differences in our brains from those of other apes is that compared to them we have a hundred times the numbers of specialised neurons, called VENS, which link our fast intuitive gut reactions to slower deliberate judgements, for example.[227] As Jean Decety explains, distinctively human abilities in the areas of complex perspective-taking and the use of language allow us to much better calm our emotions when those we care about are vulnerable and enable us to integrate these feelings with thoughts constructively. It is our emotional *control* that allows us to be more patient and better able to overcome frustrations in order to create an artefact to a certain form or depict animals in art, and better able to delay gratification, doing things today to improve things in the future.

The archaeological record provides us with good evidence of how our emotional self-control has evolved through time. Stone tool technology progressively illustrates ever better abilities to handle the frustrations of trying to impose a form on difficult materials. The basic chopping tools made through simple flaking by australopithecines demanded little patience, while careful imposition of handaxe forms

Made during the height of the ice age, Solutrean foliate points take many hours to make and a lifetime of patient learning to master the necessary skills. Rather than perform any function, they seem to have been passed along networks as gifts.

by *Homo erectus* will have meant overcoming considerable frustration. Some of the complex tool forms of the Upper Palaeolithic, such as Solutrean foliate points, take a lifetime learning of skills and several hours of careful knapping to produce. The practice of producing such objects might have helped us handle feelings, giving us a safe environment in which to develop our patience.

The extended length of our childhoods throughout human evolution may also have been prompted by a need to handle ever more demanding emotions before entering adulthood. Emotional self-control remains such a challenge to us today that it is the only cognitive skill to continue to develop into our early twenties.[228] While australopithecines probably grew to adulthood in around eight to ten years, childhoods started to get much longer around 1.8 million years ago. Nariokotome Boy wasn't an adult until around twelve years of age[229] and it took Neanderthals perhaps fifteen years to become adults.

A great deal of expensive brain tissue, effort and developmental time goes into just handling our emotions. Shouldn't it be easier to deal with our feelings? Shouldn't they bother us less? Wouldn't it be better if things were *simpler*?

You certainly wouldn't *design* our emotions to be as they are. There would be far more pleasant experiences, less to worry ourselves about. I sometimes feel just a little envious of people who study how our bodies evolved, what made our anatomy or physiology the way that it is today. Our biological evolution seems to make so much sense, different elements responding in predictable ways to evolutionary pressures, creating a working solution to problems. It all seems rather neat to explain, easy to control. Our emotional minds, on the other hand, are quite frankly a little bizarre, even ridiculous at times, a hotchpotch of differing drives and motivations which often seem to make life harder. How could the same process – natural selection – have produced both?

We might be able to explain how our minds respond, but what made our particularly human emotions evolve? Did something tie the evolution of our emotions and our changing material worlds together? Why did we put ourselves out for other people, ones we might never even meet, when no other animal would? Why would we help out a robot, even though we know that it isn't alive? Why for many thousands of years did we waste precious time and energy making stone tools look pleasing?

The darker side of our minds, the explanations for human violence and aggression and how our darker emotions affect our material worlds may hold some clues.

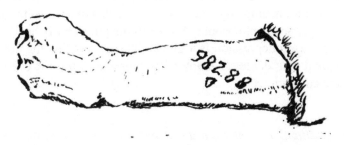

*Like a mere object, holocaust survivor Leon Greenman
was tattooed with an identification number at Auschwitz
concentration camp.*

Chapter Seven

The Darkest Depths – When People Seem Like Mere Objects

Recent breakthroughs in science show we have just the capacities we need to face our planet's challenges. We're 'soft-wired' for cooperation, empathy, fairness, along with a deep need to 'make a dent', as social philosopher Erich Fromm put it.[230] My hunch is that one reason depression is a global pandemic is that the dominant mental map denies so many of us expression of these deep needs and capacities.[231]

Sadly, although we share a deep-seated capacity for compassion, our human emotions can sometimes be stripped away and we can feel nothing for those around us, making us capable of aggression and cruelty. There are many routes to violence, whether through fear, a drive to protect our loved ones, to stand up for principles or even uniquely human hatred, but via whatever route, hurting others is never easy. Only through deep-seated dissociation from our emotions can we not feel at all. A lack of feeling can play out through the material world as well in as our relationships with people, and we are sensitive to the most subtle of signs that someone feels little and should not be trusted. Has the material world around us played a more important role in our evolutionary history than we might assume?

If an explanation for how we feel compassion for others lies inside our own minds, is there also an explanation for violence and aggression?

Sometimes people are aggressive or even cruel.

Sometimes we feel nothing for things and even nothing for people themselves. If we are capable of being so sensitive that we feel sympathy even for objects that just appear to be vulnerable, *why doesn't our evolved empathy stop us from hurting others, or why does our remorse not punish us? Have we evolved some conflicting killer ape instinct that drives us to hurt?*

In part, the answer lies in our evolved responses. Rather than any newly evolved feelings it is more usually a *stripping away* of our evolved human empathy that lies behind many acts of violence.

We respond to stress and fear in the same way as other mammals. Indeed, we all know what it is like to feel a sense of panic and find our bodies in fight or flight mode. This is when threats have made us physiologically drop back to more ancient systems. In this state, rather than connecting to others or giving any thought to how they feel, we mobilise our bodies to fight or flee. It may be no help to us to feel an urge to run away in those moments when we are most nervous: perhaps we need to present a talk in front of hundreds of people and our feelings just make it harder. In our mammalian past, running away or fighting were useful responses to predators or anything else that made us scared, so no wonder we still feel this way. If threats continue or are severe we fall back on even more primitive reptilian responses deep down in the inner part of our brain and we freeze. Our minds can go blank. Far back in the reptile world *standing completely still and doing nothing* was a useful way not to be seen and eaten, and our bodies still react in this way no matter how much we wish that they wouldn't.

As Stephen Porges explains, like all mammals in our social interactions we *play our best card first*, and in our case these are the particularly human feelings that come from our recent evolution, making us want to talk to other people, share how we and they feel, connect to them. However, if we feel threatened, our sympathetic nervous system takes over, we become scared, fight or suppress an urge to run away. Due to the influence of our conscious minds we don't necessarily act on our more primitive feelings; we usually manage to stay calm when we are scared, but often we find ourselves having to manage our feelings of wanting to either hit out or run away and hide. When our reptile brain, our parasympathetic system, takes over we dissociate from our feelings.[232] When we are under sustained fear or stress we can feel almost as if we are standing apart from our own bodies, not even really knowing how we feel. When we feel nothing at all we can't possibly experience any empathy for anyone else.

We all differ in the extent to which we can handle our difficult feelings.

No matter how good our sense of self-control though, it isn't hard to imagine humans in the past *losing it* when under threat, much like people do in the present. One-off acts of violence – the Neanderthal from St Cesaire with a head wound, or that from Shanidar shot with a projectile point – might indicate such a loss of control, instinctive self-protective anger. It is likely to be no coincidence that, as we saw in Chapter two, the only Palaeolithic cemetery showing large-scale violence is that at Jebel Sahaba, dating to a time when the drying out of the Nile likely led to widespread famines, and people were afraid of dying of hunger. Having an emotional response is not in itself an excuse for hurting people, but emotions driven by fear are *harder to overcome*.

A loss of feeling can even be more permanent. We can become emotionally dissociated as a result of a harsh upbringing. If no one understands how we feel or shows us love we close up emotionally.

If as children we are exposed to neglect, crime, conflict or violence we feel less connection, and can be more likely to exploit others when we become adults.[233] In an evolutionary sense this response, however apparently anti-social, may have had a survival function. In the wrong setting our compassion can make us exploitable, willing to be generous to those in need who might themselves have little intention of helping us in return. If there aren't any people around who are willing to develop relationships based on empathy and trust we would be foolish to be empathetic ourselves. Our sensitivity to the environment in which we grow up acts to reduce this risk. As Paul Gilbert from the University of Derby explains, being trusting, sensitive and good at being vulnerable is no help to us in an American inner city street gang. If such is the case, better for the survival of our genes if we are selfish, fiercely competitive, drop down a level of the emotional ladder, and use our lower emotional brains so our genes make it through. We might not thrive emotionally, but at least we survive. Though the wider world might well be a kind one, our evolved minds can act on the instinct that the immediate social environment we experienced as a child is a sign of what we must survive as an adult.

Even on a lesser scale our social context influences us. Paul Gilbert argues that in our modern worlds our underlying 'old brains' forged millions of years ago in competitive hierarchies like those of chimpanzees can come to the fore despite our 'new brains' that were forged in the collaborative environments of egalitarian hunter-gatherers. We can easily be triggered by apparent threats into dropping back to old-brain responses to other people, retreating and being submissive or glorying in the power of a position of authority or treating those less fortunate than ourselves with disdain. Chimpanzees behave like this a lot of the time. Different modes of thought power these different brain hormone systems and even bodily stances. Our calmer, more caring minds may well lead us to be more socially connected, resilient to depression and result in us living longer and healthier lives, yet as Paul Gilbert explains, all too often our society emphasises achievement and production and forces us into living our lives frantically oscillating between achievement and fear. Like this, we are in no state to be part of all those affiliative feelings such as ordinary kindness, playfulness or courage. Psychologists call it 'The Dark Side of Competition'.[234] We might call it 'behaving more like a chimp'.

No matter how good our evolved capacities to handle our emotions and despite those millions of VEN neurones we came across in Chapter six, our feelings often challenge us. Even the most resilient of us *fall apart* some times, as much as a result of our complex minds and our imagination of *what might happen* or *what people might think* as from actual events or real threats. Around 25 per cent of people in industrialised societies suffer the social effects of either being too swamped by their feelings to act or too closed up to feel them at all.[235] Most of us go through life with feelings we find hard to handle; perhaps they come from memories that we try to squash, or just from the day to day interactions with people around us.

We have thought of past societies as brutal, but could our modern industrialised context have in some ways made us *less sensitive* and numbed our responses to those around us? Many believe so.

Tellingly, people who live a hunting and gathering way of life are often surprised by how insensitive we seem – both to people we meet and the world around us. Is this perhaps because their collaborative way of life, interdependence and relative lack of constant stimuli encourages greater sensitivity? Certainly, modern hunter-gatherers have often been described as calmer and better able to handle their difficult emotions than we are. However, even their relative emotional balance has not merely happened. These worlds, albeit smaller than our own, have enough emotional challenges – complex changing relationships with people in their own and distant groups, ever-present threats of hunger, or risks from hunting or poor health. Much of the focus on a hunter-gatherer childhood is spent learning how to handle emotions. Jean Briggs, for example, describes the emotional challenges placed on Chubby Mata, the three-year-old Inuit child, as she learns how to navigate her feelings, and to be able to hold them in awareness. Her parents and relatives push her to feel difficult emotions, situations in which she would lose a parent, or be forced to choose who to live with. This is seemingly shocking, yet if Chubby handles these kinds of emotional challenges she can handle with calmness the day to day threats that typify survival in harsh Arctic environments.[236] As Bonnie Hewlett's study of influential craftspeople among the Baka reveals, in these simple hunter-gatherer societies those who are most respected and influential are often described as *calm* and *wise,*[237] thereby placing great emphasis on being able to feel, yet handle emotions and not react in anger. They've been through the trial by fire that is human emotions and learnt how to handle them calmly, keeping a handle on how their bodies might react to fear and push them to run away or hit out.

We often need to suppress our sensitivity, to rationalise about our world in order to cope with all the stimuli thrown at us in our societies. Do we lose our chance to learn to handle our complex and often conflicting feelings? Bruce Charlton from the University of Newcastle certainly argues that this rationalisation contributes to our modern sense of alienation from the world and leaves us with lack of meaning.[238] To our relatively *insensitive minds*, people can be seen sometimes as things, trees are only objects made of wood, rivers just moving water, our social and natural environments just something which gets in the way of producing, consuming and creating. Our worlds, despite being surrounded by living things, from people to animals and plants, can feel lonely.

Davi Kopenawa, a Yanomami shaman from the Amazon, asserts that it is our lack of feelings for the things around us which allows us to damage the environment. He says:

> I would like white people to stop thinking that our forest is dead and placed here without reason. I would like to make them listen to the voice of the xapiri [spirits] who play here incessantly … for if the forest is entirely devastated no other forest will be born.[239]

A lack of a sense of caring for things, people and the world around us can be a dangerous thing. Yet we find a certain insensitivity creeping up on us from the way we live our lives, until all that matters is the next deadline, what we need to buy or what we should achieve. We can wonder when the last time was that we were aware how others felt, had a warm feeling in our hearts or had time to care about suffering or our environment around us. Charlton comments: 'For most people, even a single day of unalloyed well-being is a rare event. Some unfortunate people probably never experience even a day of well-being, at best managing a few minutes as a kind of glimmering of what is possible.'[240]

Was the past different? Were people more sensitive, better able to feel? The values of industrialised society teach us that we are the pinnacle of humanity, so much better than what has gone before. We may well be surrounded by even more products of human ingenuity, remarkable inventions, vast stores of knowledge, but I'm still not sure that we should be quite so confident.

Sometimes our societies even create a sense of emotional dissociation deliberately when we want people to switch off from the feelings of others.

In order to make it possible for men to kill for example, military training often depersonalises and dehumanises recruits, numbing their normal emotional responses.

It is normal to find it hard, if not impossible, to kill others. Without such a natural restraint, our modern worlds would hardly be possible. Like Dart, many military commanders in both the First and Second World War mistakenly assumed that a killer instinct existed, both to kill others and to protect themselves, and found that they were wrong.

Joanna Burke describes how our natural empathy makes it remarkably difficult for any of us, all too aware of the souls of those who face us, to kill, even in wartime.[241] Many soldiers in the First World War and even in the Second were so loathe to kill that they rarely fired on the enemy.[242] When Colonel S. L. A. Marshall of the US Army interviewed men in 400 infantry companies in the Central Pacific and Europe he found that only 15 per cent of men had actually fired at enemy positions or personnel, though nearly all were at some stage within firing distance of the enemy. As Burke explains, at the battle of Makin Island in 1943 American troops with heavy artillery were attacked by Japanese wielding swords and bayonets. Half of the American guns were knocked out and half of the men in forward foxholes were killed. When Marshall interviewed the

Killing did not come naturally to soldiers in the First World War and many were loathe to fire on the enemy even when their own lives were at risk.

survivors, only thirty-five men were reported to have actively fired at the enemy with all the weapons available to them. Many men did not even use their weapons in self-defence when their lives were at stake.

Colonel Cole, of the 502nd parachute company, commented: 'When I ordered the men who were right around me to fire, they did so. But the moment I passed on they quit. I walked up and down the line yelling "God damn it start shooting!": but it did very little good. They fired only while I watched them.'[243] Marshall came to the conclusion that only around 25 per cent of men 'will ever strike a real blow unless they are compelled by almost overpowering circumstances', of which the only effective method seemed to be officers behind them insisting that they shoot.

It is not easy to switch off our innate compassionate instinct.

Military commanders found that far more effective than appealing to a killer instinct was an appeal to our mammalian instincts to protect vulnerable kin. Incitements to violence often urge us to protect our loved ones, painting another group as a threat to them, triggering our ancient mammalian desires to protect our young against attack. Propaganda deliberately fires up our desires to protect, even at the cost of our lives. Joanna Burke cites the volume 'Harry the Hun', which in the Second World War encouraged soldiers to kill through such emotional and provocative messages:

Remember that if you do not do this when they come here, the damnable barbarians since Attila will lay our country waste, indulge in mass executions, and turn our women into whores for themselves ... ask yourself how the prisoners in Germany are faring – and stab hard, and stab to kill. IT IS THE ONLY THING TO DO.

People far more often risk their lives for a common good than for their own sake.

A uniquely human motivation to *level* bullies or cheats, which evolved in the context of egalitarian hunter-gatherers, can also be deliberately brought to the fore to provoke us to be aggressive. Our *altruistic anger*, an evolved response with a distinctive neurological signature,[244] prompts us to bring down bullies, punish cheats and maintain fairness. Leaders who become dominating whether in small-scale hunter-gatherer societies, or our own, will stir our emotions, and make us willing to bring them down whether by ridicule, gossip, ostracism or physical attack, even if we don't benefit personally. It is difficult to tell if the individual acts of violence we see in the archaeological record are simple anger or fear or if motivated by this more complex desire for altruistic punishment – dominating leaders brought down by the whole group.

Altruistic punishment maintains egalitarianism in small-scale societies. However, modern conflict is rarely a simple case of good against bad or aggressor against vulnerable. Our selfless drive to fight for fairness is easily subverted by our ready trust in authorities. German and English soldiers talking to each other in 1914 during the unofficial Christmas truce were surprised to find that each believed themselves to be the ones fighting for freedom against an aggressive dominating power. Why else would they have volunteered to risk losing their lives?

Of course, we also have to recognise that another less noble but equally human emotion can also provide the basis for atrocities – that of hatred.

Tania Singer of the Max Planck Institute in Leipzig has carried out experiments which show that parts of our brain associated with pleasure can be activated at the downfall of people we see as enemies or outsiders and fundamentally different from ourselves even if they haven't done anything to us specifically. *Schadenfreude*, the pleasure we feel at someone else's pain or misfortune, is hardly a feeling to be proud of. As an evolved response, it must derive from a time in our evolutionary past when strangers must have been a threat. Portraying other human groups as subhuman, innately different from ourselves, even dangerous, and our own group as all the same and innately virtuous can sometimes subvert our empathy and drive us to want to hurt other people, and even feel pleasure when we do.[245] Our desire to belong to the group and our fear of the pain of rejection if we don't has a darker side.

An incitement to hatred and an encouragement to see some as both dangerous and subhuman was almost certainly part of the explanation for atrocities in Nazi Germany. However, here *beliefs* about what was natural to humanity also played a chilling role in atrocities. Violence was legitimised through an encouragement to see brutality as *natural*.

Nazi ideology interpreted natural selection as a process of the strong outcompeting the weak, believing that supporting the weak went somehow against nature. A strong society would have to be ruthless, would weed out the weak, those who were unhealthy, unfit or a drain on resources. Two respected German academics even saw this as a conscious choice among our ancestors, commenting in 1920, 'There was a time, now considered barbaric, in which eliminating those who were born unfit for life, or who later became so, was taken for granted.'[246] These were ideas about a human past which were no more than plucked out of the air, but they were to be dangerous. A concept of human success, derived from ancestors who discarded whoever they didn't like with no concern for how anyone felt about it, went a considerable way to legitimate atrocities in the minds of the perpetrators.

How could our natural empathy be so overrun? A view of the world in which emotions were irrelevant played a significant role. People *should* be treated like objects if the world was to progress, parts of a wider unfeeling machine, discarded if faulty so the machine worked more efficiently. To this regime *unfit for life* meant being different in many ways; it meant being a Jew or a gyspy, epileptic, schizophrenic, 'feeble-minded' or physically disabled. As Suzanne Evans explains, the Holocaust was not only about Jews, but within Germany hundreds of thousands of those who were sick and unable to recover or mentally or physically disabled were killed, often sent to special centres supposedly for their care from which they would never return.[247]

The path to evil, as Hannah Arendt explains, was often disturbingly *banal*.[248] Some perpetrators of atrocities were truly warped individuals, psychopaths perhaps, but this was not entirely true of most. More it was a case of a slippery slope which began with the idea that some people were genetically better than others, and had more of a right to live, and

156

others ought to be disposed of, like unwanted objects. From here, many involved in atrocities may have felt uncomfortable but they ignored their feelings, blindly followed authority, rationalising that the decisions made were not theirs. Some were one step removed from the killing, making it easy for them to sign forms without allowing themselves to think or feel. Those actively killing people attempted to rationalise their feelings away, persuading themselves that they were hurting some for the good of the Aryan race, carrying out a difficult task, the language of *cleansing* promoting a sense of detachment. It is hard to understand how anyone could treat someone else as a mere object in such an emotionless way. The words of one doctor in Auschwitz chillingly explain that he didn't lack human sensitivity, more he strove to override it to achieve dissociation from his feelings: 'In the beginning it was almost impossible. Afterwards it became almost routine. That's the only way to put it.'[249] Sometimes our desire to conform, to avoid rejection, can allow some of us to ignore everything our hearts are telling us is wrong.

The atrocities of the Holocaust were termed *crimes against humanity* for good reason; our emotional connection to all of humanity makes us feel ashamed of what can be possible.

An extreme form of deliberately formulated military training, designed to solve the problem of people unable to kill can also reduce us to a sense of emotional dissociation which strips us of our natural restraints. By the time of the Vietnam War, training was no longer only about how to use a weapon, but was something *dehumanising*, a long and extensive exercise in humiliation, depersonalisation and strict punishment until men would become emotionally numbed, emotionally dropped down to their pre-mammal minds. Lack of sleep, abusive language, constant gruelling physical training and relentlessly tough conditions robbed people of their sense of self, and detached them from their feelings. Philip Caputo explains that a man who could not take being shouted at and kicked was seen as someone who could not withstand the rigours of combat.[250]

The effects of such training were chilling. Atrocities became widespread. Bourke explains how Richard Boyle, a journalist working in Vietnam, picked up the air of detachment. He explains, 'I could watch a burned infant trying to nurse from its dead mother's breast, see young men with their faces blown away, witness a boy deliberately gutted.'[251] Lieutenant 'Rusty' Calley, finding himself on trial for war crimes, said:

I couldn't understand it ... I had gone to a war ... I pictured the

Only the dehumanisation and depersonalisation of Vietnam training would rob most soldiers of the tendency to see humanity in their enemy.

people of My Lai: the bodies, and they didn't bother me. I had found, I had closed with, I had destroyed the VC: the mission that day. I thought, it couldn't be wrong or I'd have remorse about it.[252]

Without the emotional compass that his natural empathy gave him, Rusty was at a loss to navigate himself in the world, with only orders to guide his actions. He seems to have killed people and committed atrocities *without feeling*. Whether he is to blame or not for how his training influences his actions, all our instincts tell us he is someone to avoid. If there was little to stop him killing innocent civilians we would hardly feel safe anywhere near him.

Was there a material expression of this lack of feeling? Certainly emotional dissociation also affected how soldiers related to objects. There were no sweetheart bears in Vietnam. Instead, there was a widespread and gruesome practice of body parts becoming trophies. A trophy skull sent by one soldier to his girlfriend appeared in *Time* magazine, apparently something to delight in, until others questioned the morality of such a trophy and its taking was more publicly condemned. Edward L. Jones, a US war correspondent in the Pacific, wrote in the February 1946 *Atlantic Magazine*: 'We boiled the flesh off enemy skulls to make table ornaments for sweethearts, or carved their bones into letter-openers.'[253] Ears tied as pendants, teeth and skulls kept as trophies, seem to our eyes acts of complete barbarism, some kind of material symbol of the power of *not caring at all*. The more efforts were put into removing the natural empathy of soldiers in Vietnam, the more capable they became of atrocities, not only to people themselves but to inanimate objects related to them, from corpses to skulls to other items associated with the dead.

During the Vietnam War, skulls of Vietnamese soldiers were boiled down and covered in graffiti as some sort of trophy.

Though we tend to think we ignore how people relate to the material things around them, we pick up many such details about people's personalities without being aware of it. In fact, we are acutely sensitive not only to the small signs of how someone might treat other people, but also how they treat objects that seem vulnerable, that are precious or that have an intimate connection to people. Where these feelings are absent we can't

159

warm to them, and instead feel suspicious that they might be a danger to us.

Joanna Burke takes an example from Bruce Petty[254] who refers to the testimony of a young American recruit coming across the dead body of a teenage Japanese soldier during the Asia-Pacific War:

> I would have guessed that the dead Japanese was only about fourteen years old and there he lay dead. My thoughts turned to some mother back in Japan who would receive word that her son had been killed in battle. Then one of the Marines, who I found out later had been through other campaigns, reached over and roughly grabbed the Japanese soldier by the belt and ripped his shirt off ... Another Marine veteran of combat saw that the dead soldier had some gold teeth, so he took the butt of his rifle and banged him on the jaw, hoping to extract the gold teeth. Whether he did or not I don't know, because at that point I turned around and walked away. I went over to where I thought no one would see me and sat down. Although my eyes were dry, inside my heart was wrenching, not at seeing the dead soldier but at seeing the way some of my comrades had treated that dead body. That bothered me a great deal. Pretty soon Al came over and sat down beside me and put his arm around my shoulder. He knew what I was feeling. When I turned to look at Al he had tears running down his face.

The haunting feeling of this moment revolves, not around any physical pain felt by a victim of simple aggression as no one is physically hurt, but around the treatment of a dead, no longer living or feeling corpse. The combat veterans seem to have become *hard-hearted,* losing their emotional triggers which would otherwise tell them that the object, the corpse, should in some ways be treated as living. The new recruit naturally sees the body as a person, and imagines how the mother would feel, and Al innately understands the shock and horror he feels, as well as, perhaps, his own powerlessness to protect him from the effects of seeing such atrocities.

We don't just feel for the new recruit and Al, but we also judge the people in this scene, creating them as personalities in our mind that we might remember. Without their saying anything, or treating any living person in any way, we form a model in our minds of their motivations, how they might react to us, anticipating how we would react to them. We can't help but feel that people that could treat a defenceless corpse with such callousness might easily harm living people, us perhaps. With no obvious physical signs that someone lacks the human feelings, such as empathy or remorse, which stop them hurting us, we are sensitive to the slightest of clues to their emotional make-up, even how they relate to the material world.

The callous acts of aggression we saw in chimpanzees were as disturbing as human violence, but how different we are from violent chimpanzees. To chimpanzees, those from other groups were never ever other than mere objects in the way. For them there is no remorse, no conflicting emotions, no need to search for a rational justification for their own actions in order to live with themselves, and no subtle signs of their motivations towards others in how they react to material things. It is hard for us to see each other in this way, not impossible, but certainly difficult and rare. We find it hard to kill, even if we are scared, even if we feel hatred or our need to protect the vulnerable or defend principles is stirred up. Only after the harshest of treatment will we lose our sense of empathy with others, and even then many will still retain their sense of humanity despite the odds.

Was it a stripping away of natural empathy which led to prehistoric cannibalism? In the earliest cases, that of the two-million-year-old australopithecine at Sterkfontein or one-million-year-old *Homo antecessor* family at Atapuerca, it seems doubtful. At this early stage our social worlds remained small and empathy for others may well have still been limited to those within the group, with no feeling at all for those outside it. Fight or flight, eat or be eaten, might have been the driving force behind relationships with strangers. As for later cases of cannibalism, we can only imagine the situation must be more complex, motives more interwoven with complex human feelings, beliefs about whether such acts were respectful or denigrating, complex emotional motivations of respect or hatred.

What of systematic violence, like the Offnet Cave massacre? Nick Thorpe from the University of Winchester argues that many prehistoric violent feuds must have been set within a context, like modern situations, in which violence didn't come naturally and had no simple cause. Instead, he suggests that the aggression had to be *incited* – men were probably hyped up into an altered mental state by fasting, special dances and ceremonies and drug-taking, and convinced that they were fighting for a just cause in order to be able to kill others, something we see in modern ethnographic contexts where violence occurs.[255] The Avatip of New Guinea, who carried out headhunting raids, believed that the ability to kill could only be imparted through magic and ritual, and was not something innate but had to be artificially constructed. Had such rituals and incitement to hate been part of the explanations for Gough's Cave? They might have been.

Was there dissent even then? Did some disagree with the symbolic desecration, the gruesome cannibalism presumably of enemies that happened at Gough's Cave? Did they talk about the event in hushed tones? Did some even try to stop it?

There are all sorts of theories but no one really knows why some people retain their sense of humanity in the worst of situations and under the greatest risks, and why for others it is eroded.

Certainly, there have been enough heroes even in the worst of situations to show that an erosion of empathy is never inevitable. In Vietnam a helicopter pilot, Hugh Thompson, in Mai Lai alongside Rusty Calley, disobeyed his orders, placing his helicopter between troops and innocent women and children to prevent them from being murdered, instead flying them to safety. Hugh risked a court martial in the process. It took a unique type of courage to follow his sense that killing innocent civilians was wrong and to defy authority despite the personal risks. In Nazi Germany Oscar Schindler and countless others saved Jews, no matter what the cost. Sometimes the very scale of atrocities and the threats makes many even more determined.

Pilar Hernàndez-Wolfe describes how trauma caused through terrorism in Columbia created in many not acceptance, but instead a determination to maintain their sense of humanity and to make a stand no matter what the cost, something she calls 'altruism through suffering'.[256] A woman who witnessed her father being murdered for making a stand against terrorists was herself driven to fight for human rights, despite the personal risks, said, 'In the end, this was about not letting them win my soul by taking away my capacity to love and trust, and turning around their ignorance and hatred and reaffirming my commitment to what I believe and to my people.'[257] People who stand up against cruelty retain their sense that 'these people are human' even when others around do not, and no matter what the situation.

One explanation for what gives people the strength to make a stand against cruelty lies in the observation that such people often believe in a shared human nature; they strongly feel that goodness is something natural to being human and the cruelty that they see is unnatural.[258] They identify with a broader humanity, maintaining a sense of a greater and intrinsically good 'we' which stretches beyond those immediately around them. It is not that they don't care about rejection or danger, but they are able to tolerate it because *their* community is a wider one than just the few around them who collude with evil, a humanity that stretches far back into the past. A faith in humanity gives them a sense of a wider whole that they can trust, and to which their actions have meaning.

Perhaps every individual has a different motive. What is certain, however, is that heroic courage in the face of cruelty inspires us.

Acts of courage and heroism have a significance beyond their immediate effects. Simply hearing about acts of altruism or a courageous willingness to make a stand makes us feel differently ourselves; it *elevates us*, makes us more likely to be heroic, generous or kind in turn.[259] Our evolved sensitive minds pick up on the possibilities that being human bring and acknowledge that the courage or kindness of others changes us. While we can scientifically measure the effect of a feeling of *elevation*, those with the emotional wisdom to defend humanity and human rights don't need to be told the science though, they *just know*.

A resistance to violence and aggression is not just about evolved emotions; it is also about *conscious choice*. We saw in Chapter four that Nim Chimpsky could not be blamed for attacking his keepers, he simply acted out the competition for dominance his species demanded in an instinctive way. We, on the other hand, are aware of how we feel, able to stand back and decide which feelings we follow, which we act on and which we ignore. Were *Homo erectus* aware of how they felt, making conscious choices? They may not have been. The Neolithic people who cared so sensitively for the Man Bac man, and the Upper Palaeolithic people who cared for the Romito dwarf, must have been conscious of following their compassionate feelings. Even the Neanderthals, so close to us in evolutionary terms, may well have been making conscious choices about the way they would influence people, the societies they would create in caring for the man at Shanidar and so many other ill or vulnerable Neanderthals. It is certainly a fascinating thought that Neanderthals may have had a social conscience, a sense of wider humanity and drive to defend its principles that situates them a long way from the callous hard-hearted brutes Coolidge and Wynn perceived, people whom they thought could abandon the injured without a second glance.

One thing that is certain is that along our evolutionary journey we have all inherited minds which are capable both of the heights of compassion and the depths of cruelty – products of the hopes, fears, compassion, connection and even ordinary kindness of our ancestors. These minds make us capable of a far-reaching influence on others through what we do. With so much at stake, it is no wonder that we put so much of our efforts into sensing, feeling and thinking about who we can really trust, and hoping to display our best qualities to others.

Has the material world played a part in how we decide who to trust? Was trust far more important to our early ancestors than we have assumed?

Only by understanding the far from obvious selection pressures on our human ancestors and the importance to evolutionary success of demonstrating trustworthiness can we begin to reconstruct an explanation.

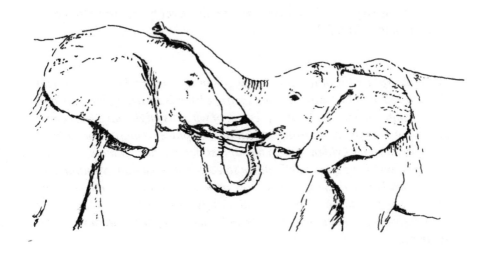

There are good evolutionary reasons why highly social and collaborative mammals, like elephants, genuinely care about each other.

Chapter Eight

Why Be Kind? Love, Morality and Why Small Things Matter

It's no use trying to be clever – we are all clever here; just try to be kind, a little kind.[260]

Since the split with other apes, changes in our brains have given us a drive to reach out to those around us from friends to strangers, pets and even inanimate objects. Yet the question of why this might have happened, and when the important transformation took place, remains unresolved. Here we consider evidence for a moral instinct in other animals, why this instinct might have been particularly selected for in human evolution and how it may have led us to become more and more sensitive to others. Signs of our trustworthiness in material things, no matter how small or seemingly insignificant, may have been far more important than we might suppose.

We like to think that we have risen above our emotions. Our feelings seem to make us vulnerable – compassion, sympathy, remorse or guilt push us to act in ways that aren't in our interests, and it seems that we almost can't help ourselves.

Could this vulnerability have been our strength? Might our peculiarly human emotions have been far more important to our success than we have assumed?

The first place to look for an explanation for human emotions is in the selection pressures we see operating on other mammals, particularly clever and social mammals like ourselves who seem to develop strong bonds with each other.

Why would any animal be motivated to do good to others at their own expense? And how does our emotional relationship to objects fit into this story?

Emotional motivations to care about, nurture and protect young are the easiest to explain. As we saw in Chapter six, mammals instinctively nurture and care for their offspring because those that did passed on their genes whereas any mammal without maternal instincts would not. Humans were no different, particularly in dangerous savannah environments where young were a tasty morsel for passing predators.

Helping one's close relatives is not so difficult to explain either. *Kin-based altruism*, a tendency to be altruistic to one's family, is also something we see in many social mammals, and is simply explained by the pay-offs of looking out for one's close kin. Helping them to survive enables them to pass on many of one's own genes. Looking after one's offspring and close relatives is easy to understand from the perspective of natural selection.

However, a tendency to care about everyone in one's group, or even farther afield, up to and including inanimate things, is much harder to explain. *Reciprocal altruism* (a return of favours to someone who is not related) is more challenging and even more so when it is *indirect* or *generalised reciprocity* (helping out someone who might not directly help you).

It doesn't make intuitive sense to help out people who neither carry our genes nor are likely to pay us back practically, one reason why we tend to assume that early humans would only think about themselves.

How then does a sensitivity to others' well-being, a drive to care about people who might not be our direct relatives, evolve? Frans de Waal from the Yerkes Primate Research Center is convinced that the answer to our tendency to care for people who aren't related to us lies in understanding the evolved *morality* of other primates. As we have seen in Chapter four, apes don't only help out their infants or family, they can help out others besides. In the wild, male chimpanzees may help out an ally in a fight or console them if they lose, friends may share meat and in bonobos strong bonds form between unrelated females. We can certainly imagine that our last common ancestor, living 7 to 8 million years ago, would already have had a certain emotional motivation to care about the well-being of those around them which went beyond maternal or kin-based instincts.

De Waal explains that a moral instinct is based on two pillars of morality which we see in ape behaviour – *fairness* and *empathy*. De Waal and his group have carried out several experiments illustrating these fundamental moral drives. In one, which demonstrates *a sense of fairness*, two capuchin monkeys who are separated by a grid through which they can see each other have learnt a task. They pass a small stone to a researcher who in return gives them a piece of cucumber. Monkeys like cucumber and are happy to carry on the task again and again. They much prefer grapes, however. When the experimenter instead gives *one* of the monkeys a grape in exchange for their stone, while the other still only receives a cucumber, this last monkey is infuriated, hurling its food back at the researcher in disgust. When the experiment is repeated with chimpanzees, they are equally as put out, but sometimes the chimp fortunate enough to be given a grape even refuses to take it, in protest. Described as 'monkeys reject unequal pay', this experiment illustrates a concern for fairness.[261] We are not the only animal to understand and care about what is fair[262] – a humbling thought when fairness may not seem like a priority to many.

Several very different animal species, such as elephants, dolphins, rats and apes – species who can cooperate in far more complex ways than others to survive – demonstrate this type of *moral instinct*. Both their *sense of fairness* and their *empathetic concern* lead them to act in ways that are moral – that is, benefitting others, even non-kin, before themselves. We have seen the empathy expressed by chimpanzees in Chapter four. Certain other complex social animals have a similar concern for others. Adult elephants will help out not only infants but also adults

Chimpanzees can focus their help towards how others need assistance – here an adult helps an infant stuck on a pole.

in their own group, seeming to genuinely care about their well-being. Rats prefer to rescue a friend than to receive a food reward, even if that food is a chocolate chip cookie.[263]

It might seem selfless to help out others in need but though animals aren't consciously aware of any calculated trade-off, such actions can pay off *in the long term*. An emotional motivation to care prompts an animal to do another a favour, or resist an injustice on their behalf. If such a favour is *remembered and returned*, the action of help has become a form of *time delayed collaboration*. The benefits of helping may be invisible in the moment but come later in the future. Since mutual exchange of favours benefits both partners, each is more likely to survive and pass on the very same genes to care and respond to another's needs. It is for this reason that a tendency to have a *moral sense* evolves in highly social animals that can keep track of how others have behaved and respond in turn.

Why should such reciprocal altruism depend on emotional motivations? Could animals not remember and add up favours, have calculated who was owed and who wasn't? Wouldn't tit-for-tat work equally well? Caring about our friends and allies, rather than just making a note of their help, is actually a *more effective* way of building up the collaborative links which might help you survive. By judging the emotional motivations of those close to us, *how much they care*, we can intuitively predict how much they would be prepared to put themselves out for us, and show how much we would put ourselves out for them likewise. We form a strong bond, without needing to wait to add up what they have done for us and perhaps lose such a valuable ally to someone else in the process.

Chimpanzees tend to build a few specific allies with whom they return favours – these alliances alone are hard enough to keep track of mentally.[264] However, they also build up something of a mental reputation of others in their group by what they observe about them, the *good or bad standing* of any chimp. Dominant chimpanzees who are too aggressive or bullying can become so *generally disliked* that a whole group can gang up on them to depose them from power, including those who have not necessarily been on the receiving end of aggression – they have made their judgement on the basis of what they see happening to others[265] and they are prepared to act on it.

Animals can be far more *moral* than we might think.

We rarely if ever attribute the levels of morality we see in our closest relatives to our distant ancestors, believing them to be more self-centred and ruthless. Nor do we pay much attention to the roots of morality in animals.

Why has natural selection been seen as only about a ruthless selfishness, even a desire to hurt others for one's own gain? One explanation may be that emotional motivations are difficult to study in a practical sense. There may be many different explanations for apparently altruistic behaviour and, in any case, few evolved emotional motivations make immediate sense. The long-term and rather messy nature of evolved emotional responses, especially those to care about others, can put scientists off studying them. The immediate effects of being competitive are easier to study.

We don't see the rationale behind emotions when we focus on what happens in the present or at least the timescales over which we do experiments or observe behaviours. Take, for example, the evolved fear of snakes or spiders common to all primates, including humans. It isn't difficult to see that a gut instinct to be startled and get quickly out of the way of anything looking even slightly like a snake would help an ancestral primate survive. Over the great span of hundreds of generations the genes of an ancestral primate scared of snake-like objects would survive while those of any companion who had no reaction to snake-like things would not, never mind all the false alarms on the way. Evolved emotions don't look very sensible watched over the short timespan, however. Most of us have at some time leapt in shock at a large but harmless spider in the bath or a slithering thing in the garden and felt foolish afterwards. The startled jumping away from apparently nothing, the heart beat racing, seems like a waste of energy and effort. Most of what we see even over the timespan of our own lives, which is short in an evolutionary perspective, appears to be a pointless reaction while we miss observing the one time that such anxiety was life-saving.

Natural selection works on the principle of *better safe than sorry* as far as emotional reactions are concerned. We rarely see the one time when either jumping away from an apparent snake or the actions of a favoured ally saved a life. Generosity looked like a foolish waste of resources.

However, there was a far greater resistance to studying why either animals or humans might be kind. As Frans de Waal explains, our competitive modern societies have gone so far as to view gut motivations to reach out to help others as some kind of invention, a fictitious idea thought up by people who were less than objective. From this perspective it can be difficult to obtain funds to study kindness, compassion or generosity.[266] Moral instincts in animals might seem more foolish than functional, something that couldn't possibly be important. Chimpanzees helped out their allies; dolphins helped human swimmers; elephants worked together for many years, all before science would focus its interest on any selfless behaviour that went beyond the immediate effects on the survival of offspring.

A tendency to deny the potential significance of an emotional motivation to help others was particularly marked where human emotions were concerned.

There were several elements to a resistance to studying human kindness from a scientific perspective. One was that emotions were seen as more of a *problem* for scientific understanding, not a valid topic of research themselves. Since our feelings push us to act in irrational and often inexplicable ways a lot of the time, from gushing over babies to giving money to charity, they could hardly contrast more with the rational logical world of scientific reason. They seemed to actively *get in the way of* the clear and rational thought so central to scientific, intellectual and technological progress. It was one thing that chimps evolved emotional reactions that might make them jump at the sight of snakes, even if they are only plastic ones put there by researchers, getting agitated and hooting and shouting at their friends and family to warn them to keep away. That most of us might still feel the same was a little ridiculous, our hearts pounding a little faster when we see snakes at the zoo, even finding ourselves screeching when we find a tiny spider in the bath. Even though it isn't difficult to see that there is a kind of wisdom to our emotional reactions, mechanisms which drove us to act in ways to keep us safe from being harmed, we hardly seem at our most sensible, scientific or logical when our emotions take hold. Being apparently *out of control* of our powers of reason was everything that objective science was opposed to.[267]

It didn't help that emotions also seemed worryingly connected to embarrassing bodily reactions. At the end of the nineteenth century William James had noted that 'When worried by any slight trouble, one may find that the focus of one's bodily consciousness is the contraction, often quite inconsiderable, of the eyes and brows. When momentarily embarrassed, it is something in the pharynx that compels either a swallow, a clearing of the throat, or a slight cough; and so on for as many more instances as might be named.'[268] Emotions seemed almost like some kind of throwback to a primitive world of bodily responses, intimately connected to embarrassing bodily functions, including tears, saliva and worse besides. Our emotions seemed to make us *more animal*, while our thoughts seemed to be what elevated us above the bodily responses found in nature.

In this light, emotions could hardly be important in the evolution of humanity, and certainly not worth studying, when they were everything we seemed to need to *put aside* in order to be successful. How often do we imagine highly clean, organised and efficient future humans who have completely overcome their emotions? Spock in *Star Trek* chastises Kirk for his illogical reactions, the whole Vulcan race driven by logic untrammelled by emotions, seemingly *more evolved* than more primitive humanity. In the cult comedy series *Red Dwarf*, the intellectuals in the future holoship have discarded the vulgarity of emotions in pursuit of rational intellectual thought. They have *risen above* their base beginnings to make a cleaner and more logical world.

Wouldn't we be more efficient, organised and ordered without our emotions? In a world focused on technological and intellectual progress powerful desires to care about others often seem things that get in the way. Feelings can be seen as embarrassingly primitive and a rather unnecessary part of our brains in comparison to intellectual thought. Nikola Tesla, the renowned physicist after whom the unit of magnetism was named, and who made vast sums from his patents, was famously disdainful of affection, preferring to focus his attentions on scientific achievement, commenting: 'I cannot think of any great inventions made by married men.'[269] To him, as to much of the scientific world of the twentieth century, our feelings towards others made us *vulnerable*, *irrational* and *out of control of our destiny* – everything a controlled, efficient and competitive world didn't want to be.[270]

That something base, vulgar and unpredictable like our feelings could have played a key role in our evolution was unthinkable. At best, any signs of sensitivity or compassion in our ancestors were a minor addition to a successful adaptation, perhaps even a minor flaw that could be overlooked.

But what if we had been wrong to ignore human feeling? What if emotions were central to our evolutionary story? If other apes shared a moral instinct, could that instinct have been an important part of

human evolution? Was there a mechanism by which natural selection might have moulded the instinctive morality of our common ancestor into human feelings *for a reason*?

Forgotten ideas from the nineteenth century would hold some important clues. Back then, Charles Darwin had seen the evolution of human emotions as key to what set humanity on its unique evolutionary path. Darwin was the first to be convinced that there was a biological basis and evolved root to even our most complex human feelings. He felt that the evolution of morality and human altruism were explicable in terms of evolutionary processes, even inevitable once any animal reached a certain threshold of both an empathy with its peers and a mental ability to *keep track of reputations.*

In *The Descent of Man* (1871), Darwin described our evolved conscience and morality as key to humanity's journey. He followed up his thinking in *The Expression of Emotions in Man and Animals* (1872), far less well known than *On the Origins of Species* (1859). In it he showed how what moved us, what lay at our very hearts, developed from basic mammalian reactions. He used photographs of people, comparing their expressions to similar reactions in animals, and showed how emotions such as fear or anger were seen throughout the world, part of our shared genetic heritage, and related to similar expressions in other species.

Of course, linking the heady world of moral sentiments, something supposedly associated with civilisation, with the reactions of animals and with the bodily world of differential reproductive success was even more challenging than linking Victorian bodies with apes, but that was no bar to his developing his ideas. Darwin wrote:

> I fully subscribe to the judgment of those writers who maintain that of all the differences between man and the lower animals, the moral sense or conscience is by far the most important. This sense, as Mackintosh remarks, 'has a rightful supremacy over every other principle of human action'; it is summed up in that short but imperious word ought, so full of high significance. It is the most noble of all the attributes of man, leading him without a moment's hesitation to risk his life for that of a fellow-creature; or after due deliberation, impelled simply by the deep feeling of right or duty, to sacrifice it in some great cause. Immanuel Kant exclaims, 'Duty! Wondrous thought, that workest neither by fond insinuation, flattery, nor by any threat, but merely by holding up thy naked law

in the soul, and so extorting for thyself always reverence, if not always obedience; before whom all appetites are dumb, however secretly they rebel; whence thy original?'

This great question has been discussed by many writers of consummate ability; and my sole excuse for touching on it, is the impossibility of here passing it over; and because, as far as I know, no one has approached it exclusively from the side of natural history. The investigation possesses, also, some independent interest, as an attempt to see how far the study of the lower animals throws light on one of the highest psychical faculties of man.

The following proposition seems to me in a high degree probable –namely, that any animal whatever, endowed with well-marked social instincts, the parental and filial affections being here included, would inevitably acquire a moral sense or conscience, as soon as its intellectual powers had become as well, or nearly as well developed, as in man.[271]

For Darwin, human morality, our conscience and a drive to care about others derived ultimately from evolutionary processes acting on *the right animal at the right time*. Humans were unique, but only as unique as any other animal. Giraffes might have an unusually long neck from the selection pressures acting on them in their environment; humans had unusually developed emotional and moral responses from the selection pressures on theirs.

It wasn't a popular message for societies convinced of how elevated they were from other animals. Darwin explained:

Firstly, the social instincts lead an animal to take pleasure in the society of its fellows, to feel a certain amount of sympathy with them, and to perform various services for them. The services may be of a definite and evidently instinctive nature; or there may be only a wish and readiness, as with most of the higher social animals, to aid their fellows in certain general ways. But these feelings and services are by no means extended to all the individuals of the same species, only to those of the same association. Secondly, as soon as the mental faculties had become highly developed, images of all past actions and motives would be incessantly passing through the brain of each individual: and that feeling of dissatisfaction, or even misery, which invariably results, as we shall hereafter see, from any unsatisfied instinct, would arise, as often as it was perceived that the enduring and always present social instinct had yielded to some other instinct, at the time stronger, but neither enduring in its nature, nor leaving behind it a very vivid impression. It is clear that many instinctive desires, such as that of hunger, are in their nature of short duration; and after being satisfied, are not readily or vividly recalled. Thirdly, after the power of language had been acquired, and the wishes of the community could be expressed, the common opinion how each member ought to act for the public good, would naturally become in a paramount degree the guide to action. But it should be borne in mind that however great weight we may attribute to public opinion, our regard for the approbation and disapprobation of our fellows depends on sympathy, which, as we shall see, forms an essential part of the social instinct, and is indeed its foundation-stone.[272]

For Darwin, as for de Waal, our social motivations were based in the instincts common to mammals which moved them to help out their allies. However, for humans these instincts would become ever more strongly selected for as higher mental faculties evolved – actions could then be remembered and language would prompt a common opinion to come to bear on anyone's behaviour or attitudes.

The ever watchful eyes of our peers, and their ability to discuss our moral worth, would be the strong force of selection for those who meant well, over those who didn't.

Darwin was not the only nineteenth-century scientist to see others' opinions of what moved us as a driving force in human evolution. William James writing not long afterwards also noticed the significance of our *motivations* on how we are judged by those around us. He argued that for humans, others' judgements are the most important selection pressure in their lives, leading to our complex emotional reactions, our keen drive to be liked and accepted. James wrote:

The most important part of my environment is my fellow-man. The consciousness of his attitude towards me is the perception that normally unlocks most of my shames and indignations and fears.

The extraordinary sensitiveness of this consciousness is shown by the bodily modifications wrought in us by the awareness that our fellow-man is noticing us at all. No one can walk across the platform at a public meeting with just the same muscular innervation he uses to walk across his room at home. No one can give a message to such a meeting without organic excitement. 'Stage-fright' is only the extreme degree of that wholly irrational personal self-consciousness which every one gets in some measure, as soon as he feels the eyes of a number of strangers fixed upon him, even though he be inwardly convinced that their feeling towards him is of no practical account. This being so, it is not surprising that the additional persuasion that my fellow-man's attitude means either well or ill for me, should awaken stronger emotions still. In primitive societies 'Well' may mean handing me a piece of beef, and 'Ill' may mean aiming a blow at *my skull*. In our 'cultured age,' 'Ill' may mean cutting me in the street, and 'Well,' giving me an honorary degree. What the action itself may be is quite insignificant, so long as I can perceive in it intent or animus. That is the emotion-arousing perception; and may give rise to as strong bodily convulsions in me.[273]

James argued that we are acutely sensitive to how others *feel towards us,* whether they are *on our side*. A desire that people might see our genuine intentions, wanting them to like us, motivates much of our lives. As he observed, what we really crave is *to be appreciated*,[274] that others will recognise our positive qualities.

Both Darwin and James had identified our uniquely human sensitivity to others' emotional motivations and a desire to display our own – they realised that this sensitivity and the judgements people made through it affected our survival, making us genetically more predisposed to be moral than any other animal. Other apes may be relatively impervious to the opinions of those around them but as humans, we spend much of our lives worrying about what people will think, hoping to be liked, working to be accepted and valued.

Why would we be so unfortunate as to be so sensitive to those around us, encumbered by a need to impress them with our worth and to monitor theirs, rather than putting the same energies into finding food and practical survival?

One explanation may lie in the unique environmental settings in which early humans evolved.

Humans were the only *ape* – armed with both an ape's moral instinct and their capacity to help constructively – to encounter environments as dangerous as the African savannah. The forest environments in which chimpanzees evolved are relatively stable with few predators, but as we now know the open savannahs and forest edges that australopithecines and early humans occupied were unstable and risky, full of dangerous predators only too willing to eat a defenceless bipedal ape or their young.[275] The hyena gnaw marks and teeth marks from big cats on the australopithecine remains found by Raymond Dart add to any already clear picture from ecological studies. This was no easy place to live.

We had to work together to survive, and that meant selective pressures on the existing mechanisms that allowed us to do so. One particularly pressing problem must have been how to protect vulnerable offspring. Helen Fischer from Rutgers University believes that a need to protect our young may have led to the evolution of distinctive human bonds between mates. It certainly seems to have been part of the story of human connection. She explains that at least 3.5 million years ago risky savannah environments put particular selection pressures on the need to form lasting partnerships – pressures leading to greater selection on parental bonds and ultimately to our capacity to *fall in love. Romantic love* between mates would ensure that they would stay together and protect their young.

Is there any evidence to support this idea? Although we share a sex drive with other mammals, only humans have a drive to *romantic love*, something that we see across the world no matter what culture. Fisher explains that while our sex drive runs on the brain hormone testosterone, and our attachment system runs on oxytocin, we also have a distinctive *attraction system* running on dopamine which drives us to search out our special mate.[276] A particular area at the base of the brain is activated when we are in love, and everything our mate or potential mate does or even the object they touch seems to have a special meaning; it is as if they shine above any other man or woman. We, and no other animal, will die for love, or sacrifice all for love. This drive appears to have its origins in an ancestral mechanism which we see in chimpanzees, prompting them to focus their attention on a mate for the temporary period when they are in oestrus. Chimpanzees, however, were under no evolutionary pressure to find a long-term mate to help rear infants, and such focus, which in humans can last a lifetime, was only temporary.

The significance of love in part explains why we might be under selective pressure to display our sensitivity. Our tendencies to care for the vulnerable would be put under pressure to become more pronounced to make us more attractive to a partner. Studies show that it is kindness that rates as the most important factor both men and women select in a mate, across all different cultures.[277]

Objects belonging to a loved one can almost shine with a special significance. Helen Fisher believes that sensitivity in its many forms, including art, story-telling, poetry and music, may also be related to mate selection, the way in which we pick our partners.[278] Certainly it is difficult to see how human babies could have become as vulnerable at birth and dependent for the increasingly lengthy periods of childhood in dangerous environments without strong bonds between parents, each selecting a partner who was kind and sensitive.

As Barbara Frederickson, Professor at the University of North Carolina, argues, feelings of love, not just for our mates but for family, friends and many others, are essential to our well-being, creating a positive spiral of emotions which affects our resilience, health and even our lifespan.[279] Love and closeness, a lightness of sharing laughter, or open-hearted connection also changes the boundaries of our minds from perceiving ourselves as a single isolated individual to being part of a greater whole.

It is not too fanciful to see evidence for love in the archaeological record. Careful burials imply a strong sense of loss. Many finely made artefacts might be signs of romantic love, from shells carried hundreds of kilometres to finely made figurines. An overspilling of sensitivity, a willingness to go far more than might be rational or sensible is certainly something we see in the growing evidence for elaborate art, movement of non-functional objects along vast distances, and other signs of going well beyond the practical, that we associate with feelings of love. Could such excesses of effort be related to love? In an ethnographic context, Barry and Bonnie Hewlett found that the main motivation for young Aka men to travel great distances to learn new skills was to impress a potential partner.[280]

There is no doubt of the significance of romantic love.

Yet is an attraction between mates who need to rear young sufficient to explain the rest of human emotions, our much wider scope or morality, and why we care so much about other people and even about things? Many other animals need both parents to defend their young without developing a moral instinct anything like that of humans, without reaching out to help objects that seem to need them.

Was there something else that tipped the balance towards some particularly human moral instinct, something on our human journey which made us different?

The timing of particular transformations may hold some important clues. The period in which our young were at their most vulnerable may have been later than Fischer proposed. It was only after 2.5 million years ago that we became truly vulnerable to the dangerous savannah.[281] Australopithecines had always maintained their arboreal adaptations – the long arms and curving fingers that allowed them to climb trees and swing between branches. They still had somewhere to hide. However, the first Homo species, emerging between 2 and 2.5 million years ago, had lost this adaptation. They had no choice but to deal with savannah predators.

Shortly after this time early humans faced a major challenge that may have been the decisive factor in placing evolutionary pressures on our emotional capacities. Between 2.5 and 1.8 million years ago several phases of markedly rapid and unpredictable oscillations in climate, each lasting several hundred thousand years, had occurred.[282] Food resources would have become less and less predictable, risks ever greater. This was a serious crunch time.

Something changed. Instead of getting smaller, retreating back to the trees, early humans did something different. Physical adaptations showed that they confronted the predators more and more often and adapted to eating more meat in their diets. Moreover, children had longer periods of childhood and adults invested greater energy into bigger and bigger brains. Most perplexingly of all, they found time to make stone tools look pleasing. They were thriving in the most risky and unpredictable of situations.

What had happened? Were early humans doing something different? Had they passed some threshold which turned them from a vulnerable ape to a force to be reckoned with?

Robert Frank argues that it was our intense social emotions which gave us a major advantage over other species. Our moral feelings, such as *empathy, sympathy, compassion, remorse, guilt, gratitude,* or *altruistic anger* would all serve an economic function making early humans far more able to weather unpredictable resources, illnesses or other risks than any other animal.

Being driven to care about and help others might seem to make us vulnerable, but could it have been the very transformation which made us successful? Frank explains that our human social emotions, motivating us to help others before ourselves, work from an economic perspective as displays of intent, *commitment devices*[283] which ensure collaboration. Those with mutual commitment give more, knowing that they can depend on each other, that over time their investment will be paid back – a lot like a legal contract. We *can't help ourselves* but reach out to those we care about when they need us because of how we feel about them, and we know they feel the same about us. The end result is that people are willing to take risks for each other, to give generously of their time or resources because they feel safe to do so, with everyone benefitting from the back-up that such willing investment provides.

Human moral feelings provide a whole new level of collaboration.

We may no longer face hungry leopards or have to survive famines together but we still base much of our lives on making commitments to others, being sensitive to their level of commitment to us, and working together on the basis of how we each feel. Friends setting up business together trust that each other will pull their weight, not exploit possibilities purely for their own ends. They have each seen reliable signs that the other was morally bound to behave in the interests of those they care about – from times when they stepped in to help without thinking of themselves; to their remorse when their actions were hurtful; to an unwitting generosity – signs of their emotional investment, that exploiting the other person would be *unthinkable*. Our emotions *handcuff* us not to exploit people we care about, to want to act in their interests, and the more visible our handcuffing to act morally, the more people will trust us.

We even have a kind of moral aversion to *adding up* the benefits of our close relationships. It is not difficult to see how trust works to buffer the effects of hard times – in a close knit society those who are trustworthy and shows signs that they care about and are willing to help others will receive vital help when they need it – but we don't even want to think

Our emotional handcuffing – being driven by our feelings to act morally – works as a commitment device ensuring that others will trust us.

about this type of payback. We wouldn't trust a close friend who consciously kept a tally and we don't keep a tally ourselves.

Most of us are hardly aware that we notice the small subtle signs of others' genuine feelings, let alone of their significance to us. However, studies of couples over many years, considering the tiny signs of trust or a lack of it, have shown how important our unconscious adding up of the accumulated moments of kindness, small signs of *an emotional turning towards others*, is.[284] John Gottman's research has shown that we can even calculate a mathematical 'trust metric', a figure that predicts how much anyone will be prepared to give or give up for others depending on the moments of genuine feeling that they have noticed. This trust metric is made up of the almost invisible moments that display how we genuinely feel which make our relationships strong, or the lack of such moments that make them weak. Close relationships almost never fall apart because of one major act of defection or betrayal, but it is the accumulated pattern of small *turning aways*, the failing to reaching out that it takes for trust to reach threshold limits where our trust metric reaches zero. Small things matter far more than we think.

We may think we are easy-going but we constantly make unconscious judgements of the instinctive morality of others and the level of their commitment to us, not a tally of what they do, but how they feel. Brené Brown draws a metaphor between our internal trust metric and jars of marbles.[285] We hold a mental marble jar for each of our family, friends, allies and colleagues. Each small gesture of reaching out when we need it, each sign of their sensitivity to us adds a marble to our jar, but of course each thoughtless act of self-interest removes one. The more marbles have been added, the more we will be prepared to willingly put ourselves out for them, and they will have noticed. We may be willing to give people we first meet the benefit of the doubt, but it takes years to build up deep-seated trust.

Isn't it all rather complicated? Certainly, we seem to need a wealth of intuition to navigate the maze of what makes people trust us or who we can trust in turn. As William James realised over a hundred years ago, other people's judgement of us is not about *what* we do but rather *why* we do it, our *motivations*. It is one thing to behave in a certain way, but displaying our motivations and being sure we are right about other people's is a tricky task. If we don't appear to be genuinely kind but instead look as though we are motivated to *curry favour*, just

How much we trust others is a little like a jar of marbles. Each small sign that they are on our side adds a marble to the jar and to our willingness to look out for them in turn.

trying to impress, even our apparent acts of goodwill will anger people; we will lose their trust – it is only genuine feeling which counts. This is one reason why it is not elaborate expression of affection or great declarations of love which inspire people to trust us. These, after all, are easy to fake. Rather, it is the small signs, such as remembered birthdays, or the care and patience put into gifts of ostrich eggshell beads, that are important.

In our modern worlds, without a threat of starvation or the danger of predators, we can forget how important people whom we trust are to us. For early humans others' commitment to them was a matter of life or death.

Might it have been 1.8 million years ago when our drive to care about each other and be cared for became so strong that having others whom we could trust to back us up became the norm? Might this be when some threshold was passed where only an unquestioning sensitivity and generosity was sufficient to keep you in the group? Andrew Whiten from the University of St. Andrews argues that human abilities to work together certainly went through a major transformation at this time. By facing predators together to find food or defend each other, by sharing food among the whole group and by maintaining egalitarianism, humans moved from being a group of small vulnerable apes to what he describes as a *highly competitive predatory organism.*[286] As he explains, neither intelligence nor technology would be enough to turn small primates into professional hunters. It was new ways to work together which moved humans into an entirely new niche. *Only changing how we feel would change who we were.*

As Randolph Nesse points out, widespread emotional commitment transforms human nature:

> The advent of commitment changes everything. As soon as one individual finds a way to convince another that he or she will act other than in simple self-interest, social life is transformed ... Reputations become important predictors of behavior, and people begin spending vast amounts of effort to convince others that they will fulfill their promises and threats ... people also can convince others that they will keep their promises by emotional displays that testify to their irrationality ... Social life becomes rich and complex.[287]

Our ancestors may have looked small and vulnerable but any group with the high levels of give and take that came from relationships driven by emotional commitments to each other would be resilient to the ups and downs of changing food supplies, illnesses or whatever else life or their environment would throw at them. They would know that the people they trust won't give in to many temptations to defect, to let them down or to pursue their own interests, which might come along – they just *couldn't* as giving up on someone because life just got practically more difficult right now would be *unthinkable*. By working together in ways no other animal could, being prepared to go to great efforts for others, policing the trustworthiness of those around them, they could iron out the risks the environment predators or prey imposed on them as individuals and all survive – as long as they had reliable signs that those around them were as handcuffed to help, and as able to do so, as they were.

Was this a sudden transformation? There must have been increasing selection pressure on human capacities to form strong bonds with others from as long as 7 to 8 million years ago. A motivation to care about allies and be prepared to help them must have been selected for as soon as our ancestors dealt with increasingly risky environments in which they needed others to help them more regularly. Being seen as sensitive and generous would also become ever more important as the risks of being excluded from the group grew greater.

However, as environments got increasingly unstable after 2.5 million years ago, very small signs of genuine emotions must have been more and more important. The more that was at stake, the more every clue mattered. Early humans will have begun to grasp the opportunities that came their way to show they were demonstrably trustworthy – a kind of hard-wired insurance policy against future trouble. Helping the ill or vulnerable, showing patience and sensitivity in tool forms, every small sign would add up in the minds of those around them. The more such expressions worked to ensure future survival, the greater the selection pressures on the genes which made us motivated to put others first and show it *unintentionally* whether this be physical signs of how we feel, like blushing or crying, or how we react to material things.

A certain threshold would have been passed beyond which evolution of emotional capacities, and other elements of mind, went particularly quickly. At some point, and we can guess at least by 1.8 million years ago, the best chances of survival would have been transformed from being strong or dominating into being *demonstrably trustworthy*. Neither individual strength nor even a stone tool would have been of much use if attacked by a huge lion or pack of hyenas. But having a past history of being particularly courageous on others' behalves, or having a reputation for being particularly generous in times of difficulty, could save your life as the rest of the group might well leap to your defence. A moral instinct made you worth taking risks for.

No other animal has developed a deep-seated collaboration such as ours which depends on moral worth, rather than mere instinct to protect kin. The value of being seen as trustworthy, generous or sensitive would put increasingly strong selection pressures on moral emotions and ways of displaying and identifying them.

Did humans have opportunities to display their intentions, to demonstrate their commitment, in ways that other animals didn't have? Was there some factor that made this type of commitment possible in our case which was missing in others? There may well have been. By 2 million years ago our ancestors had been doing something distinctive for 2 million years already – they had been using stone tools, and no doubt many other types of tools besides. Other animals used tools, but none depended on them as much as early humans did. Even this long ago, the material world around us and the things we held close and carried around with us and used much of the time already showed signs of our impact, and we already showed signs of our dependence on certain objects.

Could expressions of *feeling* about material things have played an important role in the emergence of emotional commitments?

Certain properties of material things might explain how they became uniquely significant signs of a moral instinct. Many aspects of how we make or use objects can send subtle and often rather honest messages about our character.

Thinking back to the characters we met in Chapters six and seven, there is no doubt that material things influence our judgements of whom we would trust. I imagine that I would feel safe and comfortable in the presence of Lawrence Rogers who treasured his daughter's teddy bear so carefully or David Campbell who treasured his tiny sweetheart bear through battles and the prisoner of war camp. Conversely, I would be scared to even meet the hard-hearted recruits who pulled teeth from corpses in Vietnam without any thought or feeling. Yet I know no more about either, have no more information on how to judge their character than *how they treat inanimate things*.

We often treasure mementoes, wear precious jewellery that someone has given us, keep things *close to our hearts* that make us feel more secure, reminding us of our loved ones. Perhaps we even feel a little vulnerable in doing so. Yet the importance of such things to us sends subtle signals about how we value and care about those we love without meaning to. Like blushing and crying, signs of how we feel that *we don't mean to make* are the most influential.

The messages that material things give us are intuitive but powerful. We quickly learn to tell deliberately manipulative displays from honest signs of how people feel. We assume that our emotional reaction to Palaeolithic artefacts is of no relevance to our understanding of them, but our instinctive reactions may be more important than we think.

To see the tiny Vogelherd horse, more than 30,000 years old, moves

185

us deeply – it is such a small, fragile and vulnerable piece of art. As we saw in Chapter six, our evolved emotional minds prompt us to feel a certain sensitivity and openness to people around us when we see or touch such an artefact. Our instinctive feeling that this object *must* have been made with a certain tenderness, humanity even, may be no mere romanticism but reflect the common minds of ourselves and its maker and a genuine sensitivity on our part to the feeling which went into its production.

A tiny carving of a horse made from mammoth ivory, less than 5cm long (Vogelherd Cave, 32 to 31,000bp). Were such small signs of sensitivity vitally important in the Upper Palaeolithic?

Material signals can tell us important messages about people's emotional capacities to be there for us when we need them. What we expect of people whom we feel we would trust is not straightforward sentimentality. To be overly emotional, carried away by our sensitivity or feelings of sympathy, inspires no one's trust. If someone was completely *unable* to smash the robot dinosaur PLEO in the experiment from Chapter six, or became too upset, we would feel a little unsure about their state of mind (it's only a pile of plastic after all!). We expect people to have a strong enough instinct to protect something alive and vulnerable that they should find destroying something apparently vulnerable but inanimate difficult, but, with the help of conscious control, be able to do so all the same. If they are going to be our best ally, if we are prepared to risk much for them, we want them to be brave and emotionally balanced as well as sensitive. We are nothing if not fuzzy about those who we wish to have as our best friends.

To inspire someone's trust we need to not only be sensitive but also to demonstrate the emotional well-being to handle difficult emotions, remain calm in crisis, be able to think through how to help as well as to want to help. If I'm looking for someone who would protect me or my offspring from an attacking leopard they will not only need to care deeply but to be able to keep their wits about them as well. Here, the world of carefully constructed artefacts may be particularly important since making material objects that require patience and overcoming frustration can display these types of qualities. The commitment needed to learn to make a handaxe, the emotional control to overcome the frustrations of imposing a form on stone, are no easy task and it shows. Anyone who has learnt to knap flint, spending hours just attempting to take off a few simple flakes, feels a sense of respect for the makers of handaxes.

Material things have a permanence which momentary gestures lack.

Displays of generosity, a clear willingness to help despite the cost, a sympathy when someone is in need, ordinary kindness to someone suffering are clear signs of character. However, our memory is fallible, these signs can easily be forgotten, or eclipsed by a recent action. Material signals of our trustworthy nature are more permanent, constant reminders of someone's good character. Handaxes still around today tell us something about the emotional competence of their makers who died 1.8 million years ago, but who left something of their skill and patience in permanent form.

That John Frere attached a carefully produced illustration showing the beautiful form of his handaxe when he sent his letter to the Society of Antiquaries in 1797 was significant. The artefact itself was vital – like us, he had felt a deep instinct that the object that he had found implied something special.

Are there any signs of material things playing a part in the reputations of other animals than ourselves? Very few. Young female chimpanzees have been recorded using sticks a little like dolls, taking them back to their nests, cradling them like infants.[288] Perhaps their action reflects an ancestral capacity to imagine life in something inanimate. Though we find such sensitivity to an object remarkable and are drawn instinctively to such behaviour, would other chimpanzees pick up on this overspilling of maternal instinct? Probably not. As we saw in Chapter four, their evolutionary context has made the visual memory of chimpanzees excellent – after millions of years of foraging individually in forests for their food they remember a picture of where things are better than we can. However, our minds search for the significance *to people* of the things that we see, even at the expense of remembering details. For chimpanzees, subtle indications of emotional motivation or moral instinct in how objects were used, even if they existed, were unimportant – chimpanzees are not selective in who they mate with nor find such sensitivity in their allies particularly significant.

Other animals use objects in social ways at times – the bare roots of a capacity to feel something for material things is there. White-faced capuchins play a game with pieces of bark, fruit, sticks or leaves in which the 'toy' is passed from mouth to mouth.[289] In the moment of the game, the toy and how it is passed on has a social significance, with no one eating the object. After the game, however, the toy loses its meaning and is abandoned.

Only for humans, in a context where every subtle sign of moral instinct mattered, did the material world become intimately connected to who we are.

We pick up important emotional messages through the material world that other animals just don't see.

Extra attention in material forms gives us opportunities to expresses a certain *generosity*, a willingness to go beyond the rational, practical or self-interested – the same generosity which is at the heart of give and take in human attachments. There is nothing *sensible* about aesthetically pleasing artefacts, elaborate art or the giving of finely made gifts precisely because a rational focus on immediate practical gain is exactly what they don't intend to convey. As the poet Douglas Yates observed: 'Anyone who is sensible about love is incapable of it.' Likewise, anyone too sensible about the form of their stone tools, who would always stick to only practical forms, might be equally lacking in feeling, unlikely to be carried away by their desire to help others at their own cost, not an attractive feature for someone in the Palaeolithic.

Could the very objects that we see as little more than curiosities, deviations from a more practically focused norm, intriguing mistakes even, tell us most about the human journey? Are these objects more significant than we assume? Many objects just feel peculiarly *human* because they are so impractical. An unusual artefact in the British Museum is one such case. The 350,000-year-old Furze Platt handaxe has always been an enigma. Most handaxes are around 10 to 15cm; they fit in the hand after all. This handaxe, however, found in a gravel quarry in 1919, is more than 30cm long and weighs nearly 3kg – far too huge to be of any practical purpose, it's a struggle even to pick up let alone use. Useless as a butchery tool or even a weapon, it appears an almost ridiculous display of skill and patience. There is no functional explanation for such an artefact.

Some have wondered if the handaxe could be some strange sign of aggression, some way of expressing power. However, given what we know of its maker, a *Homo heidelbergensis*, who will have spent their life working with others to hunt big animals, share food, and defend everyone

188

from predators and for whom acceptance within the group dictated survival, I can't help but see it as expressing more uniquely human emotions.

Was this artefact precisely the ultimate display of emotion over rationality that we feel it to be? It has an almost desperate sense to its production. I can't help but imagine someone making it as an elaborate display of worth, a heartfelt attempt to make up for a wrongdoing, a loss of temper perhaps, a failure to handle feelings in crisis, maybe an infidelity – saying 'I truly am trustworthy really, look what I made'?

Of course, we will never know if its message was well received.

Giant handaxes are truly impressive objects. Francis Wenban-Smith from the University of Southampton describes finding a similar handaxe in recent excavations at Cuxton in south-east England.

> About 60cm down, the level 2b sands came down onto a more gravelly layer (level 2a). As this level was being reached, the scrape of the bucket revealed the butt of a large handaxe in the bottom of the trench, with the tip buried by the recently disturbed spoil. Upon retrieval, the handaxe was found to be a monstrous ficron, 307mm long ... making it the second longest handaxe known in Britain, after the pointed specimen from Furze Platt found in 1919 ... Besides its extreme size, the workmanship of this new Cuxton find is exquisite, almost flamboyant. The narrowed waist of the ficron occurs approximately two-thirds towards the butt from the tip. From the waist to the tip, both sides are straight and perfectly symmetrical. As a final flourish, one side of the tip has been finished with two tranchet blows, creating a sharp edge extending 75mm, without affecting the overall symmetry of the plan view.[290]

The giant Furze Platt handaxe, over 30cm long, is a remarkable object – we can't help but be impressed by the skill in its production and sheer impracticality of its form.

When I asked him what he thought of such unusual artefacts he told me:

> There is something remarkable, something uniquely human, about
> these artefacts. This is an ostentatious display of skill that goes far
> beyond utilitarian; these objects are clearly communicating social
> messages in their ancient world. So what were they saying? 'Love
> me'? 'Trust me'? 'Don't mess with me'? Or merely 'Hands off my
> deer'? Or maybe in a typically human way, a fuzzy multiple-
> layered combination of sentiments to be variously received by
> different voyeurs.

Throughout the archaeological record there are examples of artefacts
which make no practical sense, behaviours like mortuary practice with
no functional basis, elaborate efforts put into pleasing forms, years of
effort put into developing creative skills. They may be telling us a more
important story than we think.

The science of human origins led us to believe that what moved us
along our unique evolutionary path was *our intelligence*. What if, instead,
it were *human feelings*, forged in the difficult and dangerous savannahs,
contexts where cleverness alone was no protection?

**Surely our intelligence must have been the defining feature of
humanity? This is certainly how we have seen ourselves in the animal
world – the most intelligent species.**

There is good reason to argue in contrast that changes in our emotional
capacities, and particularly the emergence of our peculiarly human
compassion, must have preceded any increase in intelligence.

Though we *are* cleverer than any other primate, we can't help but note
our brain expansion occurred relatively late. The Piltdown skull was
convincing because it looked like what we had expected – a primitive ape
with a very large brain. However, real finds showed that significant brain
expansion not only took place after we walked on two legs, but after we
had already begun using stone tools for millions of years and even after
we had developed a modern-like stature and appearance. A lot had
happened in our evolutionary journey before any major phase of brain
expansion.

Both our capacity for altruism and our intelligence define us as
distinctive in the primate world. We have simply assumed that intelligence

must have come first and been most important. Is that assumption perhaps because we believe that intelligence defines success today? Should we even be a little sceptical of the assumption made by intellectuals creating the narrative of our evolutionary journey that intelligence must be our first and defining feature? I can't help but wonder if modern hunting and gathering peoples, aware of their intimate dependence on each other to survive, would see the same evidence differently.

There is certainly good reason to suggest that an unusual kindness, generosity and sensitivity must have come before increases in intelligence. Martin Nowak and Karl Sigmund explain why it must have been an increasing capacity to be altruistic which preceded brain expansion.[291] As they explain, the emergence of *indirect* or *generalised reciprocity,* that is our instinct to care without expecting any return, would have been the decisive factor which led to intense pressures to become more intelligent. However, intelligence alone would not make us more altruistic.

As soon as we depend on *how much others care about us* to survive, whether they will give without counting the cost to keep us alive and if we should feel the same about them, the stakes are high. If we don't form strong bonds we are not likely to survive, but if we trust someone who doesn't care about us we might end up being exploited and have no one there when we need them. Intense selection pressures come to bear on making the right judgements about how to trust, developing the mental abilities to use all the information we have. Keeping track of reputations is taxing and mistakes about who to trust are costly. Then we need to be as intelligent as possible to keep up with who is most likely to be there for us when we need them.

While it is relatively simple for a pair of individuals to keep track of favours and return them accordingly, as our nearest living relatives do, once several individuals are involved the situation raises rather more complex problems. When the whole group collaborates to find food, defend themselves and raise offspring rather unique problems arise.

Suppose a first early human is generous to a second, but the second human exploits this generosity, perhaps by taking more than their share of food or being unwilling to take any risk on the other's behalf. This is a simple case when only two are involved. However, the situation is different when there is a whole group who needs to know who they can trust. Seeing the first being exploited by the second, a third could be annoyed and take action, punishing or chastising the exploiter, expressing their disapproval (as we sometimes see in dominant chimps who break up a fight between subordinates). But if a fourth sees only what the third human has done, and not the original exploitation, how do they know that this was an action taken for the common good on a basis of a moral instinct to punish cheats and not one that was aggressive or selfish? The reputation of the *one who intervened* is at stake, and *depending on their motivations*, they have either proved themselves trustworthy or someone not worthy of effort or support. A simple situation is already a challenge for our mental abilities to decide who is trustworthy, and yet early humans were made of many individuals all seeking to make judgements about the trustworthiness of others.

Social life became *really complicated* as soon as understanding others' motivations and, if we could really trust them, mattered.

As Nowak and Sigmund explain, a *ratchet effect* will have key changes in our brains. As the degrees of give and take driving collaboration (and so abilities to raise vulnerable young in difficult and risky environments) become greater, and collaboration against prey or predators become more effective, at each step more would be at stake. We had to become cleverer, better able to read subtle signs, including material signs of whom we could trust. However, the cleverer we became the more possibilities opened up to find elaborate ways to exploit or dupe others, and the more intelligent we needed to be in turn to detect if motivations really were genuine. Without trusting people we cannot forge the strong bonds needed to survive, but trusting people made us exploitable, and we needed to be keen to display our own trustworthiness and vigilance to detect it in others.

It couldn't have been any other way. If everyone was intelligent and rationally self-interested to be unusually kind would be foolish. Yet in a situation where the more altruistic survived, those who were also clever as well as kind were also at an advantage – they were less likely to be duped or exploited. As we saw in Chapter seven, people who are selfish or even motivated to hurt others always exist, but the altruistic majority, once in place, kept them in check,[292] often in clever ways.

Our human talents follow from an emotional drive to be altruistic but not the other way.

Robin Dunbar explains that it is our need to gossip, discuss and evaluate the motivations, trustworthiness and reputation of those close to us that drove the evolution of *language*.[293] We might have been able to coordinate a hunting trip with signals, much as chimpanzees do, but discerning why someone did something to someone else, and whether we should applaud their actions or shun them, is far more difficult and demands much more subtlety. Yet we needed to know about others' motivations and to find ways, including material ones, to persuade them of our own goodwill.

Our *theory of mind abilities*, the capacity to model in our minds why different individuals might have acted in relation to each other or how they felt about each other, had to develop to keep up. As we saw in Chapter five, the neocortex, the part of our brains concerned with social interactions, expanded fast, and with it our abilities to understand what one person might think of another's thoughts and, in turn, how each might understand *our* motivations. Because of our theory of mind abilities, we can follow a complex plot in a novel, imagining each different personality and how we interpret their actions, what moves each one of them. We needed to *keep up with the gossip*, not find we did not understand who did what to whom or why.

There is no denying that we got increasingly clever along our evolutionary journey. However, what we think of as our defining strengths – such as intelligence and language – must have evolved as the *means to cope* with the challenges brought by our need to care deeply about others to survive. *Changing how we felt* was the starting point which led onto changing how we think.

All primates are clever. In the primate world the way we stood out and were different, the factor leading to our particular success, is not likely to have been being clever but being kind, as F. J. Joakes Jackson inadvertently expressed in the opening quote.

Could we have been considering our past through eyes blinkered by what we are led to believe in our own societies?

Is the significance of human morality, compassion and a drive to care about others – its significance to what *made us human* – something we should have known all along?

Perhaps it is time for a new story of human origins.

PART THREE

A New Story

A 1.5-million-year-old Homo erectus *footprint from Ileret, Kenya. Did evolutionary pressures take the emotions of this human on an entirely new journey?*

Chapter Nine

The Path Less Travelled

Somewhere ages and ages hence:
Two roads diverged in a wood, and I—
I took the one less traveled by,
And that has made all the difference.[294]

In this chapter we reflect back on the archaeological record to consider when and where a sensitivity to others became central to human society, and when and how a willingness to give without counting the cost allowed early humans to survive where others would not. Were early human societies just like us, or were there sharp limits to who or what they could care about? We look at evidence for how sensitivity, a moral instinct, and being prepared to take risks for others developed through time, particularly considering the often overlooked evidence for sensitivity in Neanderthal society.

Robert Frost's poem above, 'The Road Not Taken', often reminds me of the many different paths in evolution, each one making all the difference, but none of them looking so different at the start.

A better understanding of our path – the environments to which our ancestors adapted and how they adjusted to them – has cast new light on the selection pressures acting on early human minds. However, we have only recently recognised the potential significance of our *emotional minds* on our success.

If we go back 7 to 8 million years ago none of the changes which would lead uniquely to humanity had yet taken place. I can't help imagining our last common ancestor at the dividing line between two paths, not knowing what lay in each direction. In one lay a future remaining in the stable environments of the forests, in the other lay the more open grasslands, full of potential, but also full of dangers, predators and risks. The path taken would dictate what happened to the minds of the two different apes, the chimpanzee/bonobo line and the human line, yet they cannot have looked so different at the start. At the origin point were individuals with a capacity to care for others, to remember who had helped them and to make judgements of them, but only along one path would that capacity to care become human love, compassion, sympathy and empathetic joy, and only one would involve an intimate emotional connection with material things.

We don't know much about the initial steps along the human path between 7 to 8 million and around 3 million years ago. By the end of this phase Dart's australopithecines were alive and the trail of footprints was made at Laetoli. Several different species living at this time might have been ancestral to humans. All were small, diminutive ape-like creatures with only slightly larger brains than any other ape, but they had reduced canine teeth, and over this period they became truly bipedal. These creatures had moved out of the forest environments that protected ancestral apes and into drier mosaic savannahs as increasing aridity caused patches of forest to dwindle. They didn't make a choice, of course, even though we term the adaptations to this new environment *a strategy* – it was more a matter of certain apes being isolated from others in drier patches and only the better adapted survived.

There was not much impressive about any of these apes. Even by 3 million years ago the australopithecines that Dart dubbed his 'killer apes' looked far more vulnerable than in any way intimidating. With hands still

Where do we go from here?

197

adapted to life swinging through trees, they probably lived in woodland alongside rivers as much as open savannah, particularly to escape predators. Cutmarks on bones suggest that as early as 3.5 million years ago australopithecines also used sharp bits of stone to scavenge meat from carcasses left behind by lions, hyenas and vultures. With time, they began to learn how to make even sharper edges, knapping flint with other stones more adeptly.

However, by 1.8 million years ago, two great pulses of extreme environmental variability, each lasting several hundred thousand years, had dominated their African environments.[295] Climates were not so much cooler, warmer, wetter or drier, but much more *unpredictable*, making resources unreliable and constantly changing.

As the environments and food sources became more risky something remarkable happened. Before 2.5 million years ago there were many different species of bipedal apes, not only the australopithecines divided into *A. africanus* and *A.afarensis*, as well *A. garhi, A. Anamenis* and *A. sediba*, but also the heavy jawed *Paranthropus* species. After 1.8 million years ago, however, there were only a few, some argue even only one, bipedal ape – the Homo lineage, including *Homo habilis, erectus* and *ergaster*. Many even lump these different species into one – *Homo erectus*.[296] It was in tandem with extreme oscillations of climate that these early humans appeared, with their notable increases in brain size, particularly in the front part of the brain which, as we saw in Chapter five, is associated with social interactions. Right when the going got toughest these early humans invested most energy in their brains, gave birth to increasingly vulnerable young, and took longer and longer to reach adulthood. They also moved into a niche in which they would need to confront dangerous big cats or hyena packs. Andrew Whiten says at that at this point human ancestors began to work as a 'single predatory organism', initially moving out from Africa into Asia but ultimately able to live in almost any environment they encountered.[297]

These new humans were not in any way intimidating alone, but they might have become a force to be reckoned with *together*. While we might expect a fight for survival in these difficult conditions, and expect to see canines get larger, and for males to get respectively bigger than females as they battled each other, this is the reverse of the biological changes that we see. Moreover, it is in this context that we see the first evidence for sustained care of the ill and the remarkable and unexplained concern with the aesthetics of finely made handaxes. If there is a significant turning point in human evolution it seems to be this one, the point at which we first use the term *Homo*, human.

The increasingly risky environments around 1.8 million years ago must have put particularly strong selective pressures on abilities to collaborate in early humans. Had humans found a particular solution to the problem of ensuring help from others? Other animals work together – ants form colonies, lions hunt as a pack – but had humans begun to rely on an entirely different form of collaboration, based not on instinctive behaviour alone, nor on genetic relatedness, but on *a sensitivity to others' well-being and motivations* and *a capacity to remember and to value the trustworthiness of others?*

Different strands of evidence brought together suggest that our feelings, the evolution of our emotional mind, more than our intellect made us human.

Studies of primates give us insights into the emotional capacities of our common ancestor; fossil bones track the changes in our brains; our own minds hold evidence for a pattern of selection to be ever more motivated by the welfare of others and ever more sensitive to subtle messages in material things. An understanding of how we evolve directs our attention to the significance of human capacities to put others first, and to make judgements about who is most worthy of our trust.

Could the turning point in a new story of human origins where compassion and sensitivity come first have been as early as 1.8 million years ago?

Some might argue that it could have been even earlier. I can't resist wondering if the australopithecine who found the Makapansgat pebble 3 million years ago already *felt something* when they saw the somewhat infantile appearance of the pebble, that they might already have a tendency to see some feeling even in an inanimate object that might engender a need to nurture the tiny stone. Did australopithecines feel a need to care that stretched to how they felt about *objects* 3 million years ago? Certainly their own infants were already proportionately larger at birth and demanded more care than the counterparts of other great apes. Selection pressures to be *better at nurturing*, to find ways to spread the cost of the increasing levels of care by *finding a more sensitive mate* must already have been felt.

Jeremy DeSilva from Boston University believes that as early as 3 or 4 million years ago we see the start of selection pressures for females and males to develop long-term monogamous bonds in order to jointly raise offspring.[298] We saw in Chapter eight that Helen Fischer argues that romantic love emerges at this time. If australopithecines, both males and females, already developed strong bonds between them, and had a heightened sensitivity to the needs of vulnerable offspring, then they were certainly a very different ape from those that Raymond Dart imagined. Is one pebble and a set of footprints in the dust, however intriguing, enough to tell us? Perhaps not, although a tendency to nurture, care for and see some kind of *life* even in objects is something we continue to see in the later evidence of early 'art' that we saw in Chapter two, such as the Tan-tan figurine or Berekhat-Ram figurine, objects also with a distinctively infant-like form.

Soon after 2 million years ago we can, however, be much more confident that we can see widespread evidence for something new in the emotional reactions of hominins.

This point is, for me, where recognisably human emotions began. Reflecting back on the different lines of evidence, it seems that this is when we can more confidently see the emergence of clearer evidence for a sensitivity to the needs of others, to what people thought and felt about each other, and a willingness to reach out to help. More than just being upset that the female *Homo ergaster* with hypervitaminosis living around 1.6 million years ago was in great pain, others in her group were *motivated* to help, protecting her over a period of weeks if not months, and feeding her. It didn't seem to matter whether she would be likely to survive to repay any debt, they just felt moved to act. More than just being aware that the Dmanisi hominin with only one tooth 1.8 million years ago was struggling to find food, others were moved to help feed him for an extended period.

Far more extensive than any help seen in other primates, these kinds of behaviours suggest that changes in the brain that occurred at this time involved changes in how we could feel about each other, and how we could *future feel*, as well as how to manage those feelings to help constructively. As I and two of my graduate students, Holly Rutherford and Andy Needham, have argued, this was when demonstrably caring for others became an important trait – one that affected *the carers' future survival* through how others treated and respected them for their actions.

It seems no coincidence that finely made handaxes, demanding an ability to control the frustrations of working stone to make a defined form also appeared at this time. Steve Mithen argues that handaxes may have been part of sexual selection, early human males vying against other males to demonstrate their ability to produce the biggest and most impressive tool. He compares early humans with grouse at a lek – fierce competition for females played out aggressively in stone.[299] I'd be surprised if he is right, and his so-called 'sexy handaxe theory' has more generally fallen out of favour. Were handaxes even made by men? With tool-making passed on to the young by the *females* in our nearest relatives, the chimpanzees, we certainly might question the assumption. But even if it *was* the males who were producing the handaxes rather than the females, the ecological setting suggests that females would have had more important priorities than looking for someone *flashy*. With their increasingly vulnerable young, the ever pressing need to secure shared food to help them survive and the importance of obtaining the help of those around them to protect them from predators, early humans must already have been sensitive about who to trust to be a reliable mate, as well as who to trust as friends and allies.

The reduced size of the canines in *Homo erectus* suggests that physical competition between males was increasingly unimportant. If there was competition it doesn't seem to have been about who would win a fight. Far more impressive than physical prowess and perhaps even harder to muster would have been the emotional willingness and capability to share food, protect and nurture young. It would have paid females bringing up vulnerable young to be very picky about their mates.

Making a handaxe to a particular form may be about far more than just showing off extra energy and resources. These finely crafted tools demonstrate an emotional awareness hitherto not seen before, both of an understanding of how others feel and also an ability to overcome frustrations and temptations rather than just acting on impulse.[300] The self-control used to impose such a difficult form on stone taps into the same parts of the brain that control our frustrations over sharing food, standing our ground with dangerous predators or prey without running away, and one's reliability as a mate who would stick around. It is a sign of someone able to handle difficult human emotions and be *trustworthy*.

Early humans must always have been watched by those around them when they made stone tools as much as in how they reacted to others' vulnerability. In a collaborative world reputation is everything. Much as those who fail to control their temper in the Inuit can be deliberately excluded, signals of being uncaring or emotionally unpredictable may well have already risked exclusion, from which there would be little chance of survival.

It would have been well worth the extra effort to make clear you were more than capable of patience, especially when the effort put into stone tools provided *a lasting reminder*. The emotional competence put into handaxes is something we can still sense, even now, over a million years after their production.

It is also by around 1.8 million years ago that we see other material evidence in the archaeological record of human remains and stone tools that these early humans were *moved by the suffering of others, sensitive to how* *others felt* and had *better ways of handling difficult feelings*. Moreover, the enlargement of the neocortex at this time also points to expanded empathetic reactions and no doubt those increasing quantities of VEN neurones in the brain that we saw in Chapter six made difficult emotions manageable.

Was it with the emergence of Homo erectus *that something new happened to human emotions?*

Are handaxes signs of an ever greater sensitivity in other ways? Greg Currie from the department of Philosophy at York University sees handaxes as the first deliberately beautiful objects, resonant with the earliest signs of an appreciation of beauty in their makers.[301] They provide, he says, 'evidence of a very deep history of aesthetic production; a history so long that it makes the Upper Palaeolithic look positively contemporary. This history extends back long before our species emerged, long before language developed, long – apparently – before any genuinely symbolic activity of any kind.'[302]

Handaxes can have a certain *elegance*. They were often made to fit the 'golden rectangle', a pleasing proportion seen in architecture, suggesting an appreciation of the aesthetic. Some finely made handaxes are made much larger than could possibly have been useful, in an apparent overspilling of a desire to make this work grander, finer and more pleasing. Highly symmetrical handaxes can reach sizes well beyond the functional, such as the 30-centimetre-long Furze Platt handaxe dating to around 350,000bp from Maidenhead, England,[303] which we considered in the last chapter. This handaxe can't possibly have been *useful* in any sense other than to look at.

Moreover, handaxes were also often made to incorporate flaws so that the final form looked pleasing rather than odd or asymmetrical. Flaws in the raw material are artificially mirrored on the other side of handaxes at the English sites of Boxgrove[304] and Elveden,[305] as well as at Isimilia, Tanzania,[306] for example. A handaxe from West Tofts in Norfolk, dating to 250,000 years ago, even features a fossil scallop shell beautifully placed at its centre. John Feliks from the University of Michigan considers that whoever made this handaxe was probably aware that this fossil was related to living scallops, perhaps fascinated by this idea.[307] Did they see the finished handaxe as somehow alive, or at least capturing in some way the spirit of a living thing? It's impossible to know.

Are finely made handaxes really the markers of the origins of art and aesthetic sense? It is certainly the first signs of a marked sensitivity to how others will feel and a willingness to take extra effort beyond the practical or functional. We saw in Chapter one that the antiquarians of the nineteenth century were struck by how the ancient handaxes they found in river gravels must have signified

The 250,000-year-old West Tofts handaxe which was crafted around a fossil scallop shell. Did the people who made it understand that the shell had once been alive?

humanity, some race of people of which they had as yet no understanding. The process involved in knapping a handaxe, how to take each piece off in a particular way, with a particular end in mind, means that when we look at them we are already transported to the moments of time in which an early human overcame frustrations, made decisions, patiently worked with care and attention to create something lasting.

Is it really the final form of finely made handaxes which is so remarkable? Their shape may be considered beautiful, but isn't it the grappling with difficult feelings, the commitment to learn, the desire to *create something appreciated and lasting* which is the beauty of these objects? As we saw in Chapter six, we can almost *read* the emotions invested in objects, and, in terms of who we trust, demonstrable patience, an ability to overcome frustration and a commitment to learn are qualities we search for.

Holding a handaxe that is over a million years old is, for me, to sense just the *craving to be appreciated*, which William James noted was, for him, 'the deepest principle in human nature'[308] in its first lasting material form. They seem to reach to us from vast depths of time to tell us something about how it felt to be human, and want to be recognised for our efforts, almost hundreds of thousands, even millions of years ago.

I have no doubt that a uniquely human feeling lies behind both the creation of finely crafted tools and an unquestioned care for the vulnerable. Were early humans almost 2 million years ago already essentially just like us?

Perhaps not quite. As we have seen, the feelings which lie at the heart of humanity, a drive to nurture those we care about, to be sensitive to how others feel, a craving to be seen as good or valuable, may have been part of our story shortly after 2 million years ago, but some of our more complex emotions may not yet have been. Gratitude, embarrassment, shame, pride, all the complex and often messy human emotions that demand a multi-level understanding of how others feel, and *how they feel about us*, may yet have only been emerging. Even more encompassing emotions, to feel for humanity, for living things around us, to be awed by a sense of the scale of our existence, demands a certain understanding of who we are in a wider whole. To *care deeply outside of our own lives and existence* may have been the starting point for being human, but the journey was only in its first few steps 1.8 million years ago.

Did the sensitivity of early humans only go so far? Were they only part way on the path to an extended human empathy? Some researchers suggest that while they may have been attentive to the needs and feelings of those in their own group, for most early humans those outside it may have meant nothing to them, mere *objects*, which sometimes got in their way.

Certainly, it is possible that one element of selection pressure towards greater collaboration in early humans came from just such a need to jointly *defend their own patch* against outsiders who were more of a threat than a source of any potential allies.[309] Much like prides of lions who cooperate to hunt and raise offspring, outside threats from other human groups might have made early humans more driven to work together, yet at the same time emphasising being hostile to strangers. Risky environments with distinctive patches of resources are certainly the types of landscapes where it might make sense to work together to defend what you had. Christopher Opie from University College London and colleagues believe that like other primates living in large groups there may also have been pressures for early humans to join together and to develop long-term monogamous bonds to protect infants from marauding males.[310]

A distinction between 'us', a focus of care, and 'them', undeserving of any feeling, may explain the evidence we saw in Chapter one from Atapuerca in northern Spain just after 1 million years ago. Here the remains of butchered *Homo antecessor*, largely females and offspring, were found deposited alongside faunal remains and have been interpreted as evidence for nutritional cannibalism, seeking out neighbouring groups of humans as *prey*. However supportive of their own, those outside their group may have mattered nothing at all to these people. Palmira Saladié and colleagues from Institut Català de Paleoecologia Humana i Evolució Social at the University of Tarragona argue that the human remains from Atapuerca are evidence for a pattern of attacks on neighbouring groups remarkably similar to those seen in chimpanzees,[311] motivated only by defending their own territories and gaining resources. Like common chimpanzees, *Homo antecessor* did not seek out strangers to harm, or feel any glory in their pain, but neither were they concerned about hurting those who got in their way. Unlike the modern humans who attacked their neighbours at Gough's Cave and made their skulls into drinking vessels, these archaic humans had no *desire* to hurt their neighbours symbolically or practically, they just saw them as a source of food.

The very *practicality* of the attitudes of *Homo antecessor* towards their neighbours strikes us as somehow inhuman. Though the end result might be the same, our moral compass suggests to us that feuding and revenge killings, wishing to hurt an enemy for personal reasons, is somehow more *human* than seeing others as simply a source of meat. The darker side to our emotional commitment, a motivation to take revenge if we are let down, might not seem pleasant but it would seem more familiar than to feel nothing at all. Saladie's research suggests that neither our tendency to care about people we don't know, nor our rather grisly pleasure in others' pain or the glorification in the misfortunes of others – that feeling of *shadenfreude* – emerged until later societies.

Deliberate cruelty may yet have been a baffling idea to *Homo erectus*. These early humans might have understood our feelings of connection to our loved ones, our tendencies to put others first without thinking, but they may well have been naive about some of the darker side to our human feelings as well as the complexities of our wider social worlds.

That early human societies were internally driven by compassion, trust and sensitivity, yet remained remarkably insensitive to those outside their group, would explain some enigmas. The distances over which people travelled to get their raw materials go no farther than we might expect home or territorial ranges to extend until at least half a million years ago, for example, no matter how valuable distant resources might have been. Who would risk entering a neighbouring territory? Moreover, a remarkable conservatism in stone tool industries for over a million years from the earliest handaxe forms has always been a mystery. These were increasingly large-brained hominins, capable of adapting to new and difficult environments, able to communicate with some form of language. Why not try something new, experiment with a new design, a new way of doing things? But who would rock the boat if to be even slightly different carried such a risk?

Perhaps the risk of a hostile reaction to anything *different or unfamiliar* explains why the design and form of stone tools remained remarkably conservative for over a million years. With little direct evidence for either inter-group violence or inter-group collaboration it is difficult to tell.

We don't know how representative the evidence from Atapuerca is of early human attitudes to their neighbouring groups, or whether it was in any way usual to exploit them as food. This type of behaviour might solve a short-term problem of food supply and deplete the area of hostile neighbours, but it was hardly one likely to improve *the long-term survival* of a species, especially if food resources fluctuated greatly and if human numbers became dangerously low at times of stress. Indeed, it is possible that that particular brand of hostility that went beyond defence to *preying on one's neighbours* was an extreme since *Homo antecessor* seems to have died out, not leading to the human line. We might be particularly grateful that *that* specific branch of human evolution didn't seem to lead anywhere.

A widening of social and emotional worlds, an opening up to new people, new perspectives, new things would have far-reaching effects.

Being more tolerant, expanding one's willingness to give without counting the cost *beyond* the immediate group, developing relationships based on high degrees of give and take with those less familiar people who lived outside a local area, would lead whoever could manage such an expansion to be even more resilient to the vagaries of environmental change. As we saw in Chapter three, exchanges of materials between regions have helped modern hunter-gatherer groups to survive, and similar exchanges are seen in the archaeological record of modern humans. Being able to depend on *distant* friends to support you in times of need seems critical to survival in many of the environments our species lived in. Yet it may have taken time to make the step to being more *tolerant of difference or unfamiliarity* whether inside or outside one's own group.

By 450,000 years ago in northern Spain evidence suggests that the beginning of this transformation had taken place. As we saw in Chapter three Benjamina, the nine-year-old child with craniosynostosis from Sima de los Huesos in Spain, looked different from other children, and with probable cognitive damage may well have thought differently as well. Yet this didn't stop her being cared for like any other child. We saw in Chapter four that when the chimpanzee McGregor, with polio, looked and acted differently he was shunned by the other chimpanzees, something that deeply upset Jane Goodall. We don't know what would have happened to a similar early human before this date, yet it seems that by at least 450,000 years ago human societies were very different. Benjamina didn't need to look, or act in a familiar way, as those around her could see through the external appearance to the *humanity underneath*. Like the Upper Palaeolithic Romito child with dwarfism, or the paraplegic Man Bac man, neither did there seem to be any expectation that Benjamina would need to be able to be independent in order to be worth supporting. She was just someone vulnerable in need of help, who would, naturally, receive it.

Our minds, focused in immediate short-term economics, can't help but wonder if the food, time and energy spent by a small group on those who were unlikely to contribute in return, was not *wasteful*. Would not a more brutal group of archaic humans survive where these tender-minded peoples might not?

I suspect that, contrary to what we might expect, such a brutal-minded group would be the first to expire. As we saw in Chapter seven, reputation would have been critical to the survival of any individual, and expressing a certain brutality a quick way to be considered *untrustworthy*. More than this, however, the emotions on which human groups depended to survive; a willingness to share their food even when hungry and to care for others when they were vulnerable; the courage to take risks on behalf of the group and to maintain a sense of fairness, would only develop in supportive contexts. The courage and self-control to face a charging animal for the sake of everyone, sensitivity to care for others or nurture children, are hard-wired *possibilities*, but as we saw in Chapter six, even in modern humans these instincts don't develop without the right environment. Only the support we see reflected in care of the vulnerable created the social context which gave such humans the confidence and courage to help each other out, knowing that care from others came *without counting costs and risks* would be taken for each other *without calculating the benefits*.

What was it like to be cared for in such societies? Did archaic humans at Atapuerca sit around the fire at night discussing how to support Benjamina without her feeling a burden? Did they wonder how to make her feel better or even if she could be cured? They may well have done. Certainly those Neanderthals who looked after the old man found at Shanidar with his plethora of injuries must have discussed how best to look after him. His care, like that of the Man found at Man Bac in Vietnam, must have involved the whole group over an extended period. There must have been discussions about what to do, and how best to help. We don't know much about what *Neanderthal medicine* might have entailed, but we do know that most of their wounds healed well. At El Sidron cave in Spain there is evidence for the use of medicinal plants, with chemicals found in deposits between the teeth of one Neanderthal coming from plants similar to yarrow and chamomile which have anti-inflammatory properties.[312] Certainly, how to care for people must have been something that Neanderthals knew about, talked about, and felt was important.

Life can hardly have been easy for archaic humans like Neanderthals living 200,000 to 30,000 years ago. Despite the frequent famines that we see in records of growth patterns in teeth, these cultures seem to have been committed to caring for the vulnerable, even someone who looked different from the norm. This can have been no easy task, not only due to frequent shortages of food but also to the gruelling physical demands of long hours travelling to find food. Yet the blind and crippled man at Shanidar was looked after for at least fifteen years. Despite what Coolidge and Wynn suggest, I get the impression that abandonment was *unthinkable* and being a little different or having little chance of repaying such kindness in a practical sense was no barrier to such care.

Neanderthals were certainly prepared to go to great lengths for each other which suggests that they felt they were part of a wider whole, not just a single individual pursuing only their own interests. Evidence from how they hunted certainly argues for an unquestioning willingness to sacrifice or take risks to bring home food for everyone. At la Cotte de Sainte Brelade in Jersey, Matthew Pope has been excavating a fascinating Neanderthal site occupied by Neanderthals between 250,000 and 60,000 years ago. Here Neanderthals hunted mammoth and woolly rhino by driving them up a narrow gorge. At the base of a cliff there are piles of bones and stone tools, the remains left after all the carcasses were butchered.[313] More than 250,000 stone tools were recovered, the results of hunting and perhaps occupation, with fires also found at the site. I can't imagine being brave enough to face a huge woolly rhinoceros, angry and only too willing to gore me through. These hunters must have been entirely confident of being *in it together* to have tackled this type of prey. Lacking the full articulation of their shoulder joints, Neanderthals hunted by getting up close and personal to animals, frequently being wounded. Were they not tempted to run away to save themselves? While we as a species maintained the running abilities first developed in *Homo ergaster*, Neanderthals lost much of that ability – they were highly inefficient runners.[314] Perhaps running away was also unthinkable.

Was it only the men who were hunting? Stephen Kuhn and Mary Stiner from the University of Arizona think not.[315] They find no evidence for any division of labour in Neanderthal society, with the many trauma patterns we see in the skeletal record from hunting large game as evident in the skeletons of women as of men. They really were all in it together. Only knowing they could count on others to care about them no matter what would have given them the courage to take the risks that they took.

As we saw in Chapter five, all too often those elusive Neanderthals seem both like us, and yet different, always standing at the point of tension between being familiar and being challenging.

Evidence from many sites, like Abri Romanic in Spain, Tor Faraj in the Levant, and Molodova in the Ukraine, show a structure to Neanderthal occupation areas which feels familiar to us.[316] At Abri Romanic eight evenly spaced hearths against the rockshelter wall must have been laid out between people to keep them warm at night,[317] with similar hearths also laid against the rock wall at Tor Faraj.[318] At Molodova in the Ukraine, a dwelling structure was even found, made of mammoth bones, with fifteen hearths inside as well as storage pits.[319] Some of the mammoth bones had a series of parallel grooves and were covered with ochre which suggests some kind of non-practical function, perhaps an aesthetic or symbolic use. We get the impression that there was *a certain way of doing things*, expressed in their domestic spaces. Being human, they must have worried if things weren't quite right.

Neanderthals clearly grieved when their loved ones died. Indeed, Neanderthals had different types of ritual practice, and it is probable that only a tiny fraction of their reactions to death were ever of the type that might have been preserved. We know that they felt the need to treat the body of the elderly man at Shanidar with a certain respect, for example, uniting to carry out some ritual to feel they had done something sensitive to even a lifeless body. Neanderthal burial includes single burials, such as at La Chapelle aux Saints in France and Teshik-Tash in the Crimea as well as multiple burials. At Sima de Las Palomas in southern Spain the bones of a Neanderthal child were associated with burned horse bones and flints, and found immediately above an adult female, laid out carefully on a slope and buried under a rock scree, reminding of us practices of burying people under mounds or cairns in later prehistory.[320] There are also locations such as those found at La Ferrassie in France and Shanidar in Iraq where people must have returned to the same spot to bury people, somewhere perhaps of great significance. Such mortuary practice speaks of an expansion of empathy from only the living to a tendency to see a soul, some kind of feeling or life even where such life no longer exists, or in the case of objects, which also seem to have been

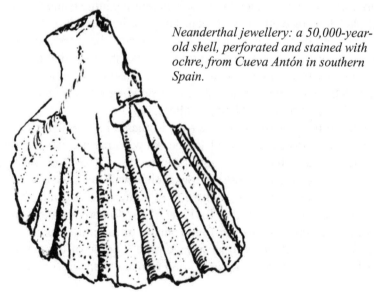

Neanderthal jewellery: a 50,000-year-old shell, perforated and stained with ochre, from Cueva Antón in southern Spain.

cared for to see a soul in places where life never existed. As we saw in Chapter three, Neanderthals seem to have some kind of attachment to objects, from using bird feathers perhaps as some kind of decoration, to what we might call art in the Roche-Cotard mask, to some kind of jewellery or decoration in the form of perforated and stained shells such as those found at Cueva Antón in southern Spain.

Nowhere is the contrast between our imagined past and the evidence greater than in Neanderthal childhoods.

Palaeolithic children rarely ever enter our imagination, yet they made up a large part of such societies, and the experience of being a child is so fundamental to adult attitudes, creativity and emotional well-being. So often in our imaginations the experience of being a Palaeolithic child must have been a harsh existence. A 'Neanderthal childhood' conjures up an image of harshness, deprivation and perhaps even cruelty. Even if they appear in reconstructions none shows any stone-age children, Neanderthals or others, as anything other than grubby, rather unkempt and always looking worried and upset. Who can imagine such children laughing and playing?

As John Shea of Stonybrook University notes, we tend to ignore evidence for even the existence of children in the Palaeolithic record.[321] Yet the Palaeolithic was full of children, and these children must have spent much time at play. Children are everywhere in modern hunting and gathering societies, enjoying years of independence. No matter what our preconceptions, a sense of fun and play must have been a central part of the childhood of archaic humans, being essential to the development of all ape young. Gorillas and chimpanzees play peek-a-boo, hiding their faces and surprising their infants, like we do,[322] and archaic humans must have been no different. Ape and human infants all suffer emotionally if they do not have enough time to play, being more insecure, and scared of taking risks.[323] Play must have been important for human children, with all those difficult emotions to learn how to handle. Being able to willingly face an enraged mammoth as an adult must have come not only from practical experiments in how to hunt as a child, but also from the years of fun and pretend-play which are needed to develop an emotional tolerance for fear and risk. In rough and tumble play we are pushed to handle a tolerable level of fear, allowing us to better handle difficult feelings as adults. It is hard to imagine archaic humans having fun, but

Neanderthal children must have been cherished and cared for.

those without chances to play with friends and adults, with the empathy and humour needed to share a sense of fun, would have been at a serious disadvantage.

The odd kind of warmth we can feel towards bundles of stuffed fur, even as adults, makes me wonder when the first human children had toys which they loved, and for whom they created a whole life story and personality. Did Neanderthals play with dolls or teddy bears? Much as I'd love to, I doubt we'll ever find an early human's teddy bear – such things would never survive. Any soft toy or bundle of furs, imagined as a companion or infant to care for that was carried around thousands of years ago, will surely have perished. But alongside the existing archaeological record of hard imperishable objects, stone tools and rare bones, apparently so functional, we certainly might imagine a long-lost forgotten soft record of cuddly things that were once loved.

There are at least some indications. Finely made miniature handaxes, thought to be made deliberately as toys, have been found at various sites. Examples only 2 to 3cm wide are found, for instance, at Wansunt Pit and Foxhall Road in southern England,[324] dated to the Lower Palaeolithic, probably made by *Homo heidelbergensis*. Another, found in Rhenen in the Netherlands, was made by Neanderthals. Carefully made, they may well have been cherished possessions.

Did a Neanderthal child scream with delight at such a present? They may well have done, and the image of an excited Neanderthal child at play is likely to be far more representative of the reality of the Palaeolithic

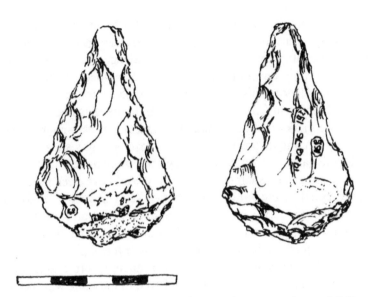

Both sides of handaxe no. 168 from Foxhall Road interpreted as a child's toy.

than those of anxious, hunched-up children, that is, if children even appear at all in reconstructions.

I have no doubt that there was a similar kind of genuine and caring bond between Neanderthal parents and their children. Their careful burial of infants at different sites, the young child buried with a red deer maxilla at Amud Cave in Israel or newborns buried under stone slabs at La Ferrassie in France, speak to us of a sensitivity to children that seems out of keeping with their conventional image. The only grave goods we find – carefully placed deer jaws or goat horns – are almost solely in children's graves. The burial of a two-year-old at Dederiyeh Cave in Syria, for example, has a triangular flint at the heart and stone slab at the head. We can't help but wonder if children held a particular significance.

How do we reconcile evidence for a home life, courageous hunting, sensitivity to the suffering of the living and even to the bodies of the diseased, and the gentle care of children, with that for cannibalism in Neanderthals? Were they so insensitive to the feelings of those in other groups that cannibalism was a practicality? Or were they at times entirely callous to their own dead, seeing them as a source of food? Were they driven to desperate measures to survive, like situations in our societies where cannibalism is recorded, as in desperate famines or plane crashes in remote places?

We can't help but feel that the explanations for Neanderthal cannibalism need to be different from those applied three-quarters of a million years earlier. Unlike at Atapuerca, there is no evidence for a selection of *the vulnerable* to prey on in human bones that have been disarticulated or defleshed by Neanderthals. Some apparent evidence for cannibalism, such as that at Krapina in Croatia or Engis in Belgium, has been discredited, shown to be marks on bones made by natural causes – another case of our leaping to conclusions about a brutal past. At many sites bones *have* been disarticulated and defleshed, though we might not be right to assume that they were eaten. Such defleshing may well have been part of some mortuary ritual, a cleaning of the bones seen in many ethnographic populations. As we saw in Chapter two, even if human flesh was eaten, this certainly happens with modern human populations with particular beliefs and it need not have been done *without feeling*.

Only at the site of Moula-Quercy in France, where two adults, two adolescents and two children were butchered in the same way as animals and their remains left with rubbish, can we suggest that humans were treated with *no special care at all*. Perhaps this was a gruesome attack or perhaps even that at Moula-Quercy there was some type of special cultural practice, driven by belief, and not any lack of understanding that

Burial of a two-year-old Neanderthal, with a triangular flint at the heart and stone slab above their head, from Dederiyeh Cave in Syria.

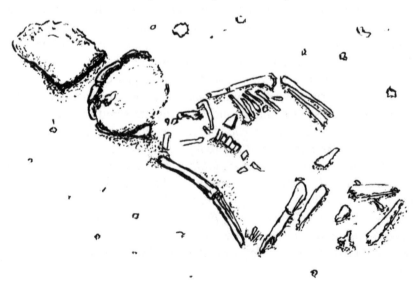

214

the bodies of the dead were once living and feeling beings. Cannibalism might always remain something of an enigma.

When we think of the cannibalism at Atapuerca, we can't help but wonder how Neanderthals felt about their neighbours. Although Neanderthals at both Saint-Césaire and Shanidar who we saw in Chapter two show evidence for interpersonal violence, this is not easy to interpret, dating as it does to the period of overlap between Neanderthals and modern humans. Was their empathy towards those that they didn't know stronger than the fears that might lead to hostilities? Were the social and emotional worlds of Neanderthals as large as ours? Did they conceive of a wider humanity, feel inspired by other's courage, elevated by tales of kindness or bravery?

Several lines of evidence suggest that, while perhaps not going as far as to have several trusted friends in distant groups, Neanderthals were unlikely to have been aggressive to outsiders. For one thing their territories were too large from an ecological perspective for it to be worth the effort defending them.[325] Moreover, evidence from raw materials suggests that they sometimes had some level of collaborative links with the groups around them. Raw materials from Solento in Italy have travelled far from the north[326] and in the Central European plain raw materials have been moved over 200km from their source.[327] While most of the raw materials Neanderthals used seem to have come from their local ranges, they were able to either move into others' territories or negotiate to exchange goods when they needed to. They must have got on, but while there are few sign of feuds or hatred, neither are there signs of the type of long-distance alliances, cemented through visits and gifts, that keep modern hunter-gatherers like the !Kung safe from famines.

Genetic evidence suggests that Neanderthals lived in small groups, probably centred around brothers, with much interbreeding.[328] This isn't the type of social structure that feels very familiar to us today. Even the most isolated groups of modern peoples live in true societies with far more movement and interaction with other groups than Neanderthals. Even at their lowest population densities, modern hunter-gatherers still meet regularly at large aggregations, trading, finding a partner, catching up with old friends. Can we imagine life without that?

Was this because of fear or a sense of threat, or just the practicality of living at low population densities in often rugged terrain that prompted Neanderthals to live their unusually isolated existence? It is an important question as in contrast to their relative isolation, modern humans entering Europe seemed to have lived in extensive social networks, with objects like beads and shells travelling over 1,000km probably in networks of gift-giving much like those we saw in the !Kung. These modern peoples were much better able to survive environmental catastrophes, with radio-carbon dates showing that they bounced back from severe climatic events, while earlier Neanderthal populations failed to thrive.[329] Was the difference in survival related to different emotional capacities? Were Neanderthals less able to forge strong links based on trust and give and take with strangers? It might not be surprising, given that evolution is likely to have dealt Neanderthals a somewhat different range of emotional capacities, living as they did in the rugged environments of Europe where meeting others was rare, travel often difficult and added to which their hefty bodies with high calorie requirements meant that group sizes had to be small. Gail Hitchens, Andy Needham and myself have argued that Neanderthals' evolutionary journey may have involved developing other emotions from those of our own species, ones that kept them together with even greater force, but failed to turn their feelings outwards to developing any stronger external links.[330]

In rather inward-looking societies were Neanderthal children even more important than we might suppose?

In my imagination the momentous meeting of different species that we know occurred when our own species entered Europe took place between two adults, men of course. I've seen documentaries in which these meetings have been portrayed as violent, each species attempting to eradicate the other with all the weapons at their disposal, though there is of course no evidence for such a brutal view much as it draws media attention. In my more tolerant mental reconstruction, a strong and serious adult entirely like us would find themselves face to face with a Neanderthal, shaking hands or exchanging spears, pondering the enormity of their meeting.

My imagined scenario may be equally wrong, and not only by imagining the meeting dominated by one gender. Our knowledge of other primates and other mammals in the same situation where similar species overlap argues that it may well have been very different. It is often *the young* of related species who make contact, play together, form alliances, tease each other and chase each other around, even while adults remain distant. Jane Goodall noted several examples of friendships between infant baboons and chimpanzees, even though adults avoided each other.[331] Somehow I'd never imagined Neanderthal and human children laughing with each other or playing chase as the momentous meeting of different species of human.

As a child I'm sure I would have leapt at the chance to play with a Neanderthal, relished the novelty of someone so different, been eager to find out more. As an adult would I have been more cautious, more worried, kept my distance until I knew more?

Of course, other factors might have come into play to determine where and how other different species met. I suspect that culture and beliefs were also more important in defining how Neanderthals or moderns were treated. In the Near East the archaeological record left by the two species is so similar that it is impossible to differentiate archaeological sites belonging to either Neanderthals or modern humans without human bones to inform us. Both Neanderthals and modern humans used and made Mousterian tools, and structured their living places in similar ways. Yet in other parts of Europe a different story unfolds. In south-west France Neanderthals appear to copy modern human personal decorations, thus suggesting that interactions between the two species occurred on some level. At the site of Grotte du Renne in France, as well as producing

Did Neanderthal and modern human children play together?

modern-type lithic implements, Neanderthal Châtelperronian industries included animal teeth suspended as necklaces and bone bracelets similar to those of the Aurignacian cultures of incoming modern humans.[332] We don't know if Neanderthals copied what they found or were taught techniques, but some cultural contact between Neanderthal and modern humans is certain. However, in Spain there is yet a different story altogether. South of the so-called 'Ebro frontier' in northern Spain, Neanderthals survived for several thousand years apparently without contact with modern humans, at least with no clear influence from them.[333] Gibraltar has been termed their last stronghold, and we imagine a species desperately surviving invaders by retreating only finally to die out.

The most likely scenario is that across different Neanderthal cultures beliefs about other peoples, and their humanity (or lack of it) already had a significant effect on how people felt about each other. It seems no coincidence that the evidence for interbreeding between the two species is limited to the Near East where tool technologies are most similar. Elsewhere was it a case of 'don't play with those odd looking children, *they aren't quite human*'? Though Neanderthals as a species died out, it is thought-provoking to consider that the small percentage of genes within us which come from Neanderthals must be from those who chose not to see differences as a barrier to integration.

Were children more important in our evolutionary history than we imagine?

As we have seen, Neanderthals were much like us, but *not the same*. The Neanderthal world we see when we look closely at the archaeological evidence is very different from the one of our imagination. The brutish thugs standing ready with clubs to hit people look so very different in the light of recent evidence. But was there, nonetheless, something remarkable about our species which made us different?

Was it a subtly different emotional intelligence than any seen previously that allowed modern humans to develop relationships based on trust with outsiders? Was there a further step to take than simply tolerating strangers?

This small bone plaquette from Raymonden, France (c. 17,000 to 11,000 years old) shows the carcass of a musk ox with figures equally placed on either side. Was this an expression of the importance of equality and collaboration to Upper Palaeolithic societies?

Chapter Ten

How Did it Feel to Live in the Palaeolithic?

Love and compassion are necessities, not luxuries. Without them humanity cannot survive.[334]

What was life like for people of our own species, living thousands of years ago? Was the frozen Ice Age a brutal time, where people focused only on survival? In this chapter we consider evidence for a sense of emotional understanding and even playfulness in Ice Age Europe. We consider how such societies may have displayed an emotional intelligence which drove the creation of safe supportive environments with a widespread sense of trust. From evidence for children's play and a sense of creativity, we consider the long-term rewards that supportiveness and tolerance might have created. Upper Palaeolithic art seems to speak to us of a sense of connection to the living world that we seem to have almost lost. Had these peoples deliberately created a certain kind of society?

Was our past, the past of our own species during the last 100,000 years really a brutal one? Was there ever a sense of fun, a warmth of human connection, playfulness, banter, the peculiar sense of warmth and safety that comes with being loved?

Popular media would tell us that there was nothing of the kind. A warmth of being understood, loved and cared for, feeling safe, is something that we imagine to have been entirely *missing* in a brutal Palaeolithic struggle for survival. Raquel Welsh, in *One million years BC*, clad in her infamous fun-fur bikini lived a constant battle for her life in a harsh and violent world. Permanently terrified, with no one to trust and narrowly escaping death on many occasions, she typifies a portrayal of our idea of a relentlessly brutal stone-age past. How traumatised we would be by the sense of social isolation and constant threat the film epitomises ... not to mention the thought of facing dangerous predators in nothing but a furry push-up bra and slippers. We would be hardly likely to be kind and generous to those around us (we are more likely to be cowering in terror).

We have moved on, haven't we? We would have thought so and yet more than forty years later the docu-soap, *Planet of the Ape-men: Battle for Earth*, depicts a life which was not much different – Neanderthals and modern humans brutally killing each other over who occupied which land, a heroine only marginally less scantily clad. A brutal death comes easily and often in such depictions and its continual threat lies over everyone. We naturally feel we are lucky to have risen above this terrifying past into a safer and kinder world.

Even museum displays and factual illustrations – the academic perspective – are not so different as we might think.

No one is smiling or laughing – there is no banter, jokes or playfulness in this world. There may be less focus on violence, but, nonetheless, illustrations are dominated by men with spears at the ready. The women who do appear keep out of the way, what children there are often

Raquel Welsh played the modern human Leona in One million years BC. The film was subtitled: This is the way it was – but was the Palaeolithic ever anything like this?

cowering with them. Diane Gifford-Gonzalez from the University of California has shown from her research on 231 depictions that women play a strange role in such illustrations – they are almost never shown as active.[335] As she notes, *they can hide, but they can't run*, rarely even standing up. Women are usually at the back of the cave crouching down over some menial task, while men are the active ones, the ones returning home with the 'deer on a stick'. In none of these depictions were men shown touching or holding children. If even present, the elderly are never doing anything useful.

Such images anger Sarah Blaffer-Hrdy from Davis University.[336] As she shows, in modern hunting and gathering societies men are involved with children and among the Baka, children spend as much time in the arms of men as in the arms of women. Moreover, women are no shrinking violets, but are active and able, making decisions and doing things.

221

Women can even be ruthless when the survival of their children is at risk. In all modern hunter-gatherer communities women, the elderly and even children have a voice and influence, women bring back their share (and often more) of the food, hunt and trap small game, and in many societies play a role in communal hunts of large animals besides. We wouldn't have survived otherwise.

What about people with disabilities? They are never displayed in such scenes. Yet we know from skeletal remains that accidents and the effects of wear and tear on bones would have been frequent and visible, few escaping life with no clear evidence of injuries. Some injuries were debilitating, from the crippling arthritis of the Neanderthal from La Chapelle aux Saints, to the withered arm and leg of the Neanderthal from Shanidar, and the pelvic injuries of the elderly *Homo heidelbergensis* at Sima de los Huesos. Others may have been easier to accommodate within everyday activities, but significant nonetheless. Almost all Lower and Middle Palaeolithic skeletons show some signs of injury, and some degree of survival from such injuries.[337] Other genetic disabilities were equally present: the torsioning of the cranium of the *Homo hiedelbergensis* child with craniosynostosis from Sima de los Huesos, the dwarfism of the child from Romito, the bent legs of the child from Sungir. Disabilities were part of life, people actively doing what they could. To have some kind of disability, from the minor to the severe, was far from unusual.

Are our imagined worlds anything like the real story of Palaeolithic life? What was it really like? How did it *feel* to live in the Palaeolithic?

There are other representations of a hunter-gatherer past. Films about an ancient hunter-gatherer past which are *made by hunter-gatherers themselves* could hardly present a greater contrast to brutal stone-age epics.

Banter is ever present in the Aboriginal film, *Ten canoes*. From the size of men's penises to fart jokes, the serious business of survival is tackled by these Aboriginal hunter-gatherers in a light-hearted way. The film focuses on a complex social story told to an adolescent boy to help him deal with his desire for the wife of one of the other hunters. There is an element of violence and conflict. An accidental killing in the film has to be avenged by a payback ceremony, relatives of the deceased carrying out a ritual where they throw spears at his killer until one strikes his body. This is a ritual which is documented anthropologically, a means of keeping conflicts contained, making sure that tensions are officially resolved, that courage is obvious. We can't help but notice that violence takes a highly controlled and socialised form in which specified means of public personal combat are used to resolve disputes. The group as a whole remains protected and feels safe.

Anatarjuat, produced by Inuit and set on Arctic pack ice, is more serious throughout. This film, after all, shows how hunter-gatherers in the past dealt with evil. However, we find that *evil* takes the form of disrespectful sharing of meat to the family of an unsuccessful hunter, and a bully in their midst who treats others with disdain. The resolution of the film lies in the bully being banished after he loses a bout of ritualised combat to the hero. The head-clubbing conflict is also documented anthropologically and matches an archaeological record of head wounds in Mesolithic Scandinavia. Hardly a constant struggle, despite the harsh pack-ice landscape, and what violence there is remains constrained by complex social norms.

Both films portray a world in which a sense of relaxed safety, mutual support and even playfulness is the norm. The struggle in both is not one against terrifying predators or attacks from other peoples, it is one against the forces which might threaten their shared sense of community. Threats to a sense of safety are talked about, tensions and conflicts are resolved through bravery. The safe, supportive and stable social world is *hard won*.

Which image of the past is nearer to the truth? What if we were not only wrong to see the Palaeolithic as a harsh, chaotic and brutal world? What if it were *our societies* which were brutal in comparison, influencing how we see *their world*?

Anthropologists have only recently turned their attention to how life as a modern hunter-gatherer *feels*. We used to see hunter-gatherers in economic terms, but we have begun to appreciate the significance of the emotional context to how they work together, and what allows them to survive.

Brian Wood from Yale University explains that food-sharing is not so much about economics or calculated exchanges, as about responding and reaching out to others.[338] Children learn to share to show their connection to others, to reinforce their interdependence. As food is shared out, passed around, given to those without it, the action of *sharing* reinforces the close relationships within the group. Displaying and promoting a sense of self-restraint is vital – grabbing, snatching or failing to share is never tolerated.

Daiji Kimura from Kyoto University reveals that what generates egalitarianism is not so much a political or economic *system*, as a way of feeling towards other people.[339] There is no edge to a hunter-gatherer group, no external system of defining equal rights. It is more that egalitarianism comes from an attitude to others as connected to oneself, a diffusion of a sense that others are as worthy. Even the people's sense of who they are, their sense of *self*, in modern small-scale hunter-gatherers is *distributed*, while we might think of ourselves as bounded individuals, entirely independent of others, they feel part of a wider whole.[340] Often the giving of gifts reinforces the relationships between people, the objects themselves being seen as having a kind of life, an ability to connect people together.[341]

Anthropologists have found that, despite the harshest of conditions, maintaining a sense of *conviviality*, a shared joyfulness and goodwill, is central to the lives of small-scale hunter-gatherers. Joanna Overing and Alan Passes from the University of St Andrews argue that there is a sort of aesthetic to the desire to create and maintain a *feeling of harmony*, an emotional environment which feels in some way beautiful.[342]

Where does this sense of harmony come from? At least in part, the conditions are created through childhood experience. As Barry Hewlett explains, life as a hunter-gatherer (forager) child is one of constant physical proximity and interdependence, while the experience of children in agricultural societies (farmers) is one where there is far less closeness.

When hunter-gatherers sit down in the camp, they are usually touching somebody. In terms of holding during infancy and early childhood, forager three to four month old infants were held 91 per cent of the day while farmer infants were held 54 per cent of the day. Forager 2-, 3- and 4-year-olds were held 44, 27 and 8 per cent of daylight hours, whereas farmer children of the same age were held 18, 2 and 0 per cent of the day.[343]

An emotional interdependence and focus on warm supportive relationships also sets hunter-gatherer children apart from those in agricultural societies:

The importance of emotional proximity to others is illustrated in two studies. In a study of conflicts between toddlers and older juveniles among hunter-gatherers and farmers, Fouts & Lamb[344] found that hunter-gatherer toddlers were substantially more likely to have conflicts over staying close to juveniles (38% of conflicts among forager toddlers versus 2% of conflicts among farmer toddlers), whereas farmer toddlers were more likely to have conflicts with juveniles over competition for objects (48% of farmer toddler conflicts versus 14% of forager toddler conflicts) or over the juvenile hitting the toddler, which never occurred among the hunter-gatherer toddlers. This study illustrates early acquisition and manifestation of cultural values—emotional proximity to others among the hunter-gatherers and the economic-material dimensions of social relations among the farmers. In another study, hunter-gatherer and farmer adolescents were asked about their experiences and feelings about the death and loss of friends and relatives.[345] Forager expressions of grief emphasized their love and emotional connections to the person, whereas farmer expressions of grief focused on material objects the lost relative gave or provided ... The development of trust of others is important to some degree in all cultures, but the socialization for trust of several others is particularly pronounced in hunter-gatherers, which relates to their extensive sharing and giving. Forager caregivers were significantly more likely than farmer caregivers to respond to infant crying, and farmer infants cried significantly longer and more frequently than did forager infants.[346] Hunter-gatherer infants and young children were held twice as often as neighbouring farmers, and this additional holding came from many different individuals—fathers, grandmothers, siblings and others.[347]

Life as a hunter-gatherer is far more warm, caring and relaxed than we assume. A widespread sense of playfulness means that anthropologists can find they are the ones perceived as overly serious. Kamei Nobutaka describes children among the Baka playing 'anthropologist', creating a mock camera made of wood and a tent, pretending to take photos of each other and record what each was doing.[348] He seemed to be the butt of a very amusing joke.

Martin Porr and Hannah Rachel Bell describe a conversation between a Bush University academic and a group of Ngarinyin men and women who found the antics of people measuring everything about them ludicrously funny:[349]

Q: In your culture are men the head of the house—you know ...
boss?

Old Man: We boss.

Old Woman: He boss ... only 'e don't know anything. Womans
... we living water. We tell 'im. He gotta listen.

Q: Is that right? (to Old Man) Is that how it works?

Old Man: We gotta listen to her. She our Mother. We fear those
womans (laughter). She make us sick if we don't listen. Get
sores. Ulcers.

Q: How do you feel when researchers come and ask you about your
culture?

Old Woman: Well, they write down all about our relations ...
but we know already where we come from. I'm think they come
to help us. But ... I dunno ... Why they do that?

Old Man: We take 'em hunting, feed 'em up. Really good
tucker. Those mob write 'im in little books. Write 'im down
all'a time! (laughter)

Mowaljarlai: You know one time that university mob come 'ere
with millions of bags ... plastic ones like supermarket bags.
They arks us, 'Can we catch your shit?' (shrieks of laughter and
shhh-ing) True story!

What they want our shit for!? Eh ... d'they arks you? They arks
me! My shit!!! (more hoots) 'You want my shit? I tell 'em. 'You
got big bag? Cos I got really big shit!'

Listening to such an exchange, we can't help but wonder if it is not
our lives which are the ones pervaded by a constant struggle, enmeshed
in social tensions and conflicts with no time for humour.

David Kopenawa, a Yanomani shaman visiting London, New York
and Paris certainly sees our world in this way. He notes:

The lives of white people who hurry around all day like xiri ants
seem sad to me. They are always impatient and anxious not to get
to their job late or be thrown away. They barely sleep and run all
day in a daze. They only talk about working and the money they
lack. They live without joy and age rapidly ... their minds empty.[350]

He would far rather be living his life.

A certain sensitivity to the world around them, a feeling of *serenity*
which modern hunter-gatherers describe, contrasts with a feeling of

disconnection and even alienation which is more common in industrialised societies.[351] A native Australian Mowaljarlai explains:

> When daylight starts, it wakes me up … It wakes the whole body. So I turn round and have a look … Morning gives you the flow of a new day—aah! … the sun is coming up, with that glow that comes straight away in the morning. The colour comes towards me and the day is waiting. You have a feeling in your heart that you're going to feed your body this day, get more knowledge. You go out now, see animals moving, a trees, a river. You are looking at nature and giving it your full attention … Your vision has opened you and you start learning now. When you touch them, all things talk to you, give you their story … You understand that your mind has been opened to all those things because you are seeing them; because your presence and their presence meet together and you recognise each other. These things recognise you. They give their wisdom and their understanding to you when you come close to them.[352]

Despite all the material goods that they lack, and the uncertainty of finding enough food, should we be just a little bit *envious* of hunter-gatherers? Are we perhaps rather loathe to let go of our idea of a brutal ancestral past because of what it might *mean for us* if our ancestors, materially poor beyond measure, might have fought to create and experience a contentment that we might have lost?

Is there any evidence for the same sense of humour, fun or playfulness, the same sense of conviviality, a climate of emotional support in the archaeological record of the Upper Palaeolithic? It seems to be the small things, so easily forgotten or ignored, which can tell us most about how it felt in the Palaeolithic.[353] Occasionally we do find glimpses of life in the Upper Palaeolithic that suggest a similar climate of conviviality.

One of the most evocative pieces of evidence is that which shows children at play. Children's drawings have been found on the walls of caves such as Rouffignac, Peche-Merle and Altamira.[354] They consist of crude lines that appear to be animals or faces drawn in the mud of the cave, lines that have been made with fingers, as evidenced by the leaving of small fingerprints. Children's footprints have been found at caves such as Chauvet and Niaux. At Chauvet Cave, a child in the cave seems to be accompanied by a dog or a wolf. They seem to be exploring, having fun, playing around. Many of the famous hand prints found at sites throughout France and northern Spain also fit the proportions of teenagers. Dale Guthrie from the University of Alaska believes that some of the hand prints which look as though fingers were missing were probably made by teenage boys as some kind of joke.[355]

Jessica Cooney from Oxford University has carried out detailed research on these finger tracings at Rouffignac, the same site as where my mammoths were discovered. Here drawings made at least 13,000 years ago by children have been identified.[356] She found that the size and shape of the finger fluting at the cave show that they were probably mostly made by two children – a girl aged two to three years of age, and another child of around five years of age. A twelve-year-old and fourteen-year-old also made some tracings. They seem to be experimenting, having fun, playing in the mud of the cave wall. The children were even sometimes held up to do drawings on the ceilings, perhaps by the older children or perhaps by adults.

My Rouffignac mammoths are most likely to have been made by an adult, not just because of the level of skill but because they were made with paint rather than in the mud. But children may well have been there with my early artist. Was he or she trying to show children something important, or even just having fun, telling them a story, the mammoths having personalities brought out by the painting?

Debris of flint knapping that has probably been made by children is common. However, some objects found in the Upper Palaeolithic may even have been toys. Thaumatropes, bones discs with images of animals etched into both sides, give the illusion that the animal was in motion

A 15,000-year-old thaumatrope from Laugerie-Basse showing a chamois (mountain goat). When the disc is spun using fibres the chamois appears to be running.

when spun on thread, perhaps to entertain. Whenever we find artefacts that are unusual we tend to interpret them as evidence of some kind of ritual but we may be wrong. Could even objects like Venus figurines have a far more prosaic interpretation as dolls? Modern hunter-gatherers like the Baka play with a range of toys, from dolls to games with sticks and missiles. Unfortunately, none of their toys would have survived in the archaeological record and we must have lost most if not all of such toys from the Palaeolithic.

One of my favourite cave art sites, Las Covalanos in northern Spain, is hard to explain by anything other than a sense of fun and humour, an adult telling us *something playful*. Unlike the famous 'painted halls' of sites like Altamira or Lascaux, the images here are not splendid and seem to have been made, not by many people, but by a single person.[357] The paintings are made in red paint, largely of deer and are full of what we can't help but see as fun trickery. A line of deer drawn in red dots appears to lead you inside a narrow cleft. Further inside within a tiny chamber, hardly big enough for more than one person, a deer has been drawn so that when you shine a flickering light it appears to be jumping down at you. Leaving the cave, as you look behind, you see a hind looking around at you, drawn so you tend to only see it looking back. We make a connection to a single person, someone with a sense of fun, who lived somewhere between 18,000 and 20,000 years ago.

Were Palaeolithic hunter-gatherers not just surviving but thriving?

We know that creating a loving, fun and supportive environment, nurturing children so that they feel safe to play, encouraging them to feel secure is essential to ensuring that children and adults are confident, secure, courageous and *kind*. Sadly, in our societies far too many of us lack this experience. Four in ten adults lack the strong bonds that allow us to handle our feelings, and make connections with others. Children who are insecure are more anxious, find it hard to relax and are more driven and aggressive.[358]

Would such an insecurity have been rare in the Palaeolithic? Might an environment of understanding and support even have been an important part of how people thrived in the Ice Age? As we saw in Chapter six, in caring and supportive environments the highest evolved levels of our brain and body reactions to stress come into play – we reach out to others for help when scared, reach to help when they are vulnerable, we feel good about being giving and generous and expect the same in return when we need it. However, in more competitive and threatening environments we drop down to lower evolutionary levels of response, retreating or aggressively defending ourselves, or even becoming completely numb to our own and others' feelings.[359] The social environment is all important to how *human* we are.

Other evidence suggests that societies in the Upper Palaeolithic had a remarkable capacity to reach out to those in need, and thrived through the support of those around them, a support that made all kinds of things possible that had not been before.

We have already seen how those with physical disabilities were supported, perhaps even accorded a particular role and significance in Upper Palaeolithic Europe.[360] The dwarf from Romito in Italy has the same nutritional status as any others in his society, and was buried carefully with much respect, even though he must have struggled to contribute in hunting or similar realms. The child from Sungir, who had a congenital deformity of her legs, was even accorded a particularly elaborate burial, covered in many necklaces, even strings of hundreds of beads made to a small childlike size, as was a child with a similar congenital deformity from Dolni Vestonice in Moravia.

People with certain mental differences may also have been tolerated, supported and integrated in the Upper Palaeolithic, even accorded particular roles according to their abilities. There is good evidence to suggest that it was sometime in the last 500,000 years that people with autism and Asperger syndrome were integrated into contemporary societies, surviving to add genes to the gene pool today. Genetic evidence for key genes associated with autism are absent from the Neanderthal genome but present in our species, remaining at a low level across the modern world.[361] Although we think of autism as a disorder, and indeed it makes life very difficult for those with severe autism, there is good reason to suspect some genes for autism bring with them a unique focus, the ability to see patterns and to drive new solutions which might have been essential to the success of modern societies.[362] A climate in which children and adults were supported and accepted, and doing what they could do to contribute, may have had lasting consequences.

Could the incorporation of autistic talents have happened in the Upper Palaeolithic? The best evidence might be some physical signs of an autistic influence on how things are made. Many suspect some elements of Palaeolithic art reflect an autistic ability to record things exactly, perhaps taught to others.[363] The extraordinary drawings of talented autistic artists such as Nadia certainly show some similarities to some of the elaborate lifelike depictions we see in caves like Lascaux.[364] Would there even be artefacts made by people with autism or Asperger syndrome, or influenced by their extraordinarily systems-focused view of the world? It is hard to be certain, but Barry Wright from the Hull York Medical School and myself have argued that some extraordinary artefacts found in the Upper Palaeolithic reflect the influence of people with Asperger syndrome. One example is the Abri Blanchard plaquette, showing the phases of the moon with different symbols in their correct position in the sky. This plaquette must have been produced by someone who set up a coordinate system and returned each night in the dark to record exactly the position of the moon in relation to their system, presumably made of carefully balanced sticks held together with plants or animal fibres. Only certain people would pursue such knowledge while the rest chatted or danced around the camp fire. They could hardly have envisaged a role for knowing the movements of the moon, simply wishing to understand a pattern which fascinated them, but it is not difficult to see how such a grasp of time and calendrical systems could be useful. Though people with Asperger syndrome typically lack emotional empathy (the empathetic feelings in relation to others), they have the same levels of cognitive empathy (a drive to help those around them) as others do. Their contributions to their communities thus tend to be focused in particular and distinctive ways.[365] A small number of individuals channelling their energies away from emotional connections and towards very specific practical concerns might well have carried an important advantage to their societies, even though their inclusion was most likely driven by tolerance rather than by any perception of usefulness.

A plaquette with a map dating to around 13,500 years ago from Abauntz Cave in northern Spain, marking rivers, marshes and hill topography with particular symbols as well as the local game animals, shows a similarly systematic view of the world.[366] We would be lost without maps today, but they might not have first been created with any practical motivation, more from a drive to understand and record the world in a peculiarly analytical way.

Evidence for large-scale supportive networks stretching across thousands of kilometres also argues that an openness to difference, a desire to incorporate others had far-reaching consequences.

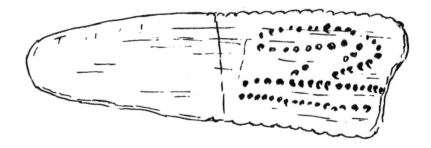

A bone plaquette from Abri Blanchard, France (c. 30,000 years old) showing the phases of the moon and its position in the sky.

A small piece of bone, dating to 13,000 years ago and found alongside some very unusual rock art at the site of Andernach-Martinsberg in Germany, doesn't look worthy of much note at first sight. Typical Magdalenian artefacts were recovered at the same site – fragments of mammoth ivory, a bone needle, remains of horse and reindeer and the debris of manufacturing stone tools. The bone, however, documents a remarkable story. This artefact was made not of horse or reindeer bone but from a *whale*. It formed part of the foreshaft of a projectile, probably a spear, and would have been thrown using a spear-thrower. While other whalebone foreshafts have been found from other sites, mostly in the Pyrenees, this was found in the Rhineland – over 1,000km from any contemporary coast. This small bone and the artefacts found with it seem to answer that question of whether it was only the objects themselves that moved through vast social networks in the Upper Palaeolithic, or people also. Associated with the whalebone foreshaft were forty-seven sea shells perforated to use as ornaments, as well as a depiction of a seal on a local slate plaque. The interpretation put forward by Michelle Langley of the University of Oxford is that the whalebone foreshaft and perforated seashells, all found in close proximity, were brought to the site by a single person, who also engraved the seal depiction on the plaque.[367] I'm inclined to agree.

Other seal depictions at nearby sites such as Gönnersdorf suggest that a journey of such magnitude to the coast was not unique. The stories behind such depictions must have been remarkable, and certainly spark our imagination. At minimum, it must have taken more than twenty weeks to reach this site from the coast. Had the same person made the journey there and back? Were long journeys some kind of rite of passage,

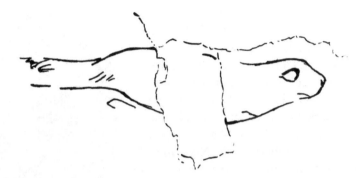

Drawing of a seal on a shale plaquette from Aldernach-Martinsberg, found with marine shells and a whalebone fragment, over 1,000km from the coast.

cementing ties between distant groups? Or did people travel to visit particular relatives? Whatever the explanation, that even distant groups could be relied upon is certain, as such a journey would be impossible were they hostile.

Could the world of the Upper Palaeolithic have been one in which a context of willing generosity and emotional support brought about fundamental changes?

It is also in this period that we see the domestication of wolves, and the beginning of a close relationship between people and their domestic dogs. There is no doubt that dogs held a special significance in this period. The earliest wolf skull which shows the shortening of the snout and wider palate and braincase typical of domesticated dogs is that from Goyet Cave, Belgium.[368] This skull, 31,700 years old, placing the domestication of dogs as happening almost as soon as modern humans enter Europe.

Dogs are treated in a special and unusual way. At Predmosti in the Czech Republi, in levels dating to 27,000bp, several dogs were found, one of which had a fragment of a bone inserted between the front teeth after death.[369] Was this a bone to take with them to an imagined afterlife? It is difficult to know, but seems a tantalising piece of evidence of a special relationship between humans and dogs. Here, and at other sites, dogs' teeth were also drilled and used as ornaments. While shells are often found perforated to use as ornaments, those made of animal teeth are rare, suggesting that dog teeth had a particular significance. Yet more evidence also points to a *special significance* of dogs. While almost all the animals forming part of people's experience in the Upper Palaeolithic appear in their art, both humans and wolves/dogs are notably very rare. Robert Losey from the University of Alberta has argued that in many hunter-gatherer societies dogs can be seen *almost as people*, with dogs buried in graves much like human's graves in the Mesolithic at Skateholm and in the Cis-Baikal in Siberia in the Neolithic.[370]

We used to assume that the domestication of dogs was motivated by practical concerns. Dogs can be very useful to hunter-gatherers, helping with hunting either by herding game or barking, even being used with sleds for carrying meat.[371] More recently, however, it has been argued that their domestication was rather more prompted by a human emotional affinity to wolves, a drive to nurture wolf puppies and to protect them. Certainly, the tendency to care for vulnerable animals, particularly young animals, is well attested in the modern hunter-gatherer record.

A 27,000-year-old dog's skull from Predmosti, with a bone inserted between its teeth.

James Sherpell from the University of Pennsylvania School of Veterinary Medicine explains that hunter-gatherer camps are often full of a whole variety of animals which are cared for and looked after, seen more as guests than pets. The nineteenth-century English naturalist, Bates, described 'twenty-two species of quadrupeds' living tame within Amazonian hunter-gatherer communities.[372] Any consideration of economic advantage is seen as bizarre, reflecting our way of thinking not theirs. Guests, even animal ones, could not be eaten.[373] While animals outside the home might be killed for food, with the belief that the spirits of the animals willingly gave themselves up in this way, *within the home* animals seen to come under the umbrella of *unconditional support* for their needs.

Johnathan Bradshaw from the University of Bristol believes that our desire to nurture vulnerable animals has been selected for as a *sign of sensitivity*, a reliable indicator that a potential partner might be a sensitive and nurturing parent.[374] I'm sure that he is right, and we saw in Chapter five that in a modern-day context most of us are sensitive not only to cute and vulnerable animals but also to the apparently vulnerable inanimate

Was it hard to resist looking after an orphaned wolf puppy?

objects. I suspect, however, that the role that dogs play in supporting us emotionally also played a part. Dogs seem a particular case, responding quickly to living with people, and forming close attachments. Many hunter-gatherer groups are recorded as loving their dogs. With all our difficult evolved emotions, embarrassment, remorse, guilt or compassion, and challenged by living in a wide social world, people in the Upper Palaeolithic may have found that dogs helped them cope *emotionally*. Dogs can be security figures,[375] giving support in times of emotional need, a sense of safety. In an environment where reputation mattered above everything else and it was important to be calm, wise and have self-control, dogs may have been part of the emotional support of complex and often conflicted humans. Many of us today are sure that our dogs help keep us sane.

By far the most famous evidence for a certain sensitivity in the Palaeolithic is that for elaborate art and sophisticated music. It is not difficult to see that artistic and musical talents may have been important in displaying one's reputation, a certain sensitivity to others' feelings and a level of patience that we saw in Chapter eight was vital to developing trust.

Did music and art also fulfil a role in helping to handle complex and often conflicting emotions? Both art and music have connections to emotional well-being today. Like the role of domestic dogs, these supports to help handle complex emotions might have been particularly important in large-scale connected societies of Upper Palaeolithic Europe.

The earliest secure evidence for music in the form of bone flutes is also found in Europe shortly after modern humans arrive, and in association with evidence for large-scale networks in the form of personal ornaments made from distant raw materials. At Hohle Fels and Vogelherd in Germany an almost complete bone flute and fragments of three ivory flutes date to more than 35,000 years ago.[376] Lines on the bone flute, made from the radius of a griffon vulture, show that the distance between the holes must have been measured, a deliberate construction of a musical instrument demonstrating an understanding of how different notes would interact with each other. Similar flutes at Geißenklösterle date to over 40,000 years ago.

The Hohle fels bone flute, at least 35,000 years old.

More than twenty other flutes have been found at a number of Upper Palaeolithic sites, with the largest collection coming from Isturitz in the Pyrenees. The similarity of these flutes provides further evidence for a large-scale and long-term *connection* between hunter-gatherers in ice-age Europe. Francesco D'Errico, from the University of Bordeaux, carrying out detailed analysis of the microwear on these instruments, concluded that they may have been played much like an oboe, with a reed mouthpiece.[377] Bevelling at the finger holes has been used to create a better seal, and from the angle and the use-wear, the instrument would have been played almost vertically, probably at 5 to 15 degrees, rather than horizontally like a flute. The very precise construction of these instruments suggests a developed history of musical instruments and, by implication, song and dance at this time. Sharing music was probably part of everyday life, as it is for modern hunter-gatherers. Like art, there must have been a certain *craft* to making music. Musical instruments, like finished drawings, required skill and patience in their production and demanded that techniques were learnt and sensitively applied.

Like music, elaborate art appears early. The Hohlenstein-Stadel lion-headed man, like the depictions at Chauvet and Cosquer Caves, appears almost as soon as our species arrives in Europe. Art appears to be everywhere, what we find deep in caves only a relic of what would have been seen at the surface. Many cave art sites like El Miron in northern Spain have fine line drawings, carvings or deep bas relief on their walls, which would once have been coloured with paints. Art must have filled living spaces. Passing only briefly to re-make their weapons at Creswell Crags in Derbyshire, ice-age artists stopped to draw deer and other animals. Tools like spear-throwers are often covered in elaborate art.

Showing that one was sensitive and generous in making and giving gifts was essential and much of that reputation-building seems to have come out through art. We feel the same sort of awed tenderness holding the tiny Vogelherd horse as we might do with vulnerable baby animals or infants. Perhaps we also feel a little more connected to other people who feel the same way.

Why is European Upper Palaeolithic art so immediate, so moving? I can't help but wonder if the *scale of human connections and interdependence in ice-age Europe* provides an explanation. Much art produced by modern hunter-gatherers is highly stylised, heavily symbolic, difficult to decipher to those living outside these contexts. Without the story behind the symbols in such art we don't feel the same in response. Yet the art of the Upper Palaeolithic has some kind of universal appeal, a natural response we feel to the sensitivity of figurative depiction of lions hunting or deer swimming across a river.

Might the *power to transport* of such art, a sense of being there, feeling the awe of experiencing closeness to majestic animals, have been the way it is because it *needed to cross different cultures?* Travelling from the Rhineland to the coast, would people need art to convey their sensitivity, their trustworthiness to others, to cross ethnic boundaries? There are enigmatic symbols in Upper Palaeolithic art, but we know that these are local in origin,[378] perhaps even only understood within the regional group. However, finely drawn figurative depictions carry an emotional message of a certain sensitivity which needs no particular knowledge. As a system of communicating common feeling, a shared understanding, these depictions even move us today, and must have crossed language and ethnic barriers in the past.

The Hohlenstein-Stadel lion-headed man is around 40,000 years old: sensitive and elaborate art such as this appears almost as soon as our own species arrives in Europe.

I can't help but wonder if Neanderthals even have played a role in the emergence of Upper Palaeolithic art? Hand prints found in El Castillo cave in Spain have been dated to over 37,000 years old, well before modern humans arrive in the region, and must have been made by Neanderthals.[379] Several hand prints at the cave were dated, and a red disc shape in paint proved to be even older. Were art and perhaps even music used as a medium of communication between modern humans and Neanderthals? Could the sensitivity shown in ice-age figurative art have been a means of communicating *being trustworthy* that would also cross species divide? It might have been. Despite the thousands of years between us, and the differences in our cultures, we are certainly moved by the humanity of Upper Palaeolithic art, and Neanderthals might have felt the same.

Was the tolerance, conviviality, openness and support that we have seen reflected in art, music, and large-scale social worlds the key to survival, even to *thriving*, through the Ice Age? It certainly seems to have been.

We can see that the transformations created by a climate of tolerance and support contributed to the success of Upper Palaeolithic populations. Not only did generosity make them better able to withstand famines and catastrophes through the give and take of strong relationships, but new transformations made by integrating people who might have been excluded or animals which might have been abandoned, also made societies more resilient. None of the long-term consequences could ever have been economically calculated.

As Daiji Kimora stresses, hunter-gatherers don't have an *observer's eye*, no rational economic perspective on their worlds. Instead, they are acutely sensitive to the feelings of others, to displaying their own worth, to policing cheats or bullies, to be seen to share. We've seen in Chapter eight how a *reputation* for being willing to help others contributes to individual survival, particularly when that survival depends on everyone else. However, on the large scale, *societies* structured by the need for display and reputation for altruism are also stronger ones.

Was there more to how a sense of conviviality, a warmth, a certain supportive environment was maintained? Did people in the Palaeolithic consciously create the societies they lived in?

One artefact that suggests to me such a consciousness of the societies people were deliberately creating is the small bone plaquette shown at the start of this chapter, dating to 17,000 to 11,000 years ago from the site of Raymonden in France. This piece of bone depicts a cartoon-like carcass of a musk ox, with several people shown equally distributed on either side of the meat bearing parts. Is this an expression of the idea of sharing equally?

Modern hunter-gatherers certainly express a conscious understanding of the societies they play a part in creating and the significance of how people *feel* to a thriving society.

A feeling of equality matters. A !Kung elder comments: 'When a young man kills much meat, he comes to think of himself as a chief or big man, and he thinks of the rest of us as his servants or inferiors. We can't accept this. We refuse one who boasts.'[380] A climate of warmth and conviviality cannot have been easy to maintain.

Evidence for violence is sometimes seen as a sign of brutality in the Upper Palaeolithic. We saw in Chapter seven that we are all capable of anger and aggression, hatred, even feeling nothing for the welfare of others. The evidence from Gough's Cave seems shocking, as does the violence at a time of famine at Jebel Sahaba in the Nile Valley. However, it may be that our record of Palaeolithic violence reflects more clearly a pattern of a conscious attempt to control conflicts and maintain equality. Though drawing our attention, the level of violence overall is low[381] in past hunter-gatherer contexts and in keeping with that seen in ethnographically recorded egalitarian hunter-gatherers.[382] The traumas are typically non-lethal and predominantly affect men. In fact, patterns of traumatic injury in Upper Palaeolithic burials reflect far better a hard-won peace than any long-term brutality. As in the Mesolithic period, the recorded patterns of violence are typical of an overthrowing of those who are bullies or who are dominating, or of bouts of ritualised conflict – in other words, socialised violence, challenging contests that demand much courage in which conflicts remain contained, everyone else feels safe. How hard must it be to have the courage to wait for another to have their turn to throw a spear at you or aim their club at your head? It was only this kind of willingness to submit to the need to be considerate of the wider order that maintained peace.

Everything suggests that the Upper Palaeolithic world was more similar to the portrayals that have been created by hunter-gatherers themselves than how *we* have imagined it to be. This was no paradise. People fell into the temptation of seeking power and were resisted; others argued; equality was fought for. Human emotions were problematic, conflicting, calmed with connections to animals, and with art and music.

People were supported come what may, even when this can't have been easy, and only in that way did everyone feel safe. The environments in which conviviality, sensitivity and playfulness were the norm would have been hard won – but, nonetheless, they may have created a type of contentment and connection we rarely experience.

I can't help but wonder if the motivation to create *the convivial*, that emotional wisdom to appreciate why feelings matter, is something we might have lost? Could it be more important than we think?

The Beagle, setting sail from Plymouth in 1831.

Conclusions
A Return to the Cave

Together [we] address ourselves to the two-million-year-old man that is in all of us ... In the last analysis, most of our difficulties come from losing contact with our instincts, with the age old forgotten wisdom stored up in us. [383]

Does it matter what happened in our past? Does it make any difference to who we are, or who we can be? Here we consider how the attitudes of modern societies have influenced what we feel ought to have been important in our origins and how a more subtle understanding tells us a rather different story. Are we prepared to listen to what the evidence can tell us about what we could be? Do modern hunter-gatherers also have something important to tell us? Those who first encountered hunting and gathering peoples never considered that there might be something which we could learn from them. Are we any different today? Are we prepared to listen to the perspectives of people who live outside our world and see it through different eyes?

Are our *origins* important to the present, or even to the future?

We are not the first to wonder about such a question. Occasionally in excavations of early prehistoric sites we find stone tools which belong, not to one, but to both of *two* entirely different periods. Though first created in one period, these artefacts have been discarded and then found again by peoples living many thousands of years later who have reworked them. On my excavations in the Pennines we unearthed an early Mesolithic core which must have been found eroding from sediments by people of the Late Mesolithic several thousand years later and used to make a new tool. Handaxes from hundreds of thousands of years ago are sometimes reworked in later periods, made into something that fitted the new style of flintwork. The peoples who reused these stone tools will have recognised how they were produced, known that they were made by someone like themselves who must have lived a very long time ago.

242

We can't help but wonder what they thought as they held such artefacts in their hands. How did they feel about their predecessors, clearly able to make and work stone tools as they did, so similar and yet clearly so different, making tools in a way that was unfamiliar to them, perhaps even seeming primitive? What myths and stories did they invent to explain the existence of peoples like themselves many years earlier? Like Palaeolithic cave artists painting over depictions from thousands of years earlier, they must have had explanations for these different ancestors, how they were related to them, how they lived and how they came to exist. Certainly, wherever we go in the world today all peoples have stories about peoples in the past which explain to them who they are, where they came from and what makes them *human*.

Our own story of *who we are* has changed radically over the last two centuries of our existence. Those changes have not been comfortable ones. Palaeolithic people finding early stone tools, much like the geologists of the nineteenth century who first held handaxes, may have found themselves in awe of the existence of another time beyond their own. But at least for these peoples such finds didn't necessarily challenge their beliefs about how they came to exist; they could still believe that earlier tools were made by spirits or ancestral beings, perhaps. Knowing how to date such remains, how to piece together what led to their deposition has forced us to let go of the myths or religious narratives which explained our origins. What we are left with is a jigsaw of often conflicting pieces of evidence that we have wanted, even *needed*, to make sense of. We need a *story* of our past to make sense of who we are, and where we are heading.

There is little doubt that in our drive to create a new origin story we have often created the past that we feel we *ought to have*, seen what we think *should be there* or what seems *comfortable to us* based on who we feel ourselves to be today. Raymond Dart, in the aftermath of violent wars in Europe, saw a killer ape in the crushed hyena bones at Makapansgat; others have seen brutality in the lifestyles of Neanderthals or a state of constant war in patterns of wounds in hunter-gatherer cemeteries. Coming from our modern worlds and focused on production and competition, the majority of us have seen a hard-hearted rational self-interest in human adaptations. It has seemed so much more comfortable to see ourselves in the past as strong and independent, self-interested, rational in our thinking, economically motivated. We can't help but fill in the gaps in our knowledge with our own assumptions, with what feels right from our own experience. It is disarmingly easy to recreate our past in our own image, even though doing so blinkers us, and having done so we so often feel so sure that we *must* be right.

But what if this image has been an imposition of our own economically driven rational world, our sense that we must make it alone? We know that isolation was never an option for our ancestors. In the dangerous savannahs, vulnerable early humans surrounded by predators would have depended on others. To survive involved not just some vague group cohesion but it involved having a good *reputation* – for kindness, self-control, a willingness to help out, a sensitivity to the vulnerable. By being driven to help, people would have forged the bonds that meant others were willing to help them in turn, *come what may*. From what we can infer from the evidence, the pressure of group opinion was far more significant to survival than individual strength or even intellect. Displaying a certain *sensitivity* became important; hard-heartedness was hardly a way to ensure long term survival.

We seem to pay little attention to evidence for the sensitivity of early humans. All too often we seem to focus our attention on the moments of violence in our evolutionary past, ignoring the far greater and more subtle evidence for care for others and for compassion. A moment of violence leaves its immediate and obvious trace, while only weeks, months or even decades of care and compassion can be identified archaeologically. Violence is also more thrilling, and we have evolved to pay great attention to such possible danger. The Gough's Cave skull cups, the Offnet Cave massacre, and early cannibalism, both repel us and entice us to know more, stirring up our emotions. Our minds have been constructed to pay more attention to such dangers than to everyday kindness.

But what if we look more carefully at the subtle traces left to us of a far gentler humanity? Underneath the cruelty we know we are capable of, is there not a very human ordinary compassion, a particular tenderness, an almost irresistible desire to reach out to help which remains with us in all but the most brutal and callous of contexts?

A rather different story of our origins is told by the bones of those cared for despite the odds, evidence of nurturing of vulnerable infants, grief at the passing of loved ones, and by artefacts telling us about sensitivity to forms. This new story may elevate our ancestors, but what does it mean for us? What if, instead of living in ways that proved successful and that were natural to us for thousands of generations, we are instead coping with an alien way of life, an experiment in competition, isolation and a greed for more and more possessions? What if our societies are triggering the earlier primate response, a struggle for dominance which came before the more egalitarian Palaeolithic world? Could we have ignored this alternative story, perhaps even because the implications make us uncomfortable?

If only we could go back to find out. Gazing at the Rouffignac mammoths as a child I so wished I could be transported to this past world. Our popular culture of cavemen seemed so out of keeping with this art and I so wanted to know what the reality had been. Were the peoples who drew so expertly on cave walls with such sensitivity really as brutal as they have been portrayed? If we could travel back in time to the Upper Palaeolithic or even earlier periods, would we learn something important, would it change who we are?

We can't go back, of course.[384] The best we have are a few preserved remains, and our efforts to interpret them. Yet I can't help but imagine that these peoples sometimes consciously wanted to communicate something. Could they, at least sometimes, have been as aware of their descendants, ourselves, wishing to tell us something about humanity, both its capacity for great kindness and great cruelty and how one or the other might thrive? Did they ever draw on cave walls, or place ancient artefacts they had reworked, thinking of what might come after them? I like to think that sometimes they did, and that sometimes what we find are artefacts deposited deliberately. Perhaps someone even dared to hope that the care they gave to the Dmanisi toothless *Homo erectus*, Benjamina the *Homo heidelbergensis* who had craniosyntosis, the crippled Neanderthal from Shanidar or the paraplegic man from Vietnam amounted to something, that carefully depicted art might survive to be seen thousands of years later, or that the bones of a child like the Neanderthal, so carefully placed in a ledge in Amud Cave, might tell us a story that it was important to hear.

I'd like to think that if only we could *really know* our ancestors we might be better for it, a little more wise to what is important, a little less ready to assume that brutality and competition were natural and inevitable. I'm sure the prehistoric past was no golden age and that these times held their share of suffering, even cruelty. But if any of the early humans who first touched the finds we study today could be transported to our world would there not be some wisdom they could impart? As we have seen, everything seems to argue that basic human kindness, compassion, a spirit of helping others out was not just there, but everywhere, vital to survival, the heart of later changes in mind. If we could visit our ancient past would we listen to this story, or would we be so wrapped up in our own success, our apparent progress, that we would have no time or inclination to pay attention, believing there is nothing that we need to know? Would we instead be quick to assume that peoples clad only in skins, with no written language, no civilisation, no knowledge of our world could have nothing to tell us?

Sadly, we have all too often treated modern hunter-gatherers, who at least live similar lifestyles to those of the Upper Palaeolithic, with cruelty and a lack of understanding, seeing our hunting and gathering past as a brutal phase that we have risen above and can't wait to shed. Our history of contact with modern hunter-gatherers has been one of many missed opportunities to learn something important. Certainly, there was little doubt in the minds of the early explorers who came across indigenous peoples that they themselves were the most evolved, cultured and civilised, and the poorly clothed savages that they came across were hardly worthy of note.

Travelling on his famous voyage on the *Beagle*, the very same journey on which he would come to formulate his theory of evolution by natural selection, Darwin came across many indigenous peoples. No matter what far flung corner of the world they travelled, there seemed to be people already there, living their own lives in their own way. Did this famous scientist look beyond the material to what might structure their society, what might allow them to survive despite the odds? Did he see something significant in their way of life? Unfortunately, coming from polite society, for him they were savages, on some lower rung of an evolutionary ladder. Whereas Captain Fitzroy was fascinated by them, Darwin said of the peoples of Tierra del Fuego after a brief encounter: 'if their dress and appearance is miserable, their manner of living is yet more so'.[385] Perhaps their lives were too challenging to attempt to understand, animals and birds far easier to study. Certainly, it was all too easy to feel entirely different from these thin and almost naked peoples, to feel a sense even of revulsion that we might be essentially *the same*. Tragically, many saw indigenous populations as so removed from their own humanity as to be little more than obstacles to expansion.

Some of the most shocking of the objectifications of hunting and gathering peoples were *human zoos*.[386] Only a few decades after Darwin's visit, eleven people, mostly Selk'nam, were taken back to Europe to be exhibited. Photographs of these terrified people huddled together on the

Like a 'human zoo'. An exhibit of Selk'nam from Tierra del Fuego and their keeper were photographed in Paris in 1889 and sold as postcards.

boat remain to this day. Alongside modern hunting and gathering peoples from around the world, they were weighed, measured and photographed, set in front of a backdrop to illustrate their homeland, and shown in Paris, London, Brussels and other European cities during the nineteenth century. People passed by the exhibit, fascinated by what they saw. They bought postcards, like those showing the Selk'nam with their keeper, almost like a lion tamer with his stick. Like the other *exhibits*, most of the Selk'nam died, with only one nine-year-old boy known to return. We don't know their names and nobody even once asked their opinions or ideas or what they might tell us.

At the time of Darwin's voyage to Tierra del Fuego in 1832, there were around 3,000 Selk'nam, the inland tribe of the islands, but by 1919 there were only 300.[387] They would not survive much longer. When I visited Tierra del Fuego in the mid 1990s to carry out research, the last had died over twenty years before. Though the remains of some their ritual huts or *choza* were still standing, almost as if they might one day return, the peoples themselves had disappeared, the only signs of their presence recorded in El Museo del Fin del Mundo (the museum at the end of the world) in Ushuaia. They had got in the way, died through a combination of deliberate genocide and European diseases. Edward Lucas Bridges, the English son of a missionary who was initiated into the Selk'nam, recalls climbing to a ridge with his Selk'nam friend, looking out across a landscape filled by colonists' intrusions and hearing him sigh resignedly at the destruction saying, 'Yak haruin' (My land).[388] When I was talking to the few descendants of the Tehuelche, the tribes to the north of Tierra del Fuego, I sensed a tremendous sadness for a world and peoples that were entirely lost.

A group of Selk'nam photographed walking along a beach in 1908. By the end of the century none had survived.

The missed opportunity to understand from modern peoples why the way of life which typified humanity for hundreds of millennia worked, not just practically but in social and emotional terms, seems even more poignant in Darwin's case. So careful to observe Galapagos finches, so much to learn from birdlife, yet he seemed to feel that he had so little to learn from these people. Darwin's missed opportunity was made even more acute because he had a chance to learn what few had experienced. On his voyage he travelled with a human bridge between two cultures, a man called Jemmy Button, someone who could have told him everything about Fuegian life. Jemmy was an indigenous Fuegian from a coastal population in Tierra del Fuego, who had lived in England, spoke fluent English and was returning to his homeland. We know from Darwin's accounts that they talked, yet nothing of their conversations was deemed worthy to document.

What was a native Fuegian doing coming back to Tierra Del Fuego on the *Beagle*? Jemmy's story is one of the most remarkable tales of both *connection* and *alienation* between modern hunter-gatherers and a world that saw itself as civilised.[389] Fascinated by the idea that underneath their dirty and unkept exterior lay a familiar humanity, Captain Fitzroy had devised an ambitious human experiment on the Fuegians. In 1830 he took Jemmy, whose Fuegian name was *o'run-del'lico*, away from his homeland with three other Fuegians, one of whom died on the voyage. Fitzroy wanted to transform the Fuegians into *civilised people*, make them emissaries for the civilised world among their own peoples, and illustrate that, no matter how lowly, such populations were capable of *being human*. His motives seem moral yet in many ways he had seen the Fuegians as expendable, human experiments to *civilise* and return back to their homeland.

Jemmy was plucked from his canoe when he was only fourteen, supposedly bought from his mother for the price of a pearl button. We can't help but doubt whether Jemmy or his mother had any understanding of what was happening. We know from later accounts that his mother searched the coasts for many weeks in the hope that he had been left behind, while Jemmy was stuck on a boat with only people from tribes he didn't know for company. What must he have felt arriving at Plymouth? Seeing buildings, monumental architecture, more people than he could ever have imagined? It is hard to think ourselves into the mind of someone who has seen none of these things.

Remarkably, Fitzroy's great experiment, a kind of extreme Pygmalion, worked even more successfully than he had imagined. A drawing made of Jemmy 'before and after' his transformation supposedly shows the effects being *civilised* had on his whole demeanour. Jemmy and the other Fuegians went to a religious school, sat at desks, learnt English and sang hymns. Jemmy was particularly popular in polite society and even had an audience with King William IV, whom he impressed. Jemmy seemed to *take* to modern culture, loving the clothes he wore and parading in front of a mirror. Polite society marvelled at how a 'savage' could be civilised. Rather than marvel at common humanity, the essential sameness of Europeans to these peoples living isolated for thousands of years, Jemmy's transformation was taken as a message of the value of civilised society, and its potential to *improve*. No one asked Jemmy what he felt, the learning and the listening went only in one direction. What might he possibly have to say of any use or interest?

As the three Fuegians were sent back to Tierra del Fuego, sailing with so many butter dishes and goblets and other trappings of civilisation transported for them that there were worries that the boat was overloaded, still no one, not even Darwin himself, asked for Jemmy's story or if there was anything we could learn from his culture.

We can only infer Jemmy's views from what we know of how he acted. As soon as he had a chance Jemmy simply discarded his modern clothes, ran off and rejoined his tribe. When he was seen later he was described as pitiably thin, and unclothed. The sailors were mystified, and Captain Fitzroy was shocked and appalled. They had rescued Jemmy from his pitiable existence, provided him with the best finery and the most appealing trappings of modern civilisation and yet he had abandoned it. In subsequent years Jemmy once again met with British sailors. Each time he was offered a passage back to Britain, back to his old life, with all its comforts, and every time he refused. It seemed not only inexplicable but almost *offensive* that he should prefer such an apparently savage existence.

Jemmy 1831

A contemporary drawing of Jemmy Button contrasted his 'savage' with his 'civilised' appearance.

For the nineteenth-century sailors, Jemmy's disappearance only added to the baffling behaviour of these peoples. An apparent disregard for the wealth and values of Western society seemed to be everywhere. Did they not understand the value of material things? Natives would appear delighted by gifts, yet later hold possessions in little esteem, abandoning them or tending to share everything out, give everything away. Shipwrecked sailors in Tierra del Fuego would be cared for by indigenous peoples, given food and looked after, but not until after they had been stripped of all their

Jemmy 1834

possessions, which would be shared out. Natives would destroy clothing, tearing it into equal pieces, rather than one of them own something useful, holding fairness in much higher regard than ownership.

When I asked Ivan Briz i Godino of the University of Ushuaia in Tierra del Fuego what motivated this type of behaviour he told me, 'These were highly collaborative societies where to share is the most important thing, for the Yamana for anyone to have and not to give away would be egotistical.'[390]

Few Europeans saw past the outward appearance of a lack of material

250

goods and a disdain for accumulating possessions, to wonder if there was some kind of hidden wealth, a certain mutual generosity, invisible to the eye. The only clue we have to any deeper consideration of the lives of the Fuegians, and some reference that there was something precious to this existence, is a note in Fitzroy's narrative which reads:

> Disagreeable, indeed painful, as is even the mental contemplation of a savage, and unwilling as we may be to consider ourselves even remotely descended from human beings in such a state, the reflection that Caesar found the Britons painted and clothed in skins, like these Fuegians, cannot fail to augment an interest excited by their childish ignorance of matters familiar to civilised man, and by their healthy, independent state of existence.[391]

Perhaps, after all, Fitzroy had wanted to know something from Jemmy, even if he never could quite bring himself to ask.

Would we be more open to wanting to understand the Fuegians today?

I'd like to think so. But fascinated though we are by our ancestors, *past* hunter-gatherers, with their mystical worlds, peoples whom we feel must have been *special* in some way, we rarely stop to try to understand if modern hunter-gatherers might have anything to tell us. We might like them to feel some sense of respect, admiration, some awe for our achievements, or for the depths of our knowledge, but would such peoples feel this way or would our lives horrify them? Would they, like Jemmy, prefer the lives that they led, despite the physical hardships, the shortages of food?

Davi Kopenawa, a Yanomami shaman from the Amazon, certainly makes it clear that he too prefers his own way of life, refusing even to use manufactured goods. His reflections remind us of Jemmy's choices, and perhaps how Jemmy might have felt. We like to think that hunting and gathering peoples who have so little would be impressed with our societies, awed by the things we have created, by our inventions and our mastery of the world. Instead, they seem almost appalled by the extent of our *stuff*. Rather than look at the material things, they focus more on the small and subtle signs of how people feel, and are deeply concerned that something is very wrong.

Davi says:

They probably find themselves very clever to produce a multitude of goods. They were tired of walking and wanted to go faster, so they invented the bicycle. Then eventually they found it still too slow. Next they built motorcycles, then cars. Then they found that all that was still not fast enough, and they created airplanes. Now they possess a great number of machines and factories. Yet that still isn't enough for them. Their thought remains constantly attached to their merchandise. They make it relentlessly and always desire new goods. But they probably are not as wise as they think they are. I fear that this euphoria of merchandise will have no end and they will entangle themselves with it to the point of chaos.[392]

Davi, visiting Paris, New York and London to petition governments to stop destroying the rainforest, could barely believe that in these cities some could live with such wealth, food, shelter and comfort while others suffered, a condition seeming to him to be deeply unnatural. Of New York, he writes:

Yet while the houses in the center of the city are tall and beautiful, those on its edges are in ruins. The people who live in those places have no food, and their clothes are dirty and worn. When I took a walk among them, they looked at me with sad eyes. It made me feel upset. These white people who created merchandise think they are clever and brave. Yet they are greedy and do not take care of those among them who have nothing. How can they think they are great men and find themselves so smart? They do not want to know anything about these needy people, though they too are their fellows. They reject them and let them suffer alone. They do not even look at them and are satisfied to keep their distance and call them 'the poor'. They even take their crumbling houses from them. They force them to camp outside in the rain, with their children. They must tell themselves 'They live on our land, but they are other people. Let them stay far away from us, picking their food off the ground like dogs! As for us, we will pile up more food and more weapons, all by ourselves!' It scares me to see such a thing.[393]

252

Could we be the ones who are more brutal? Tjiniman Murimbata, a modern Aboriginal hunter-gatherer attending a conference in Tucson, was equally non-plussed by the accumulation of our knowledge and our wealth of possessions and instead shocked by the lack of humanity in how people treated each other. He says:

Among my own people no one laughs at anyone who seems to be ignorant or foolish but only at those who are conceited, or who try to take power that is not given to them by others. Those are the ones who are truly foolish because we cannot live except through each other. That is what you white people have forgotten and why you have such antisocial customs.[394]

Tjiniman bemoans the lack of heart of many people who simply use their heads, seemingly insensitive to their own feelings and to those of people around them. '[They] have lost their heart-soul and have only their head-soul left.'[395] He quotes a fellow hunter-gatherer's description of a Western person: 'he does not take notice of things around him, and he does not 'feel' anyone that is near him. His bodily senses have been out of use for so long that they do not function any more.'[396]

Are these modern hunter-gatherers right? Do we feel less than we should? If our worlds *are* numb and insensitive compared to theirs, are they equally as numb and insensitive in comparison to our Palaeolithic past? Has an everyday numbing of our feelings, an immunity to suffering, a depression of emotion affected everything about us, making us a little less courageous, less kind, less caring than we were?

Many people suspect that modern hunter-gatherers are right to question the very basis of our rather alienating societies, to see them as something rather new and strange in the long span of human existence. We appear to be so much better off, appear to have progressed. Yet, as Randolph Nesse points out, even among those who have succeeded beyond measure in getting what they wanted, 'vast numbers of people remain deeply unhappy, and many of the rest lead lives that feel frantic or meaningless or both. What we have been doing to increase happiness is no longer working, and there is no consensus about what to do next.'[397]

When modern hunter-gatherers sit around their camp fires listening to the stories which explain their existence we can see that they feel proud of their past. Creation myths reassure them of their place in nature, their right to be in the world and their responsibility to protect it. Epic tales encourage and inspire. *Their* past was a world full of heroic deeds, the ever-present potential for cruelty balanced by the perpetual power of ordinary kindness. This was a place populated by humble heroes battling not just the outer world but inner conflicts – facing temptations which they resisted, or by which they were thwarted, making their way with human strengths and vulnerabilities, not least their desires to display a certain wisdom or to be loved.

Our past seems clinical in comparison, devoid of heroes or human feeling. Does it need to be? Have we become too scared of what we might find out about the people who played their part in our origins, too ready to assume a certain aggression or brutality, to even look for these features? We seem to strive to separate ourselves from nature, worried that our connection to the animal world might make us less in control. Reminders of our past, like modern hunter-gatherers, can seem almost an embarrassment. For Darwin, the material impoverishment and the lack of laws of the natives of Tierra del Fuego was a past we must continue to battle against, and modern attitudes can sometimes be little different. When we look at the real finds which our ancestors crafted, the bones of their bodies we have excavated, we see them only as objects, evidence for behaviours, bones and artefacts with no heart or soul.

In taking the emotions away from our past have we deprived ourselves of something important? Shouldn't the everyday experience of our ancestors – their kindness to the vulnerable, courage to face dangers for each other, a certain tenderness despite the odds – count for something?

The more I find out about our origins the more convinced I am that the archaeological evidence truly does tell us a *human* story. There *is* something special in the dusty bones and ancient artefacts we find. This real evidence is as much a product of that certain heroism, an ordinary kindness, a capacity to fall from grace or to rise above it that *made us human* as we might find in any myth. Each time a glimpse of the past is preserved within our world, from the care of the *Homo ergaster* female to that of the Neanderthal at Shanidar, from the Makapansgat pebble to the Rouffignac mammoths, we can't help but feel the unmistakable melody of humanity if we are prepared to listen.

Perhaps now is the time for a new story.

It should be the same wherever you look
so tightly was the beginning folded

time's not what it was but a place of dispersal
we sit facing each other in the blur
reach out as the past the future
increasingly intervene.[398]

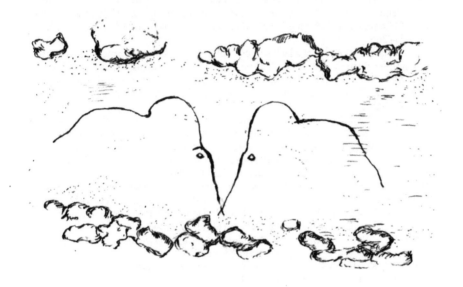

Notes

CHAPTER ONE

1. Manderson, D. (2008) Desert island disks: Ten reveries on inter-disciplinary pedagogy in law. *Public Space: The Journal of Law and Social Justice* 2:1–19, p. 5. Cited in Porr M. and H. R. Bell (2002) 'Rock-art', 'Animism' and Two-way Thinking: Towards a Complementary Epistemology in the Understanding of Material Culture and 'Rock-art' of Hunting and Gathering People. *Journal of Archaeological Method and Theory* 19: 161–205.
2. Bruce Charlton argues that a lack of a cosmology to explain our existence places great psychological stress on us. See Charlton, B. G. (2007) An evolutionary cosmology for scientists – and the modern world in general. *Medical Hypotheses* 69(4): 713–717.
3. Frere, J. (1800) Account of flint weapons discovered at Hoxne in Suffolk. *Archaeologia* 13:204–205.
4. Lyell, C. (1863) *The geological evidences of the antiquity of man with remarks on the origin of species by variation.* 3rd edition, revised. London: John Murray, p. 1.
5. Buckland, W. (1824) *Reliquiae diluvianae, or Observations on the organic remains contained in caves, fissures and diluvial gravel and on other geological phenomena attesting the action of an universal deluge.* London: John Murray, p. 169.
6. Russell, M. (2003) *Piltdown Man: The secret life of Charles Dawson.* Tempus: Stroud.
7. Dart, R., and D. Craig. (1959) *Adventures with the missing link.* New York: Harper. See also: Wolberg, D. L. (1970) The Hypothesized Osteodontokeratic Culture of the Australopithecinae. *Current Anthropology* Vol. 11(1): 23–37.
8. Ardrey, R. (1961) *African genesis: A personal investigation into the animal origins and nature of man.* New York: Atheneum Books, p. 29.
9. Brain, C. K. (1981) *The hunters or the hunted?: an introduction to African Cave Taphonomy.* Chicago: University of Chicago Press.
10. Grosman, L. C. D. (1996) *On killing: The psychological cost of learning to kill in war and society.* New York: Back Bay Books.
11. Isaac, G. L. (1978) Food sharing and human evolution: archaeological evidence from the Plio-Pleistocene of East Africa. *Journal of Anthropological Research* 34(5): 311–325.
12. Binford, L. R. (1981) *Bones: ancient men and modern myths.* New York: Academic Press.
13. Potts, R. (1984) Home Bases and Early Hominids: Reevaluation of the fossil record at Olduvai Gorge suggests that the concentrations of bones and stone tools do not represent fully formed campsites but an antecedent to them. *American Scientist* 72(4): 338–347.
14. Rose, L., and F. Marshall. (1996) Meat eating, hominid sociality, and home bases revisited. *Current Anthropology* 37: 307–338.
15. Steve Mithen explains that Upper Palaeolithic cave art performed the function of reminding societies of how to hunt certain animals that might not usually have been exploited and it illustrated the particular ways of hunting. He saw art as a functional communication device. See: Mithen, S. J. (1988) Looking and learning: Upper Palaeolithic art and information gathering. *World Archaeology* 19(3): 297–327.
16. Clive Gamble interpreted the movement of non-functional items in Upper Palaeolithic societies as a means of creating mutual obligations, obliging those who received gifts to support the donors in times of crisis and so providing a buffer against changing

256

resources. See: Gamble, C. (1982) Interaction and alliance in Palaeolithic society. *Man* 17 (1): 92–107.

17. Heinrich, J., Heine, S. J., and A. Norenzayan (2010) Most people are not WEIRD. *Nature* 466(7302): 29.

18. Warneken, F., and M. Tomasello. (2009). The roots of human altruism. *British Journal of Psychology* 100(3): 455–471.

19. Frank, R. H. (1988) *Passions within reason: The strategic role of the emotions*. W. W. Norton & Co.

20. Green, A., and J. G Janmaat. (2011) *Regimes of social cohesion: Societies and the crisis of globalization*. Basingstoke: Palgrave Macmillan.

21. See Carol's Dweck's research such as:
Dweck, C. S. (1986) Motivational processes affecting learning. *American Psychologist* 41(10): 1040.
Heyman, G. D., and C. S. Dweck. (1998) Children's thinking about traits: Implications for judgments of the self and others. *Child Development* 64(2): 391–403
Heyman, G. D., Dweck, C. S., and K. M. Cain (1992) Young children's vulnerability to self-blame and helplessness: Relationship to beliefs about goodness. *Child Development*, 63(2): 401–415.

22. Spikins, P. A., Rutherford, H. E., and A. P. Needham. (2010) From homininity to humanity: Compassion from the earliest archaics to modern humans. *Time and Mind*, 3(3), 303–325.

23. Hublin, J. J. (2009) The prehistory of compassion. *Proceedings of the National Academy of Sciences* 106(16): 6429–6430.

CHAPTER TWO

24. LeGuin, U. K. (2004) *Four keys to happiness*, New York: Harper Collins, p. 156.

25. Nariokotome boy and other skeletal material may be attributed to either *Homo ergaster* or *Homo erectus*. For simplicity, both are referred to here under the term *Homo erectus*. Many argue that different forms in Africa and Asia should described as such, although opinions vary. See Lordkipanidze, D., de León, M. S. P., Margvelashvili, A., Rak, Y., Rightmire, G. P., Vekua, A., and C. P. Zollikofer (2013) A complete skull from Dmanisi, Georgia, and the evolutionary biology of early Homo. *Science* 342 (6156): 326–331.

26. Gracia-Téllez, A., Arsuaga, J. L., Martínez, I., Martín-Francés, L., Martinón-Torres, M., Bermúdez de Castro, J. M., ... and J. Lira (2012) Orofacial pathology in *Homo heidelbergensis*: The case of Skull 5 from the Sima de los Huesos site (Atapuerca, Spain). *Quaternary International* 295: 83–93; De Castro, J. M. B., and P. Pérez (1995) Enamel hypoplasia in the Middle Pleistocene hominids from Atapuerca (Spain). *American Journal of Physical Anthropology* 96(3): 301–314.

27. Berger, T. D., and E. Trinkaus (1995) Patterns of trauma among the Neandertals. *Journal of Archaeological Science* 22(6): 841–852.

28. Bermúdez de Castro, J-M., Martinón-Torres, M. L., Sarmiento S. M., and A. Muela (2004) Paleodemography of the Atapuerca: Sima De Los Huesos Hominin Sample: A revision and new approaches to the Paleodemography of the European Middle Pleistocene population. *Journal of Anthropological Research* 60(1): 5–26.

29. Ogilvie, M.D., Curran, B. K., and E. Trinkaus (1989) Incidence and patterning of dental enamel hypoplasia in Neanderthals, *American Journal of Physical Anthropology* 79(1): 25–41; Stapert, D. (2007) Neanderthal children and their flints. *Pal/Arch's Journal of Archaeology of Northwest Europe* 1(2): 1–39.

30. Stock, J., and C. Shaw (2012) Evidence for long distance terrestrial locomotion among early modern humans and Neanderthals relative to Holocene foragers and modern

human athletes. *Proceedings of the European Society for Human Evolution* 1, 175; Shaw, C. N., and J. T. Stock (2013) Extreme mobility in the Late Pleistocene? Comparing limb biomechanics among fossil *Homo*, varsity athletes and Holocene foragers. *Journal of Human Evolution* 64(4): 242–249.

31. Cowgill, L. W., Trinkaus, E., and M. A. Zeder (2007) Shanidar 10: a Middle Paleolithic immature distal lower limb from Shanidar Cave, Iraqi Kurdistan. *Journal of Human Evolution*, 53(2): 213–223.

32. See Zollikofer, C., Ponce de León, M. S., Vandermeersch, B., and F. Lévêque (2002) Evidence for interpersonal violence in the St. Césaire Neanderthal. *Proceedings of the National Academy of Sciences* 99(9): 6444–6448.

33. Churchill, S. E., Franciscus, R. G., McKean-Peraza, H. A., Daniel, J. A., and B. R. Warren (2009) Shanidar 3 Neanderthal rib puncture wound and Palaeolithic weaponry. *Journal of Human Evolution* 57(2): 163–178.

34. Berger, T. D., and E. Trinkaus (1995) Patterns of trauma amongst the Neanderthals. *Journal of Archaeological Science* 22(6): 841–892.

35. Trinkaus, E. (2012) Neandertals, early modern humans, and rodeo riders. *Journal of Archaeological Science* 39(12): 3691–3693.

36. Croxall, E., and E. H. M. Sterck (2012) Neanderthal territoriality: an ecological approach. *Proceedings of the European Society for Human Evolution* 1:62.

37. Brookfield, J. F. Y. (2003) Human evolution: a legacy of cannibalism in our genes? *Current Biology* 13(15): 592–593.

38. Pickering, T. R., White, T. D., and N. Toth (2000) Brief communication: Cutmarks on a Plio-Pleistocene hominid from Sterkfontein, South Africa. *American Journal of Physical Anthropology* 111(4): 579–584.

39. See description of cannibalism in Pettitt, P. (2011) *The Palaeolithic origins of human burial.* Abingdon: Routledge.

40. Aubry, C. (2002) Consuming Grief: Compassionate Cannibalism in an Amazonian society, *Anthropological Quarterly* 72(2): 433–436.

41. Carbonell, E., Caceres, I., Lozano, M., Saladie, P., Rosell, J., Lorenzo, C., Vallverdu, J., Huguet, R., Canals, A., and J. M. Bermudez de Castro (2010) Cultural cannibalism as a Palaeoeconomic system in the European Lower Pleistocene. *Current Anthropology* 51(4): 539–549.

42. Defleur, A., White, T., Valensi, P., Slimak, L., and E. Cregut-Bonnoure (1999) Neanderthal cannibalism at Moula-Guercy, Ardeche, France. *Science* 286(5437): 128–131.

43. Lalueza-Fox, C., Rosas, A., and M. D. L. Rasilla (2012) Palaeogenetic research at the El Sidrón Neanderthal site. *Annals of Anatomy-Anatomischer Anzeiger* 194(1): 133–137.

44. Bello, S. M. Parfitt, S. A., Cáceres, I., Saladié, P., and A. Rodriguez-Hidalgo (2012) Upper Palaeolithic ritualistic cannibalism: Gough's Cave (Somerset, UK) from head to toe, *European Society of Human Evolution* 1: 38

45. Bourke, J. (2000) *An intimate history of killing: Face to face killing in twentieth century warfare.* New York: Basic books.

46. Frayer, D. (1997) Ofnet: evidence for a Mesolithic massacre. In D. W. Frayer (ed.), *Troubled times: violence and warfare in the past.* Amsterdam: Gordon and Breach Publishers, pp. 181–216.

47. Nash, G. (2005). Assessing rank and warfare-strategy in prehistoric hunter-gatherer society: a study of representational warrior figures in rock-art from the Spanish Levant, southeastern Spain. *Warfare, Violence and Slavery in Prehistory.* Oxford: BAR, 1374: 75–86.

48. Roksandic, M., Djurić, M., Rakočević, Z., and K. Seguin (2006) Interpersonal violence

at Lepenski Vir Mesolithic/Neolithic complex of the Iron Gates Gorge (Serbia-Romania), *American Journal of Physical Anthropology* 139(3): 339–348.

49. Jones, T. L., Brown, G. M., Raab, L. M., McVickar, J. L., Spaulding, W. G., Kennett, D. J., ... and P. L. Walker (1999). Environmental imperatives reconsidered: demographic crises in western North America during the medieval climatic anomaly. *Current Anthropology* 40(2): 137–170.

50. Wendorf, F. (1968). Site 117: a Nubian final paleolithic graveyard near Jebel Sahaba, Sudan. In F. Wendorf (ed.), *The prehistory of Nubia, Volume 2*. Texas: Southern Methodist University Press, pp. 954–995.

51. Peterson, N. (2013) Anthropological Perspectives on Peace and Violence. *Conference on Hunting and Gathering Societies* (CHAGS), Liverpool.

52. Everett, E., Lucas, H., and K. Hakami (2013) Comparing two hunter-gatherer societies (Piraha and Maniq) on theoretical grounds. *Conference on Hunting and Gathering Societies* (CHAGS), Liverpool.

53. Gurven, M., Wesley, A-A., Hill, K., and M. Hurtado (2000) 'It's a wonderful life': signalling generosity among the Ache of Paraguay. *Evolution and Human Behaviour* 21(4): 263–282.

54. Weissner, P. (2002) Taking the risk out of risky transactions: A forager's dilemma. In A. Salter (ed.) *Risky transactions: Trust, kinship and reciprocity*. New York: Berghahn Books, pp. 21–46.

55. Hewlett, B. S., Fouts, H. N., Boyette, A. H., and B. Hewlett (2011) Social learning among Congo basin hunter-gatherers. *Philosphical Transactions of the Royal Society B*. 336(1537): 1168–1178.

56. Wood, B. (2013) The role of food-sharing in Hadza's children's social development. Presentation. *Conference on Hunting and Gathering Societies* (CHAGS), Liverpool.

57. Wiessner, P. (1982) Risk, reciprocity and social influences on !Kung San economics. In E. Leacock and R. Lee (eds.), *Politics and History in band societies*. Cambridge: Cambridge University Press, pp. 61–84.

58. Konner, M. (2010) *The evolution of childhood, relationships, emotion, mind*. Cambridge MA: Harvard University Press.

59. Charlton, B. (2000) *Psychiatry and the human condition*. London: Radcliffe Medical.

60. Brody, H. (2002) *The other side of Eden: Hunters, farmers, and the shaping of the world*. London: Macmillan.

61. Briggs, J. L. (1970) *Never in anger: Portrait of an Eskimo family* (Vol. 12). Harvard: Harvard University Press.

62. Boehm, C., and C. Boehm (2009) *Hierarchy in the forest: The evolution of egalitarian behavior*. Harvard: Harvard University Press. See also, Boehm, C. (2012) *Moral origins: The evolution of virtue, altruism, and shame*. New York: Basic Books.

63. Lee, R. B. (1979) The !Kung San: *Men, women, and work in a foraging society*. Cambridge: Cambridge University Press, pp. 244–246.

64. Boehm, C., and C. Boehm (2009) *Hierarchy in the forest: The evolution of egalitarian behavior*. Harvard: Harvard University Press, p. 72.

65. Heinrich, J. and F. J. Gil-White (2001) The evolution of prestige. Freely conferred deference as a mechanism for enhancing the benefits of cultural transmission. *Evolution and Human Behaviour* 22(3): 165–196.

66. Spikins, P. A. (2008) The boastful and the bashful. Prestigious leaders and social change in Mesolithic societies. *Journal of World Prehistory* 21: 173–193; Shultziner, D., Stevens, T., Stevens, M., Stewart, B. A., Hannagan, R. J., and G. Saltini-Semerari (2010) The causes and scope of political egalitarianism during the Last Glacial: a multi-disciplinary perspective. *Biology and Philosophy* 25(3): 319–436.

CHAPTER THREE

67. Holmes, O. W., The professor at the breakfast table, first published in *The Atlantic Monthly*, May 1859.

68. Bednarik, R. G. (1998) The 'australopithecine' cobble from Makapansgat, South Africa. *South African Archaeological Bulletin* 53: 4–8.

69. Bednarik, R. G. (2003) A figurine from the African Acheulian. *Current Anthropology* 44: 405–413.

70. Bednarik, R. G. (1994) Art Origins. *Anthropos* 89: 169–180. See also:
D'Errico, F., and A. Nowell (2000) A new look at the Berekhat Ram figurine: Implications for the origins of symbolism. *Cambridge Archaeological Journal* 10: 123–167.

71. Porges, S. W. (2003) The polyvagal theory: Phylogenetic contributions to social behavior. *Physiology & Behavior* 79(3): 503–513.

72. Barham, L. S. (2002) Systematic pigment use in the Middle Pleistocene of south central Africa. *Current Anthropology* 43(1): 181–190.

73. Roebroeks, W., Sier, M. J., Nielson, T. K., De Loecker, D., Parés, J. M., Arps, C. E. S., and H. J. Mücher (2012) Use of red ochre by early Neanderthals, *Proceedings of the National Academy of Sciences* 109(6): 1889–1894.

74. D'Errico, F., and M. Soressi (2002) *Systematic use of manganese pigment by Pech-de-l'Aze' Neandertals: Implications for the origin of behavioral modernity.* Paper presented to the Palaeoanthropology Society, Denver (www.paleoanthro.org/pdfs/2002abst.pdf).

75. Zilhão, J., Angelucci, D. E., Badal-García, E., D'Errico, F., Daniel, F., Dayet, L., Douka, K., Higham, T. F. G., Martínez-Sánchez, M. J., Montes-Bernárdez, R., Murcia-Mascarós, S., Pérez-Sirvent, C., Roldán-García, C., Vanhaeren, M., Villaverde, V., Wood, R., and J. Zapata (2010) Symbolic use of marine shells and mineral pigments by Iberian Neanderthals. *Proceedings of the National Academy of Sciences* 107(3): 1023–1028.

76. Peresani, M., Fiore, I., Gala, M., Romandini, M., and A. Tagliacozzo (2011) Late Neandertals and the intentional removal of feathers as evidenced from bird bone taphonomy at Fumane Cave 44 ky B.P., Italy. *Proceedings of the National Academy of Sciences* 108(10): 3888–3893.

77. Marquet, J.-C. and M. Lorblanchet (2003) A Neanderthal face? The proto-figurine from La Roche-Cotard, Langeais (Indre-et-Loire, France). *Antiquity* 77: 661–70.

78. Gowlett, J. A. (2011) Special Issue: Innovation and the Evolution of Human Behavior – The Vital Sense of Proportion: Transformation, Golden Section, and 1: 2 Preference in Acheulean Bifaces. *PaleoAnthropology* 174: 187.

79. See Pettitt, P. (2013) The Palaeolithic origins of human burial. London: Routledge.

80. Cameron, D. W. and C. P. Groves (2004) *Bones, stones, and molecules: 'Out of Africa' and human origins.* Amsterdam: Elsevier/Academic.

81. Walker, A., and P. Shipman (1996) *The wisdom of bones: In search of human origins.* London: Weidenfeld and Nicolson. See also:
Walker, A., Zimmerman, M. R., and R. E. F. Leakey (1982) A possible case of hypervitaminosis A in *Homo erectus*. *Nature* 296: 248–250.

82. Walker, A., and P. Shipman (1996) *The wisdom of bones: In search of human origins.* London: Weidenfeld and Nicolson, p. 134.

83. Cameron, D. W. and C. P. Groves (2004) *Bones, stones, and molecules: 'Out of Africa' and human origins.* Amsterdam: Elsevier/Academic, p. 158.

84. Lordkipanidze, D., Vekua, A., Ferring, R., Rightmire, G. P., Agusti, J., Kiladze, G., Mouskhelishveli, A., Nioradze, M., Ponce de León, M. S., Tappen, M. and C. P. E. Zollikofer (2005) Anthropology: The earliest toothless human skull. *Nature* 434(7034): 717–718.

85. Bonmatí, A., Gómez-Olivencia, A., Arsuaga, J. L., Carretero, J. M. Gracia, A., Martínez, I., and C. Lorenzo (2011) El caso de Elvis el viejo de la Sima de los Huesos. *Dendra Médica Revista de Humanidad*es 10: 138–147.
86. Gracia, A., Arsuaga, J. L., Martínez, I., Lorenzo, C., Carretero, J. M., Bermúdez de Castro, J. M., and E. Carbonell (2009) Craniosynostosis in the Middle Pleistocene human Cranium 14 from the Sima de los Huesos, Atapuerca, Spain. *Proceedings of the National Academy of Sciences of the USA* 106(16), 6573–6578.
87. Gracia, A., Arsuaga, J. L., Martínez, I., Lorenzo, C., Carretero, J. M., Bermúdez de Castro, J. M., and E. Carbonell (2009) Craniosynostosis in the Middle Pleistocene human Cranium 14 from the Sima de los Huesos, Atapuerca, Spain. *Proceedings of the National Academy of Sciences of the USA* 106(16), 6573–6578, on p. 6577.
88. Hublin, J. –J. (2009) The Prehistory of Compassion. *Proceedings of the National Academy of Sciences* 106(16): 6429–6430.
89. Klein, R. G. (1999) *The human career, human biological and cultural origins*. Chicago: University of Chicago Press, p. 333.
90. Klein, R. G. (2009) *The human career: human biological and cultural origins*. University of Chicago Press, p. 584.
91. Solecki, R. S. (1972) *Shanidar: the humanity of Neanderthal man*. London: Allen Lane the Penguin Press.
92. Klein, R. G. (1999) *The human career, human biological and cultural origins*. Chicago: University of Chicago Press.
93. Trinkaus, E. and M. R. Zimmerman (1982) Trauma among the Shanidar Neanderthals. *American Journal of Physical Anthropology* 57:1. 61–76.
94. Trinkaus, E. and M. R. Zimmerman (1982) Trauma among the Shanidar Neanderthals. *American Journal of Physical Anthropology* 57:1. 61–76.
95. Franciscus, R. G. and S. E. Churchill (2002). The costal skeleton of Shanidar 3 and a reappraisal of Neandertal thoracic morphology. *Journal of Human Evolution* 42(3): 303–356.
96. Berger, T. B. and E. Trinkaus (1995) Patterns of Trauma among the Neanderthals. *Journal of Archaeological Science* 22(6) 841–852. See also:
Klein, R. G. (2009) *The human career: human biological and cultural origins*. University of Chicago Press, p. 584.
97. Klein, R. G. (2009) *The human career: human biological and cultural origins*. University of Chicago Press, p. 584. See also:
Dawson, J. E. and E. Trinkaus (1997) Vertebral osteoarthritis of the La Chapelle-aux-Saints 1 Neanderthal. *Journal of Archaeological Science* 24(11): 1015–1021.
98. Lebel, S., Trinkaus, E., Faure, M., Fernandez, P., Guérin, C., Richter, D., Mercier, N., Valladas, H., and G. A. Wagner (2001) Comparative morphology and paleobiology of Middle Pleistocene human remains from the Bau de L'Aubesier, Vaucluse, France. *Proceedings of the National Academy of Sciences USA* 98(20): 11097–11102.
99. Zollikofer, C. P., de León, M. S. P., Vandermeersch, B., & Lévêque, F. (2002) Evidence for interpersonal violence in the St. Césaire Neanderthal. *Proceedings of the National Academy of Sciences* 99(9): 6444–6448.
100. Walker, M. J., López-Martínez, M., Ortega-Rodrigánez, J., Haber-Uriarte, M., López-Jiménez, A., Avilés-Fernández, A., Polo-Camacho, J. L., Campillo-Boj, M., García-Torres, J., García. J. S. C., Nicolás-del Toro, M. S., Rodríguez-Estrella, T. (2012) The excavation of buried articulated Neanderthal skeletons at Sima de los Palmos, Murcia, Spain. *Quaternary International* 259: 7–21.
101. Pettitt, P. 2013. *The Palaeolithic Origins of Human Burial*. London: Routledge.
102. Hovers, E., Kimbel, W. H., and Y. Rak (2000) The Amud 7 skeleton – still a burial. Response to Gargett. *Journal of Human Evolution* 39(2): 253–260.
103. Algoe, S. B., and J. Haidt (2009) Witnessing excellence in action: the 'other focusing'

emotions of elevation, gratitude and admiration. *Journal of Positive Psychology* 4 (2): 105–127.

104. Keltner, D., Marsh, J., and J. A. Smith (eds.) (2010) *The compassionate instinct: The science of human goodness.* W. W. Norton & Company.

105. Bone, J. D., Hey, J. D., and J. R. Suckling (2010) Do People plan ahead? *Applied economics Letters* 10 (5): 277–280.

106. De Waal, F. (2009). *Primates and Philosophers: How Morality Evolved: How Morality Evolved.* Princeton: Princeton University Press.

107. Oxenham, M. F., Tilley, L., Matsumara, H., Nguygen, L. C., Nguyen, K. T., Nguyen, K. D., Domett, K. and D. Huffer (2009) Paralysis and severe disability requiring intensive care in Neolithic Asia. *Anthropological Science* 117(2): 107–112. See also: Tilley, L., and M. F. Oxenham (2011) Survival against the odds: Modeling the social implications of care provision to seriously disabled individuals. *International Journal of Palaeopathology* 1(1): 35–42.

108. Formicola, V. (2007) From the Sunghir Children to the Romito Dwarf. *Current Anthropology* 48(3): 446–453.

109. Toda. M. (2013) Caring in inter-ethic communities: Physical disabilities among the Baka people of Southeastern Cameroon. *Conference on Hunting and Gathering Societies* CHAGS, Liverpool.

110. Wiessner, P. (2002) Taking the risk out of risky transactions: a forager's dilemma. In F. K. Salter (ed.) *Risky Transactions: Trust, Kinship, and Ethnicity.* Oxford: Berghan Books, pp. 21–43.

111. White, R. (2007) Systems of personal ornamentation in the Early Upper Palaeolithic: Methodological challenges and new observations. In P. Mellars, K. Boyle, O. Bar-Yosef and C. Stringer (eds.) *Rethinking the human revolution: New behavioural and biological perspectives on the origin and dispersal of modern humans.* Cambridge: McDonald Institute for Archaeological Research, pp. 287–302.

112. Gamble, C. (1999) *The Palaeolithic societies of Europe.* Cambridge: Cambridge University Press, p. 333.

113. Emmons, R. A. and M. E. McCullough (eds.) (2004) *The psychology of gratitude.* Oxford: Oxford University Press.

114. Nesse, R. M. (2007) Runaway social selection for displays of partner value and altruism. *Biological Theory* 2(2): 145–155.

115. Fischer, M. L. and J. J. Exline (2006) Self-forgiveness versus excusing: The roles of remorse, effort, and acceptance of responsibility. *Self and Identity* 5(2): 127–146.

116. Liotti, G. and P. Gilbert (2011) Mentalizing, motivation, and social mentalities: Theoretical considerations and implications for psychotherapy. *Psychology and Psychotherapy: Theory, Research and Practice* 84(1): 9–25.

CHAPTER FOUR

117. Quote from Jane Goodall in an interview with Robin McKie, published in 'Chimps with everything: Jane Goodall's 50 years in the jungle', the *Observer*, 24 June 2010.

118. Langergraber, K. E., Prüfer, K., Rowney, C., Boesch, C., Crockford, C., Fawcett, K., ... and L. Vigilant (2012) Generation times in wild chimpanzees and gorillas suggest earlier divergence times in great ape and human evolution. *Proceedings of the National Academy of Sciences* 109(39): 15716–15721.

119. Morell, V. (1993) Called Trimates: Three bold women shaped their field. *Science* 260(5106): 420–425.

120. Jane Goodall Public lecture. Cambridge Personal Histories, Oral Histories of Primatology, Cambridge, 11 December 2011.

121. Jane Goodall Public lecture. Cambridge Personal Histories, Oral Histories of Primatology, Cambridge, 11 December 2011.
    —Goodall, J. (2010) *Through a window: My thirty years with the chimpanzees of Gombe*. Boston, MA: Houghton Mifflin. See also:
122. Goodall, J. (2010) *Fifty years at Gombe*. New York: Stewart, Tobori and Chang.
123. Goodall, J. (1986) *The chimpanzees of Gombe: patterns of behavior*. Cambridge, MA: Belknap Press of Harvard University Press.
124. Boesch, C., Bole, C., Eckhardt, N., and H. Boesch (2010) Altruism in forest chimpanzees: The case of adoption. *PLoS One* 5(1), e8901.
125. Biro, D., Humle, T., Koops, K., Sousa, C., Hayashi, M., and T. Matsuzawa (2010) Chimpanzee mothers at Bossou, Guinea carry the mummified remains of their dead infants. *Current Biology* 20(8): R351–R352.
126. Goodall, J. (1986) *The chimpanzees of Gombe: patterns of behavior*. Cambridge, MA: Belknap Press of Harvard University Press.
127. Anderson, J. R., Gillies, A., and L. C. Lock (2010) Panthanatology. *Current Biology* 20(8): R349–R351, p. 20.
128. Kahlenberg, S. M. and R. W. Wrangham (2010) Sex differences in chimpanzees' use of sticks as play objects resemble those of children. *Current Biology* 20(24): R1067–R1068.
129. See among other publications:
    —de Waal, F. B. M. (2009) The age of empathy: Nature's lessons for a kinder society. New York: Harmony Books.
    —de Waal, F. B. M., and P. F. Ferrari (2012). The primate mind: Built to connect with Other minds. Cambridge, MA; Harvard University Press.
    —de Waal, F. B. M. (2013) The bonobo and the atheist: In search of humanism among the primates. New York: W. W. Norton & Company.
130. Fábrega, H. (1997) *Evolution of sickness and healing*. Berkeley CA: University of California Press.
131. Boesch, C. (1992) New elements about a theory of mind in wild chimpanzees. *Behavioral and Brain Sciences* 15(1): 149.
132. Warneken, F., Hare, B., Melis, A. P., Hanus, D., and M. Tomasello (2007) Spontaneous altruism by chimpanzees and young children. *PLoS biology* 5(7), e184.
133. de Waal, F. B. M. (2009) *The age of empathy: Nature's lessons for a kinder society*. New York: Harmony Books.
134. Beran, M. J. (2002). Maintenance of self-imposed delay of gratification by four chimpanzees (Pan troglodytes) and an orangutan (Pongo pygmaeus). *The Journal of General Psychology* 129(1): 49–66. See also:
    Rosati, A. G., Stevens, J. R., Hare, B., and M. D. Hauser (2007) The evolutionary origins of human patience: temporal preferences in chimpanzees, bonobos, and human adults. *Current Biology* 17(19): 1663–1668.
135. Flack, J. C., and F. B. De Waal (2000) Any animal whatever. Darwinian building blocks of morality in monkeys and apes. *Journal of Consciousness Studies* 7(1–2): 1–2.
136. Schino, G., and F. Aureli (2010) Primate reciprocity and its cognitive requirements. *Evolutionary Anthropology: Issues, News, and Reviews* 19(4): 130–135.
137. Matsuzawa, T. (2013) Evolution of the brain and social behavior in chimpanzees. *Current Opinion in Neurobiology* 23(3): 443–449.
138. Slocombe, K. E., and N. E. Newton-Fisher (2005) Fruit sharing between wild adult chimpanzees (Pan troglodytes schweinfurthii): a socially significant event? *American Journal of Primatology* 65(4): 385–391.
139. Goodall, J. (1986) Social rejection, exclusion, and shunning among the Gombe chimpanzees. *Ethology and Sociobiology* 7(3): 227–236.

140. Goodall, J. (1971) *In the Shadow of Man.* Boston: Houghton Mifflin, pp. 223–224.
141. Boesch, C. (1992) New elements of a theory of mind in wild chimpanzees. *Behavioral and Brain Sciences* 15(1): 149.
142. Goodall, J. (1986). Social rejection, exclusion, and shunning among the Gombe chimpanzees. *Ethology and Sociobiology* 7(3): 227–236.
143. Mitani, J. C., Amsler, S., and M. Sobolewski (2010) Chimpanzee minds in nature. In E. Lonsdorf, S. Ross, and T. Matsuzawa (eds.) *The chimpanzee mind.* Chicago: University of Chicago Press, p. 181.
144. Goodall, J. (1994) *With love: Ten heart warming stories of chimpanzees in the wild.* New York/London: North-South books.
145. Mitani, J. C., Watts, D. P. and S. J. Amsler (2010). Lethal intergroup aggression leads to territorial expansion in wild chimpanzees. *Current Biology* 20(12): R507–R508.
146. Hess, E. (2008) *Nim Chimpsky: The chimp who would be human.* New York: Bantam.
147. Field research among wild chimpanzees has given us a far greater understanding of the roots of language than the experiments with Nim. Katie Slocombe from the University of York has revealed the significance of gestures in how chimpanzees communicate with each other, for example. This suggests that the origins of language are not only in vocal communication but something more 'multimodal'. See:
Fedurek, P., and K. E. Slocombe (2011) Primate vocal communication: a useful tool for understanding human speech and language evolution? *Human Biology* 83(2): 153–173
Slocombe, K. E., Waller, B. M., and K. Liebal (2011) The language void: the need for multimodality in primate communication research. *Animal Behaviour* 81(5): 919–924.
148. Overing, J. and A. Passes (eds.) (2002) *The anthropology of love and anger: the aesthetics of conviviality in native Amazonia.* London and New York: Routledge.
149. Foley, R. (1995) The adaptive legacy of human evolution: A search for the environment of evolutionary adaptedness. *Evolutionary Anthropology: Issues, News, and Reviews* 4(6), 194–203.
150. Whiten, A. and D. Erdal (2012) The human socio-cognitive niche and its evolutionary origins. *Philosophical Transactions of the Royal Society B: Biological Sciences* 367(1599): 2119–2129.
151. de Waal, F., and F. Lanting (1997) *Bonobo: The forgotten ape.* Berkeley: University of California Press.
152. de Waal, F., and F. Lanting (1997). *Bonobo: The forgotten ape.* Berkeley: University of California Press, p. 34.
153. Anderson, J. R., Kuroshima, H., Takimoto, A., and K. Fujita (2013) Third party social evaluation of humans by monkeys. *Nature communications* 4: 1561.
154. Clay, Z. and F. B. M. De Waal (2013) Development of socio-emotional competence in bonobos. *Proceedings of the National Academy of Sciences* 110(45): 18025–18026.
155. Hare, B., Melis, A. P., Woods, V., Hastings, S., and R Wrangham (2007). Tolerance allows bonobos to outperform chimpanzees on a cooperative task. *Current Biology* 17(7), 619–623.
156. Hare, B., Wobber, V., & Wrangham, R. (2012) The self-domestication hypothesis: evolution of bonobo psychology is due to selection against aggression. *Animal Behaviour* 83(3): 573–585. See also:
Hare, B. (2007) From nonhuman to human mind. What changed and why? *Current Directions in Psychological Science* 16(2): 60–64.

CHAPTER FIVE
157. Paul Mills, unpublished, from 'Shall the bones live?'

158. Stapert, D. (2007) Neanderthal children and their flints. *PalArch, Journal of the Archaeology of Northwest Europe* 1(2): 16–38.
159. Spikins, P. (2002) *Prehistoric People of the Pennines: Reconstructing the lifestyles of Mesolithic hunter-gatherers on Marsden Moor*. Wakefield: West Yorkshire Archaeology Service. See also:
    Spikins, P. (1999) *Mesolithic Northern England: environment, population and settlement*. BAR British Series 283. Archaeo-press, Oxford.
    Bailey, G., and P. Spikins (eds.) (2008) *Mesolithic Europe*. Cambridge: Cambridge University Press.
160. Spikins, P., Conneller, C., Ayestaran, H., and B. Scaife (2002) GIS based interpolation applied to distinguishing occupation phases of early prehistoric sites. *Journal of Archaeological Science* 29(11): 1235–1245.
161. Evans, D. (2001) *Emotion: The science of sentiment*. Oxford: Oxford University Press.
162. Aiello, L. C. and P. Wheeler (1995) The expensive tissue hypothesis. *Current anthropology* 36(2): 199–221.
163. Wrangham, R. (2009) *Catching fire: how cooking made us human*. New York: Basic Books.
164. Dunbar, R. I. M. (2003) The Social Brain: mind, language and society in an evolutionary perspective. *Annual Review of Anthropology* 32: 163–181. See also:
    Dunbar, R. I. M. (2009) The social brain hypothesis and its implications for social evolution. *Annals of human biology* 36(5): 562–572.
165. Humphrey, N. (1984) *Consciousness Regained*. Oxford: Oxford University Press.
166. Bryne, R., and A. Whiten (1988) *Machiavellian intelligence*. London: Clarendon.
167. Jablonka, E., Ginsburg, S., and D. Dor (2012) The co-evolution of language and emotions. *Philosophical Transactions of the Royal Society B* 367(1599): 2152–2159.
168. Dunbar, R. (1998) *Grooming, gossip and the evolution of language*. Harvard: Harvard University Press.
169. Falk, D. (2004) Prelinguistic evolution in early hominins: Whence motherese? *Behavioral and Brain Sciences* 27(4): 491–503.
170. Greenspan, S. I., and S. G. Shanker (2004) *The first idea: how symbols, language, and intelligence evolved from our primate ancestors to modern humans*. Cambridge: Da Capo Press (Perseus Books Group) See also:
    Gross, J. J., and R. A. Thompson (2006) Emotion regulation: Conceptual frameworks, in J. J. Gross. *Handbook of emotion regulation*. London: Guildford Press, pp. 3–26.
171. For a more detailed description see Zollikofer, C. P. E., and M. S. Ponce de León (2013) Pandora's growing box: Inferring the evolution and development of Hominin brains from Endocasts. *Evolutionary Anthropology* 22: 20–33.
172. Pearce, E., Stringer, C. and R. Dunbar (2013) New Insights in the differences in brain organisation between Neanderthals and anatomically modern humans. *Proceedings of the Royal Society B* 280, 1758: 1471–2194.
173. For the emotional differences in tolerance between bonobos and common chimpanzees, see Hare, B. (2007) From non-human to human mind: What changed and why? *Current Directions in Pyschological Science* 16(2): 60–64
    Hare, B. (2007) Tolerance allows bonobos to outperform chimpanzees on a cooperative task. *Current Biology* 17: 619–623.
    Stevens, J. R., Hallinam, E., and M. D. Hauser. (2005). The ecology and evolution of patience in two New World monkeys. *Biology Letters* 1: 223–226, discuss different levels of patience in response to feeding behaviours in New World monkeys.
174. Mithen, S. (1996) *The prehistory of the mind: A search for the origins of art, religion and science*. London: Thames and Hudson, p. 1.

175. Van Reybrouck, D. (1998) Imaging and imagining the Neanderthal: the role of technical drawings in archaeology. *Antiquity* 72(275), 56–64.
David Van Reybrouck, in his recent volume *From primitives to primates: a history of ethnographic and primatological analogies in the study of prehistory* (2013, Havertown: Sidestone Press), highlights that many preconceptions have influenced our image of human ancestors. He also argues that in recent years primates have replaced modern hunter-gatherers as the 'primitives' in our imagined past.
176. Wynn, T., and F. Coolidge (2012) *How to think like a Neanderthal*. Oxford: Oxford University Press.
177. Pettitt, P. (2000) Neanderthal lifecycles: Developmental and social phases in the lives of the last Archaics. *World Archaeology*, Vol. 31, No. 3, pp. 351–366, on p. 355.
178. Spikins, P., Hitchens, G., and A. Needham (2014) The cradle of thought? Growth, learning, play and attachment in Neanderthal children. *Oxford Journal of Archaeology* 33(2): 111–134.
179. Zollikofer, C. P. E., and M. S. Ponce de León (2010) The evolution of human ontogenies. *Seminars in Cell and Developmental Biology* 21: 441–452.
180. Colombet, P., Bayle, P., Crevecoer, I., Ferrié, J.-G., and B. Maureille (2012) New Mousterian neonates from the south-west of France, *PESHE* 1: 57.
181. Berger, D., and E. Trinkaus (1995) Patterns of trauma amongst Neanderthals. *Journal of Archaeological Science* 22: 841–852.
182. Hrdy, S. B. (1999) *Mother nature: A history of mothers, infants, and natural selection*. New York: Pantheon.
183. Speth, D. 2004. Newsflash: Negative evidence convicts Neanderthals of gross mental incompetence. *World Archaeology* 36(4): 519–526, on p. 525.

CHAPTER SIX
184. Doyle, A. C. (1892). *The Adventures of Sherlock Holmes*. London, England: George Newnes Ltd. Adventure 3: A Case of Identity, p.8.
185. Created by Kacie Kinzer.
186. Rosenthal-von der Pütten, A. M., Krämer, N. C., Hoffmann, L., Sobieraj, S., and S. C. Eimler (2013) An experimental study on emotional reactions towards a robot. *International Journal of Social Robotics* 5(1): 17–34.
187. Rosenthal-von der Pütten, A. M., Schulte, F. P., Eimler, S. C., Sobieraj, S., Hoffmann, L., Maderwald, S., Brand, M., and N. C. Krämer (2014) Investigations on empathy towards humans and robots using psychophysiological measures and fMRI. *Computers in Human Behaviour,* 33: 201–212.
188. Paper in preparation: 'Self-compassion and material objects' (Spikins, P. A., Slocombe, K., and A. Needham) funded by Chronic Diseases and Disorders Fund (Wellcome Trust) at the University of York under the project title. '"Lost in Translation": Autism and material culture'.
189. Emma Swain, 'The bear essentials in a time of war', *Maitland Mercury*, 10 November 2012.
190. Kahlenberg, S. M., and R. W. Wrangham (2010) Sex differences in chimpanzees' use of sticks as play objects resemble those of children. *Current Biology* 20(24): R1067–R1068.
191. Decety, J., Norman, G. J., Berntson, G. G., and J. T. Cacioppo (2012) A neurobehavioral evolutionary perspective on the mechanisms underlying human empathy. *Progress in Neurobiology* 98(1): 38–48
Decety, J., and M. Svetlova (2012) Putting together phylogenetic and ontogenetic perspectives on empathy. *Developmental Cognitive Neuroscience* 2(1): 1–24.
192. The anterior cingulate cortex, anterior midcingulate cotex, supplementary motor area,

amygdala, brainstem and periaqueductal gary from a circuit which responds to the perceptions of other's distress (see Decety et al., 2012)

193. Miller, S. C., Kennedy, C., DeVoe, D., Hickey, M., Nelson, T., and L. Kogan (2009) An examination of changes in oxytocin levels in men and women before and after interaction with a bonded dog. *Anthrozoos: A Multidisciplinary Journal of The Interactions of People & Animals* 22(1): 31–42.

194. Kurdek, L. A. (2008) Pet dogs as attachment figures. *Journal of Social and Personal Relationships* 25(2): 247–266; Kurdek, L. A. (2009) Pet dogs as attachment figures for adult owners. *Journal of Family Psychology* 23(4): 439.

195. The great apes or higher primates include humans, chimpanzees, gorillas and orang-utans. Gibbons are also closely related and some would include gibbons within the great apes. We are all large tailless primates with highly manipulate hands and large brains.

196. Preston, S. D., and F. De Waal (2002) Empathy: Its ultimate and proximate bases. *Behavioral and Brain Sciences* 25(1): 1–20.

197. Warneken, F., and M. Tomasello (2006) Altruistic helping in human infants and young chimpanzees. *Science* 311(5765): 1301–1303.

198. Silk, J. B., Brosnan, S. F., Vonk, J., Henrich, J., Povinelli, D. J., Richardson, A. S., Lambeth, S. P., Mascaro, J., and S. J. Schapiro (2005) Chimpanzees are indifferent to the welfare of unrelated group members. *Nature* 437 (7063): 1357–1359.

199. See, for example, Batson, C. D. (2014) The altruism question: Toward a social-psychological answer. *Psychology Press* for a comprehensive review, as well as Goleman, D. (2006) *Social intelligence.* New York: Bantam Books.

200. Henrich, J., Boyd, R., Bowles, S., Camerer, C., Fehr, E., Gintis, H., and R. McElreath (2001) In search of homo economicus: behavioral experiments in 15 small-scale societies. *American Economic Review*, 91(2): 73–78.

201. See Decety et al., 2012.

202. Goleman, D. (2006) *Social intelligence.* New York: Bantam Books.

203. Keltner, D., Marsh, J., and J. A. Smith (eds.) (2010) *The Compassionate Instinct.* New York and London: W. W. Norton & Company.

204. Lobmaier, J. S., Sprengelmeyer, R., Wiffen, B., and D. I. Perrett (2010) Female and male responses to cuteness, age and emotion in infant faces. *Evolution and Human Behavior* 31(1): 16–21.

205. Sherman, G. D., Haidt, J., and J. A. Coan (2009) Viewing cute images increases behavioural carefulness. *Emotion* 9(2): 282–286. See also Sherman, G. D., Haidt, J., Iyer, R. and J. A. Coan (2013) Individual differences in the physical embodiment of care: Prosocially oriented women respond to cuteness by becoming more physically careful. *Emotion* 13(1): 151–158.

206. Chaminade, T., Zecca, M., Blakemore, S. J., Takanishi, A., Frith, C. D., Micera, S., Dario,P., Rizzolatti,G., Gallese, V., and M. A. Umiltà (2010) Brain response to a humanoid robot in areas implicated in the perception of human emotional gestures. *PloS one* 5(7): e11577.

207. Sherman, G. D., and J. Haidt (2011) Cuteness and disgust: the humanizing and dehumanizing effects of emotion. *Emotion Review* 3(3): 245–251.

208. Hodder, I. (2012) *Entangled: An archaeology of the relationships between humans and things.* Maldon, MA: Wiley Blackwell.

209. Mikulincer, M, Shaver, P. R., Gillath, O., and R. A. Nitzberg (2005) Attachment, Caregiving and Altrusim: Boosting Attachment security increases attachment and helping. *Journal of Personal and Social Psychology* 89(5): 817–839
Mikulincer, M. Gillath, O., Halevy, V., Avihou, N., Avidan, S., and N. Eshkoli (2001) Attachment theory and reactions to other's needs: Evidence that activation of the sense of attachment security promotes empathetic responses. *Journal of Personality and Social Psychology* 81(6): 1205–1224.

210. Steklis, H. D., and R. D. Lane (2012) The Unique Human Capacity for Emotional Awareness: Psychological, Neuroanatomical, Comparative and Evolutionary Perspectives. In S. Watanabe and S. Kuczaj (eds.) *Emotions of Animals and Humans*. Japan: Springer, pp. 165–205.

211. Depue, R. A. and J. V. Morrone-Strupinsky (2005) A neurobehavioural model of affiliative bonding: implications for conceptualising a human trait of affiliation. *Behavioral and Brain Sciences* 28(3): 313–350.

212. White, R. (2007) Systems of personal ornamentation in the Early Upper Palaeolithic: Methodological challenges and new observations. In C. Stringer (ed.) *Rethinking the Human Revolution: New Behavioural and Biological Perspectives on the Origin and Dispersal of Modern Humans.* Cambridge: McDonald Institute for Archaeological Research, pp. 287–302.

213. Changeux, J. -P. (2009) Presentation: Neurobiology, Neurology and Art and Aesthetics, Evolutionary Origins of Art and Aesthetics, UCTV University of California CARTA online series. See also, Changeux, J.-P. (1994) Art and neuroscience. *Leonardo* 27: 189–201.

214. Hodgson, D. (2011) The first appearance of symmetry in the human lineage: where perception meets art. *Symmetry* 3(1): 37–53.

215. Freedberg, D., and V. Gallese (2007) Motion, emotion and empathy in aesthetic experience. *Trends in Cognitive Sciences* 11(5): 197–203.

216. See, for example, Damasio, A. (1994) *Descartes' error: Emotion, reason and the human brain.* New York: Putnam.

217. Bechara, A., Damasio, H. and A. R. Damasio (2000) Emotion, decision making and the orbitofrontal cortex. *Cerebral Cortex* 10(3): 295–307
Sanfey, A. G., Rilling, J. R., Aronson, J. A. Nystrom, L. E., and J. D. Cohen (2003) The neural basis of economic decision-making in the Ultimatum Game. *Science* 300(5626): 1755–1758.

218. Bone, J., Hey, J. D., and J. Suckling (2009) Do people plan? *Experimental Economics* 12(1): 12–25.

219. Gilbert, P. (2003) Evolution, social roles, and the differences in shame and guilt. *Social Research: An International Quarterly* 70(4): 1205–1230.

220. McCullough, M. E., Kilpatrick, S. D., Emmons, R. A., and D. B. Larson (2001) Is gratitude a moral affect? *Psychological bulletin* 127(2): 249
Bartlett, M. Y., and D. DeSteno (2006) Gratitude and prosocial behaviour: helping when it costs you. *Psychological science* 17(4): 319–325.

221. Fehr, E. and S. Gächter (2002) Altruistic punishment in humans. *Nature* 415(6868): 137–140. See also:
De Quervain, D. J. F., Fischbacher, U., Treyer, V., Schellhammer, M., Schnyder, U., Buck, A., and E. Fehr (2004). The neural basis of altruistic punishment. *Science.* 305(5688): 1254–1258.

222. Zell, E., Warriner, A. B., and D. Albarracín (2012) Splitting of the Mind: When the You I Talk to is Me and Needs Commands. *Social psychological and personality science* 3(5): 549–555.

223. Wiessner, P. (2002) Taking the risk out of risky transactions: a forager's dilemma. In F. K. Salter (ed.) *Risky Transactions: Trust, Kinship, and Ethnicity. Oxford: Berghahn Books*, pp. 21–43.

224. Grant, A. M., and F. Gino (2010) A little thanks goes a long way: Explaining why gratitude expressions motivate pro-social behaviour. *Journal of Personality and Social Psychology* 98(6): 946–955. See also:
DeSteno, D., Bartlett, M. Y., Baumann, J., Williams, L., and L. Dickens (2010) Gratitude as moral sentiment: emotion guided cooperation in economic exchange. *Emotion* 10(2): 289–293

McCullough, M. E., Kilpatrick, S. D., Emmons, R. A., and D. B. Larson (2001) Is gratitude moral affect? *Psychological Bulletin* 127(2): 249–266.

225. Nowak, M. A., and S. Roch (2007) Upstream reciprocity and the evolution of gratitude. *Proceedings of the Royal Society B: Biological Sciences* 274(1610): 605–610.

226. McCullough, M. E., Kilpatrick, S. D., Emmons, R. A., and D. B. Larson (2001) Is gratitude moral affect? *Psychological Bulletin* 127(2): 249–266.

227. Steklis, H. D., and R. D. Lane (2012) The Unique Human Capacity for Emotional Awareness: Psychological, Neuroanatomical, Comparative and Evolutionary Perspectives. In S. Watanabe and S. Kuczaj (eds.) *Emotions of Animals and Humans*. Japan: Springer, pp. 165–205.

228. Gailliot, M. T., and R. F. Baumeister (2007) Self-regulation and sexual restraint: Dispositionally and temporarily poor self-regulatory abilities contribute to failures at restraining sexual behaviour. *Personality and Social Psychology Bulletin* 33(2): 173–186. See also:
Metchalfe, J., and W. Mischel (1999) A hot/cool system analysis of delay of gratification: Dynamics of willpower, *Psychological Review* 106(1): 3–19.

229. Graves, R. R., Lupo, A. C., McCarthy, R. C., Wescott, D. J., and D. Cunningham (2010) Just how strapping was KNM-WT 15000? *Journal of Human Evolution* 59(5): 542–554.

CHAPTER SEVEN

230. Erich, F. (1973) *The Anatomy of Human Destructiveness.* New York: Holt, Rinehart and Winston.

231. France Moore Lappe on 'Creating an Ecology of Hope', interview by Mark Karlin for *Truthout*, Monday 26 December 2011.

232. Porges, S. W. (2003) The polyvagal theory: Phylogenetic contributions to social behavior. *Physiology & Behavior* 79(3): 503–513.

233. McCullough, M. E., Pedersen, E. J., Schroder, J. M., Tabak, B. A., and C. S. Carver (2012) Harsh childhood environmental characteristics predict exploitation and retaliation in humans. *Proceedings of the Royal Society B Biological Sciences* 280(1750): 2012–2104.

234. Gilbert, P., McEwan, K., Bellew, R., Mills, A., and C. Gale (2010) The dark side of competition: How competitive behaviour and striving to avoid inferiority are linked to depression, anxiety, stress and self-harm. *Psychology and Psychotherapy: Theory, research and practice* 82(2): 123–136.

235. See Mikulincer, M., and P. R. Shaver (2007). *Attachment in adulthood: Structure, dynamics, and change.* New York NY: Guilford Press.

236. Briggs, J. L. (1998) *Inuit Morality Play, the emotional education of a three-year-old.* Yale: Yale University Press.

237. Hewlett, B. S., Fouts, H. N., Boyette, A. H., and B. L. Hewlett (2011) Social learning among Congo Basin hunter-gatherers. *Philosophical Transactions of the Royal Society B* 366(1567): 1168–1178.

238. Charlton, B. G. (2007) Alienation, recovered animism and altered states of consciousness. *Medical Hypotheses* 68(4): 727–731.

239. Kopenawa, D. (2013) *The Falling Sky: Words of a Yanomami shaman.* Harvard: Belknap, p. 12.

240. Charlton, B. (2000) *Psychiatry and the human condition.* London: Radcliffe Medical.

241. Bourke, J. (2000) *An intimate history of killing: Face to face killing in twentieth century warfare.* New York: Basic Books.

242. Bourke, J. (2000) *An intimate history of killing: Face to face killing in twentieth century warfare.* New York: Basic Books, p. 75.

243. Marshall, S. L. A. (2000) *Men against fire: the problem of battle command.* Oklahoma: University of Oklahoma Press, p. 72.
244. De Quervain, D. J. F., Fischbacher, U., Treyer, V., Schellhammer, M., Schnyder, U., Buck, A., and E. Fehr (2004) The neural basis of altruistic punishment. *Science* 305(5688): 1254–1258.
245. Sherman, G., and J. Haidt (2011) Cuteness and disgust: The humanizing and dehumanizing effects of emotion. *Emotion Review* 3(3): 245–251.
246. Binding, K. And A. Hoche. (1992) Permitting the Destruction of Unworthy Life: Its Extent and Form. *Issues in Law and Medicine*, Vol. 8(2): 231–265, on p. 231.
247. Evans, Suzanne E. (2004) *Forgotten Crimes: The Holocaust and People with Disabilities.* Chicago: Ivan R. Dee. See also:
    Kessler, K. (2007) Physicians and the Nazi euthanasia program. *International Journal of Mental Health* 36(1): 4–16.
248. Arendt, H. (2006) *Eichmann in Jerusalem: A Report on the Banality of Evil.* New York: Penguin classics.
249. Colaianni, A. (2012) A long shadow: Nazi doctors, moral vulnerability and contemporary medical culture. Journal of medical ethics, 38(7), 435–438 cites Lifton, R. J. (2000) *The Nazi doctors: Medical killing and the psychology of genocide.* New York: Basic Books, p. 195.
250. Caputo, P. (1999) *A rumor of war.* London: Random House.
251. Boyle, R. (1972) *The flower of the dragon: The breakdown of the US army in Vietnam.* San Francisco: Ramparts Press.
252. Bourke, J. (1999) *An intimate history of killing: Face-to-face killing in twentieth-century warfare.* New York: Basic Books, p. 172.
253. Iserson, K. V. (1994) *Death to dust: What happens to dead bodies?* Tucson, AZ: Galen Press, p. 382.
254. Petty, B. M. (ed.) (2002) *Saipan: Oral Histories of the Pacific War.* Jefferson, N.C: McFarland, p. 119.
255. Thorpe, I. J. (2003) Anthropology, archaeology, and the origin of warfare. *World Archaeology* 35(1): 145–165.
256. Hernández-Wolfe, P. (2011) Altruism born of suffering: How Columbian human rights activists transform pain into pro-social action. *Journal of Humanistic Psychology* 51(2): 229–249.
257. Hernández-Wolfe, P. (2011) Altruism born of suffering: How Columbian human rights activists transform pain into pro-social action, *Journal of Humanistic Psychology* 51: 229.
258. Oliner, S. P. (2004) *Do unto others: Extraordinary acts of ordinary people.* Boulder CO: Westview Press. See also:
    Bocchiaro, P., and P. G. Zimbardo (2010) Defying unjust authority: An exploratory study. *Current Psychology* 29(2): 155–170
    Zimbardo, P. (2011) Why the world needs heroes. *Europe's Journal of Psychology* 7(3): 402–407.
259. Schnall, S., Roper, J., and D. M. Fessler (2010) Elevation leads to altruistic behavior. *Psychological Science,* 21(3): 315–320. See also:
    Algoe, S. B., and J. Haidt. (2009) Witnessing excellence in action: The 'other-praising' emotions of elevation, gratitude, and admiration. *The Journal of Positive Psychology* 4(2): 105–127
    Haidt, J. (2003) Elevation and the positive psychology of morality. In C. L. M. Keyes and J. Haidt (ed.) *Flourishing: Positive psychology and the life well-lived.* Washington DC: American Psychological Association, pp. 275–289.

CHAPTER EIGHT

260. Advice to a new young tutor at Cambridge by F. J. Foakes Jackson (Dean of Jesus College, Cambridge, 1895–1916).

261. Brosnan, S. F., and F. B. De Waal (2003) Monkeys reject unequal pay. *Nature* 425(6955): 297–299.

262. Brosnan, S. F. (2013) Justice-and fairness-related behaviors in nonhuman primates. *Proceedings of the National Academy of Sciences* 110 (Supplement 2): 10416–10423.

263. Bartal, I. B. A., Decety, J., and P. Mason (2011) Empathy and pro-social behavior in rats. *Science* 334(6061): 1427–1430.

264. Schino, G., and F. Aureli (2010) Primate reciprocity and its cognitive requirements. *Evolutionary Anthropology: Issues, News, and Reviews* 19(4): 130–135.

265. Flack, J. C., and F. B. De Waal (2000) Any animal whatever. Darwinian building blocks of morality in monkeys and apes. *Journal of Consciousness Studies* 7(1–2): 1–2.

266. De Waal, F. (2011) What is an animal emotion? *Annals of the New York Academy of Sciences* 1224(1): 191–206.

267. De Waal, F. (2011) What is animal emotion? *Annals of the New York Academy of Sciences* 1224(1): 191–206.

268. James, W. (1884). II.—What is an emotion? *Mind*, (34): 188–205, on p. 193.

269. Pickover, C. (1999) *Strange brains and genius: The secret lives of eccentric scientists and madmen.* London: Harper Perennial, p. 33.

270. Genius though he was, Tesla's attitude towards affection didn't seem to inspire much human love. In many ways he was a sad figure. He once claimed a pigeon loved him as could any woman, spending $2,000 on mending its wing. He didn't marry or have children, and rather lacked close friends, dying alone of coronary thrombosis in the hotel room in which he lived. He wasn't found until two days later.

271. Darwin, C. (1982 [1871]) *The descent of man.* New York: Appleton, pp. 71–2.

272. Darwin, C. (1871) *The descent of man.* 2 vols. London, p. 85.

273. James, W. (1884). II.—*What is an emotion? Mind.* (34): 188–205, on pp. 195–196.

274. James, W. (1890) *The principles of psychology.* Cambridge MA: Harvard University Press, p. 31.

275. While early ideas about the environments in which hominins evolved were dominated by the idea of entirely open grasslands, we have come to appreciate not only that the environments of early homo species were likely to have been more open, a more mosaic savannah environment, but that those of *Australopithecus* and early species may well have been substantially wooded. See Dominguez-Rodrigo, M. (2014) Is the 'Savanna hypothesis' a dead concept for explaining the emergence of the earliest hominins? *Current Anthropology* 55(1): 59–81. There is no doubt, nonetheless, that the environments, particularly of early homo species, were much more open, more risky and more dangerous places to live.

276. Acevedo, B. P., Aron, A., Fisher, H. E., and L. L. Brown (2012) Neural correlates of long-term intense romantic love. *Social cognitive and affective neuroscience* 7(2): 145–159.
    Fisher, H (2006) The drive to love: The neural mechanism for mate selection. In R. J. Sternberg and K. Weis (eds.) *The new psychology of love.* 2nd Edition. New Haven: Yale University Press, pp. 87–115.

277. Buss, D. M. (2003) *The evolution of desire: Strategies of human mating.* New York: Basic Books.

278. Miller, G. (2000) *The mating mind.* New York: Doubleday.

279. Fredrickson, B. L., Cohn, M. A., Coffey, K. A., Pek, J., and S. M. Finkel (2008) Open hearts build lives: positive emotions, induced through loving-kindness meditation, build consequential personal resources. *Journal of Personality and Social Psychology* 95(5): 1045–1062; Garlan, E. L., Fredrickson, B., Kring, A, M., Johnson, D. P. Meyer, P. S. and D. L. Penn (2010) Upward spirals of positive emotions counter downward spirals of negativity: Insights from the broaden-and-build theory and affective neuroscience on the treatment of emotion dysfunctions and deficits in psychopathology. *Clinical Psychology Review* 30(7): 849–864.

280. Hewlett, B., and B. Hewlett (2013) Hunter-gatherer adolescence. *Conference on Hunting and Gathering Societies* (CHAGS), Liverpool.

281. Dominguez-Rodrigo, M. (2014) Is the 'Savanna hypothesis' a dead concept for explaining the emergence of the earliest hominins? *Current Anthropology* 55(1): 59–81.

282. Potts, R. (2013) Hominin evolution in settings of strong environmental variability. *Quaternary Science Reviews* 73: 1–13.

283. Frank, R. H. (1988) *Passions within reason: The strategic role of the emotions.* New York: W. W. Norton & Company.

284. Gottman, J. M. (2011) *The science of trust: Emotional attunement for couples.* New York: W. W. Norton & Company. See also, Driver, J. L., and J. M. Gottman (2004). Daily marital interactions and positive affect during marital conflict among newlywed couples. *Family Process* 43(3): 301–314.

285. Brown, B. (2012) *Daring greatly: How the courage to be vulnerable transforms the way we live, love, parent, and lead.* New York: Gotham Books.

286. Whiten, A., and D. Erdal (2012) The human socio-cognitive niche and its evolutionary origins. *Philosophical Transactions of the Royal Society B: Biological Sciences* 367(1599): 2119–2129.

287. Nesse, R. M. (2001) Natural selection and the capacity for subjective commitment. In R. M. Nesse (ed.) *Evolution and the Capacity for Commitment,* Vol. 3. New York: Russell Sage Foundation, pp. 1–44.

288. Kahlenberg, S. M., and R. W. Wrangham (2010) Sex differences in chimpanzees' use of sticks as play objects resemble those of children. *Current Biology* 20(24): R1067–R1068.

289. Perry, S., Godoy, I., and W. Lammers (2012) The Lomas Barbudal Monkey Project: two decades of research on Cebus capucinus. In Kappeler, P. M. and D. P. Watts (eds.) *Long-term field studies of primates.* Long-Term Field Studies of Primates. New York, NY: Springer, pp. 141–163.

290. Wenban-Smith, F. (2004) Handaxe typology and Lower Palaeolithic cultural development: ficrons, cleavers and two giant handaxes from Cuxton. *Lithics* 25: 11–21, on p. 14.

291. Nowak, M., and K. Sigmund (2005) Evolution of indirect reciprocity. *Nature Reviews* 437(27): 1291–1298.

292. See Gintis, H., Bowles, S., Boyd, R., and E. Fehr (2003) Explaining altruistic behavior in humans. *Evolution and Human Behavior* 24(3): 153–172.

293. Dunbar, R. (2004) Gossip in evolutionary perspective. *Review of General Psychiatry* 8(2): 100–110.

PART THREE
CHAPTER NINE
294. From 'The Road Not Taken' by Robert Frost (1920).

295. Potts, R. (2013) Hominin evolution in settings of strong environmental variability. *Quaternary Science Reviews* 73: 1–13.

296. As I have done in this text for simplicity.

297. Whiten, A., and D. Erdal, D. (2012) The human socio-cognitive niche and its evolutionary origins. *Philosophical Transactions of the Royal Society B: Biological Sciences* 367(1599): 2119–2129.

298. DeSilva, J. (2011) A shift towards birthing relatively large infants early in human evolution. *Proceedings of the National Academy of Sciences* 108(3): 1022–1027.

299. Kohn, M., and S. Mithen (1999) Handaxes: products of sexual selection? *Antiquity* 73: 518–26.

300. Spikins, P. A. (2012) Goodwill Hunting? Debates over the meaning of handaxe form reconsidered. *World Archaeology* 44(3): 378–392.

301. Currie, G. (2011) The Master of the Masek Beds: Handaxes, art and the minds of early humans. In E. Schellekans and P. Goldie (eds.) *The Aesthetic Mind: Philosophy and Psychology*. Oxford: Oxford University Press, p. 9.

302. Currie, G. (2009) Art of the Palaeolithic. In S. Davies, K. M. Higgins, R. Hopkins,R. Stecker, and D. Cooper (eds,) *A Companion to Aesthetics* Vol. 68. Oxford: Wiley-Blackwell, p. 6.

303. Hodgson, D. (2011) The first appearance of symmetry in the human lineage. *Symmetry* 3(1): 37–53, on p. 35.

304. Pope, M., Russel,es K., and K. Watson (2006) Biface form and structured behaviour in the Acheulean. *Lithics: The Journal of the Lithic Studies Society* 27: 44–57.

305. Ashton, N., and M.J. White (2003) Bifaces and raw materials: flexible flaking in the British Earlier Palaeolithic. In M. Soressi and H. Dibble (eds.) *From Prehistoric bifaces to human behaviour: multiple approaches to the study of bifacial technology.* Philadelphia: University of Pennsylvania Museum of Archaeology and Anthropology, pp. 109–123.

306. Wynn, T. (1995) Handaxe enigmas. *World Archaeology* 27: 10–24, on p. 13.

307. Feliks, J. (1988) The impact of fossils on the development of visual representation. *Rock Art Research* 15: 109–134.

308. James, W. (1890) *The principles of psychology*. Cambridge MA: Harvard University Press, p. 31.

309. Bowles, S. (2006) Group competition, reproductive leveling, and the evolution of human altruism. *Science* 314(5805): 1569–1572.

310. Opie, C., Atkinson, Q. D., Dunbar, R., and S. Shultz (2013) Male infanticide leads to social monogamy in primates. *Proceedings of the National Academy of Sciences* 110(33): 13328–13332.

311. Saladié, P., Huguet, R., Rodríguez-Hidalgo, A., Cáceres, I., Esteban-Nadal, M., Arsuaga, J. L., Bermúdez de Castro, J.- M., and E. Carbonell (2012) Intergroup cannibalism in the European Early Pleistocene: The range expansion and imbalance of power hypotheses. *Journal of Human Evolution* 63(5): 682–695.

312. Hardy, K., Buckley, S., Collins, M. J., Estalrrich, A., Brothwell, D., Copeland, L., and A. Rosas (2012). Neanderthal medics? Evidence for food, cooking, and medicinal plants entrapped in dental calculus *Naturwissenschaften* 99(8): 617–626.

313. Scott, B., Bates, M., Bates, R., Conneller, C., Pope, M. I., Shaw, A., and G. Smith (2014) A new view from La Cotte de St. Brelade, Jersey. *Antiquity*: 88(339): 13–29.

314. Raichlen, D. A., Armstrong, H., and D. E. Lieberman (2011) Calcaneus length determines running economy: implications for endurance running performance in modern humans and Neandertals. *Journal of Human Evolution* 60(3): 299–308.

315. Kuhn, S. and M. Stiner (2006) What's a Mother to Do? *Current Anthropology* 47(6): 953–981.

316. Hayden, B. (2012) Neanderthal social structure? *Oxford Journal of Archaeology* 31(1): 1–26.

317. Vaquero, M., Vallverdú, J., Rosell, J., Pastó, I., and E. Allué (2001) Neandertal

behavior at the middle Palaeolithic site of Abric Romani, Capellades, Spain. *Journal of Field Archaeology* 28(1–2): 93–114.

318. Henry, D. O. (2003) *Neanderthals in the Levant: behavioral organization and the beginnings of human modernity.* New York: Continuum International Publishing Group.

319. Demay, L., Péan, S., and M. Patou-Mathis (2012) Mammoths used as food and building resources by Neanderthals: Zooarchaeological study applied to layer 4, Molodova I (Ukraine). *Quaternary International* 276: 212–226.

320. Walker, M. J., López-Martínez, M., Ortega-Rodригánez, J., Haber-Uriarte, M., López-Jiménez, A., Avilés-Fernández, A., Polo-Camacho, J. L., Campillo-Boj, M., García-Torres, J., García. J. S. C., Nicolás-del Toro, M. S., and T. Rodríguez-Estrella (2012) The excavation of buried articulated Neanderthal skeletons at Sima de los Palmos, Murcia, Spain. *Quaternary International* 259: 7–21.

321. Shea, J. J. (2006) Child's play: reflections on the invisibility of children in the Paleolithic record. *Evolutionary Anthropology: Issues, News, and Reviews* 15(6): 212–216.

322. Cordoni, G. and E.Palagi (2011) Ontogenetic trajectories of chimpanzee social play: similarities with humans. *PloS one* 6(11): e27344.

323. Lindsey, E. W., & Colwell, M. J. (2003) Preschoolers' emotional competence: Links to pretend and physical play. *Child Study Journal* 33(1): 39–52.

324. Pettitt, P. and M. White (2012) *The British Palaeolithic: Human Societies at the Edge of the Pleistocene World.* New York: Routledge, p. 200.

325. Croxall, E., and E. H. M. Sterck (2012) Neanderthal territoriality: an ecological approach. *PESHE* 1: 62.

326. Spinapolice, E. E. (2012) Raw material economy in Salento (Apulia, Italy): new perspectives on Neanderthal mobility patterns. *Journal of Archaeological Science* 39(3): 680–689.

327. Féblot-Augustins, J. (1993) Mobility strategies in the late Middle Palaeolithic of central Europe and western Europe: elements of stability and variability. *Journal of Anthropological Archaeology* 12(3): 211–265.

328. Lalueza-Fox, C., Rosas, A., Estalrrich, A., Gigli, E., Campos, P. F., García-Tabernero, A., ... and M. de la Rasilla (2011) Genetic evidence for patrilocal mating behavior among Neandertal groups. *Proceedings of the National Academy of Sciences* 108(1): 250–253.

329. Hublin, J. J. and W. Roebroeks (2009) Ebb and flow or regional extinctions? On the character of Neandertal occupation of northern environments. *Comptes Rendus Palevol* 8(5): 503–509.

330. Spikins, P., Hitchens, G., Needham, A. and H. Rutherford (2014) The cradle of thought: growth, learning, play and attachment in Neanderthal children. *Oxford Journal of Archaeology* 33(2): 111–134.

331. Goodall, J. (2010) *Through a window: My thirty years with the chimpanzees of Gombe.* New York: Houghton Mifflin Harcourt.

332. Hublin, J. J., Talamo, S., Julien, M., David, F., Connet, N., Bodu, P., and M. P. Richards (2012) Radiocarbon dates from the Grotte du Renne and Saint-Césaire support a Neandertal origin for the Châtelperronian. *Proceedings of the National Academy of Sciences* 109(46): 18743–18748.

333. Zilhão, J. (2000). The Ebro frontier: a model for the late extinction of Iberian Neanderthals. In C. Stringer, N. Barton and C. Finlayson (eds.) (2000). Neanderthals on the Edge. Oxford: Oxbow, pp. 111–121.

CHAPTER TEN

334. Tenzin Gyatso, 14th Dalai Lama.

335. Gifford–Gonzalez, D. (1993) You can hide, but you can't run: Representations of women's work in illustrations of Palaeolithic life. *Visual Anthropology Review* 9(1): 22–41.

336. Hrdy, S. B. (2000) *Mother nature: Maternal instincts and how they shape the human species*. London and New York: Ballantine Books.

337. Shang, H. and E. Trinkaus, E. (2008) An ectocranial lesion on the Middle Pleistocene human cranium from Hulu Cave, Nanjing, China. *American Journal of Physical Anthropology* 135(4): 431–437.

338. Wood, B. (2013) The role of food-sharing in Hadza's children's social development. *Conference on Hunting and Gathering Societies* (CHAGS), Liverpool.

339. Kamura, F. (2013) Rethinking egalitarianism, *Conference on Hunting and Gathering Societies* (CHAGS), Liverpool.

340. Lambek, M., and A. Strathern (eds.) (1998) *Bodies and persons: Comparative perspectives from Africa and Melanesia*. Cambridge: Cambridge University Press.

341. Fowler, C. (2004) *The archaeology of personhood: an anthropological approach*. London: Routledge.

342. Overing, J., and A. Passes (eds.) (2002) *The anthropology of love and anger: the aesthetics of conviviality in native Amazonia*. London: Routledge.

343. Hewlett, B. S., Fouts, H. N., Boyette, A. H., and B. L. Hewlett (2011) Social learning among Congo Basin hunter–gatherers. *Philosophical Transactions of the Royal Society B: Biological Sciences* 366(1567): 1168–1178, on pp. 1171–1172.

344. Fouts, H. N., & Lamb, M. E. (2009) Cultural and developmental variation in toddlers' interactions with other children in two small-scale societies in Central Africa. *International Journal of Developmental Science* 3(4): 389–407.

345. Hewlett, B. L. (2005) Vulnerable lives: death, loss and grief among Aka and Ngandu adolescents of the Central African Republic. In B. S. Hewlett and M. E. Lamb (eds.) *Hunter-gatherer childhoods: evolutionary, developmental and cultural perspectives*. New Brunswick, NJ: Aldine Transaction, pp. 322–342.

346. Hewlett, B. S., Lamb, M. E., Leyendecker, B., & Schölmerich, A. (2000). Internal working models, trust, and sharing among foragers 1. *Current Anthropology* 41(2): 287–297.

347. Hewlett, B. S., Fouts, H. N., Boyette, A. H. and B. L. Hewlett (2011) Social learning among Congo Basin hunter-gatherers. *Philosophical Transactions of the Royal Society B: Biological Sciences* 366(1567): 1168–1178, on pp. 1171–1172.

348. Kobutaka, K. (2013) Hunting gathering culture and school education, comparative studies on Baka children in 1990s and 2010s. *Conference on Hunting and Gathering Societies* (CHAGS), Liverpool.

349. Porr, M., & Bell, H. R. (2012) 'Rock-art', 'Animism' and two-way thinking: Towards a complementary epistemology in the understanding of material culture and 'rock-art' of hunting and gathering people. *Journal of Archaeological Method and Theory* 19(1): 161–205 citing Bell, H. R. (2009) *Storymen*. Cambridge: Cambridge University Press

350. Kopenawa, D. (2012) *The Falling Sky: Words of a Yanomami shaman*. Harvard: Belknap, pp. 354–355.

351. Charlton, B. G. (2007) Alienation, recovered animism and altered states of consciousness. *Medical Hypotheses* 68(4): 727–731.

352. Mowaljarlai, D., and J. Malnic (1993) *Yorro Yorro—Everything standing up alive. Spirit of the Kimberley*. Broome: Magabala Books Aboriginal Corporation, p. 54.

353. James Deetz used the phase 'In small things forgotten' as the title for his classic work on the importance of small, apparently unimportant clues such as shards of pottery, inscriptions on gravestones and cutlery to understanding what early American life was really like. See Deetz, J. (1977) *In small things forgotten*. New York: Doubleday.

354. Stapert, D. (2007) Finger flutings by Palaeolithic children in Rouffignac Cave: comments on a paper by Sharpe and Van Gelder. *Antiquity* 81(312): 343–363.

355. Guthrie, R. D. (2005) *The nature of Paleolithic art*. Chicago: University of Chicago Press.

356. Van Gelder, L., and K. Sharpe, K. (2009). Women and girls as Upper Palaeolithic cave 'artists': Deciphering the sexes of finger fluters in Rouffignac Cave. *Oxford Journal of Archaeology* 28(4): 323–333. See also Sharpe, K., and L. Van Gelder, L. (2006) Evidence for cave marking by Palaeolithic children. *Antiquity* 80(310): 937–947.

357. Bahn, P. (2007) *Cave art: A guide to the decorated ice age caves of Europe*. Francis Lincoln Limited: London, p. 135.

358. Moullin, S., Waldfogel, J., and E. Washbrook (2014) *Baby bonds: Parenting, attachment and a secure base for children*. Report for The Sutton Trust, London.

359. For more details, see: Porges, S. W. (2003) The polyvagal theory: Phylogenetic contributions to social behavior. *Physiology & Behavior* 79(3): 503–513; Porges, S. W. (2011) *The Polyvagal Theory: Neurophysiological foundations of emotions, attachment, communication, and self-regulation (Norton Series on Interpersonal Neurobiology)*. New York: W. W. Norton & Company.

360. Formicola, V. (2007) From the Sunghir children to the Romito Dwarf. *Current Anthropology* 48(3): 446–453.

361. Green, R. E., Krause, J., Briggs, A. W., Maricic, T., Stenzel, U., Kircher, M., ... and J. C. Mullikin (2010). A draft sequence of the Neandertal genome. *Science* 328(5979): 710–722.

362. Spikins, P. (2009) Autism, the integrations of 'difference'and the origins of modern human behaviour. *Cambridge Archaeological Journal* 19(2): 179–201.

363. Trehin, P. (2003, November) Palaeolithic art and autistic savant syndrome. In *Autism Europe Congress, Lisbon*;

364. Humphrey, N. (1998) Cave art, autism, and the evolution of the human mind. *Cambridge Archaeological Journal* 8(2): 165–191.
Selfe, L. (1977) *Nadia: A case of extraordinary drawing ability in an autistic child*. London: Academic Press.

365. Dziobek, I., Rogers, K., Fleck, S., Bahnemann, M., Heekeren, H. R., Wolf, O. T., and A. Convit (2008) Dissociation of cognitive and emotional empathy in adults with Asperger syndrome using the Multifaceted Empathy Test (MET). *Journal of Autism and Developmental Disorders* 38(3): 464–473.

366. Utrilla, P., Mazo, C., Sopena, M. C., Martínez-Bea, M., and R. Domingo (2009). A Palaeolithic map from 13,660 calBP: engraved stone blocks from the Late Magdalenian in Abauntz Cave (Navarra, Spain). *Journal of Human Evolution* 57(2): 99–111.

367. Langley, M. C., and M. Street (2013) Long range inland–coastal networks during the Late Magdalenian: Evidence for individual acquisition of marine resources at Andernach-Martinsberg, German Central Rhineland. *Journal of Human Evolution* 64(5): 457–465.

368. Germonpré, M., Sablin, M. V., Stevens, R. E., Hedges, R. E. M., Hofreiter, M., Stiller, M., and V. R. Després, (2009) Fossil dogs and wolves from Palaeolithic sites in Belgium, the Ukraine and Russia: osteometry, ancient DNA and stable isotopes. *Journal of Archaeological Science* 36(2): 473–490.

369. Germonpré, M., M., Lázničková-Galetová, M., and M. Sablin (2012) Palaeolithic dog skulls at the Gravettian Předmostí site, the Czech Republic. *Journal of Archaeological Science* 39(1): 184–202.

370. Losey, R. J., Bazaliiskii, V. I., Garvie-Lok, S., Germonpré, M., Leonard, J. A., Allen, A. J., Katzenberg, M. A., and M. V. Sablin (2011) Canids as persons: Early Neolithic dog and wolf burials, Cis-Baikal, Siberia. *Journal of Anthropological Archaeology* 30(2): 174–189

371. See Lupo, K. (2011) A dog is for hunting. In U. Albarella and A. Trentacoste (eds.) *Ethnozooarchaeology*. Oxford: Oxbow Press; Ruusila, V., and Pesonen, M. (2004, August), pp. 4–12. Interspecific cooperation in human (Homo sapiens) hunting: the benefits of a barking dog (Canis familiaris). In *Annales Zoologici Fennici* Vol. 41, No. 4, Helsinki: Suomen Biologian Seura Vanamo, 1964–, pp. 545–549

372. Sherpell cites Galton, F. (1922) *Inquiry into human faculty and its development*. London: Macmillan, pp. 246–253.

373. Serpell, J. A. (1987) Pet-keeping in non-western societies: some popular misconceptions. *Anthrozoos: A Multidisciplinary Journal of The Interactions of People & Animals* 1(3): 166–174.

374. Bradshaw, J. W. S. and E. S. Paul (2010) Could empathy for animals have been an adaptation in the evolution of homo sapiens? *Animal Welfare* 19(Supplement 1): 107–112.

375. Kurdek, L. A. (2008) Pet dogs as attachment figures. *Journal of Social and Personal Relationships* 25(2): 247–266.

376. Conard, N. J., Maria M. and S. C. Münzel (2009) New flutes document the earliest musical tradition in southwestern Germany. *Nature* 460(7256): 737–740.

377. D'Errico, F., Henshilwood, C., Lawson, G., Vanhaeren, M., Tillier, A. M., Soressi, M., ... and M. Julien (2003) Archaeological evidence for the emergence of language, symbolism, and music–an alternative multidisciplinary perspective. *Journal of World Prehistory* 17(1): 1–70.

378. Conkey, M. W. (1980) The identification of prehistoric hunter-gatherer aggregation sites: the case of Altamira. *Current Anthropology* 21(5): 609–630.

379. Pike, A. W., Hoffmann, D. L., García-Diez, M., Pettitt, P. B., Alcolea, J., De Balbin, R., ... and J. Zilhão (2012) U-series dating of Paleolithic art in 11 caves in Spain. *Science* 336(6087): 1409–1413.

380. Lee, R. B. (1979) *The !Kung San: Men, women and work in a foraging society*. Cambridge: Cambridge University Press, p. 246.

381. Roksandic, M. (2006) Violence in the Mesolithic. *Documenta Praehistorica* 33: 165–182. Peter-Röcher, H. (2002) Krieg und Gewalt. Zu den Kopfdepositionen in der Großen Ofnet und der Diskussion um kriegerische Konflikte in pra"historischer Zeit. Praehistorische Zeitschrift 77: 1–28.

382. Knauft, B. M., Abler, T. S., Betzig, L., Boehm, C., Dentan, R. K., and T. M. Kiefer (1991). Violence and sociality in human evolution. *Current Anthropology* 32(4): 391–428.

CHAPTER ELEVEN

383. Jung, C.C. (1977). C.J. Jung Speaking. Princeton, New Jersey: Princeton University Press.

384. In *Psychiatry and The Human Condition* (Oxford, UK: Radcliffe Medical Press, 2000), Bruce Charlton from the University of Newcastle, comments:

The Golden Age for humans – such as it was – was the life of a nomadic hunter gatherer. This was the time when more of the people were happier for more of the time than at any other point in human history...There is little doubt that, conceived in this way, psychiatric impairment is the norm. Mental health and well-being are so rare as to be remarkable. For most people, even a single day of unalloyed well-being is a rare event. Some unfortunate people probably never experience even a day of well-being, at best managing a few minutes as a kind of glimmering of what is possible.

But why should this be? Why should the world be a place of illness and drugs – surely that is unnatural? The answer is that the modern world is indeed unnatural and has been so, for the majority of humankind, for many thousands of years. Unnaturalness is profound, inevitable, unavoidable. It is time that we recognized that 'naturalness' is not an option, and worked hard on how best to cope with it.

385. Charles Darwin's diary aboard the *Beagle*, notes from 18 December 1832.
386. Corbey, R. (1993) Ethnographic showcases, 1870–1930. *Cultural Anthropology* 8(3): 338–369.
387. Gusinde, M. (1982) *Los Indios de Tierra del Fuego. Los Selk'nam. Tomo 1.* Buenos Aires: Centro Argentino de Etnologia Americana.
388. From the records of Edward Lucas Bridges. Bridges, E. L. (1988) *Uttermost part of the earth: Indians of Tierra del Fuego.* New York: Dover Publications.
389. Hazlewood, N. (2000) *Savage: The Life and Times of Jemmy Button.* London: Hodder and Stoughton.
390. See also research on the significance of collaboration to the Yamana. Briz i Godino, I. B., Santos, J. I., Galán, J. M., Caro, J., Álvarez, M., and D. Zurro (2013) Social cooperation and resource management dynamics among late hunter-fisher-gatherer societies in Tierra del Fuego (South America). *Journal of Archaeological Method and Theory*: 1–21.
391. FitzRoy, R., King, P. P., and Darwin, C. (1966) *Narrative of the surveying voyages of His Majesty's ships adventure and Beagle: Proceedings of the second expedition, 1831–1836, under the command of Captain Robert Fitz-Roy* (Vol. 2). H. Colburn.
392. Kopenawa, D. (2012) *The Falling Sky: Words of a Yanomami shaman.* Belknap: Harvard, p. 338.
393. Kopenawa, D. (2012) *The Falling Sky: Words of a Yanomami shaman.* Belknap: Harvard, pp. 349–350.
394. Murimbata, T., and C. Whitehead (2000) Why consciousness conferences are not really getting us anywhere. *Journal of Consciousness Studies* 7(6): 81–85, on p. 82.
395. Murimbata, T., and Whitehead, C. (1998) A stone age anthropologist looks at Tucson III. *Journal of Consciousness Studies* 5(4): 505.
396. Murimbata, T., and Whitehead, C. (1998) A stone age anthropologist looks at Tucson III. *Journal of Consciousness Studies* 5(4):505, quote taken from Ryan, W. M. (1969) *White Man, Black Man* (Milton, Queensland: Jacaranda Press) in Knight, C. (1987) 'Menstruation and the Origins of Culture', Doctoral Thesis, Department of Anthropology, University College, London.
397. Nesse, R. (2004) Natural selection and the elusiveness of happiness, *Philosophical Transactions of the Royal Society of London B.* 359(1449): 1333–1347.
398. Paul Mills, unpublished, from 'Inflation Impromptu'.

Throughout the book I've illustrated key artefacts, art, reconstructions and even drawings or photographs with my own line drawings. I wanted the reader to be able to see the evidence through my eyes, as well as wanting to give a certain coherence that would be lacking had I used various photographs or other illustrations from different sources. These drawings have been done by eye usually from a number of different sources, as well as my memory of the art or artefacts themselves; they are broadly correct, but I would encourage a researcher to look for a detailed technical illustration for any analytical purposes.

Cover drawing: Chloe Brown